# CHINESE LYRICISM

*Prepared as one of the Companions to Asian Studies*
*Wm. Theodore de Bary, Editor*

# CHINESE LYRICISM

*Shih Poetry from the Second to
the Twelfth Century, with translations,
by Burton Watson*

COLUMBIA UNIVERSITY PRESS

NEW YORK & LONDON

Burton Watson, Associate Professor of Chinese at Columbia University, is the author of *Ssu-ma Ch'ien: Grand Historian of China* (1958) and *Early Chinese Literature* (1962), and the translator of *Records of the Grand Historian of China, translated from the* Shih chi *of Ssu-ma Ch'ien,* 2 vols. (1961), *Su Tung-p'o: Selections from a Sung Dynasty Poet* (1965), *Basic Writings of Mo Tzu, Hsün Tzu, and Han Fei Tzu* (1967), *The Complete Works of Chuang Tzu* (1968), and *Cold Mountain: A Hundred Poems by Han Shan* (1962; reissued 1970).

Portions of this work were prepared under a grant from the Carnegie Corporation of New York and a contract with the U.S. Office of Education for the production of texts to be used in undergraduate education. The draft translations so produced have been used in the Columbia College Oriental Humanities program and have subsequently been revised and expanded for publication in the present form.

*To Ogawa Tamaki*

# ACKNOWLEDGMENTS

THE TRANSLATIONS and comments in this volume owe much to the hours spent reading Chinese poetry with my students at Stanford and Columbia over the past five years, and my thanks go first to them. Gary Snyder and Philip Whalen, who read most of the translations in draft form, supplied encouragement and help when it was needed. Though only Western language publications are cited in the notes and bibliography, I have of course drawn gratefully upon numerous Chinese and Japanese commentaries and studies; particularly useful were the volumes in the *Chūgoku shijin senshū* series (Selected works of Chinese poets) published by Iwanami Shoten, Tokyo, many of them the work of old friends from Kyoto days. My debt to Professor Yoshikawa Kōjirō of Kyoto University I have acknowledged in earlier publications. The dedication of this volume reflects my deep gratitude to his colleague, Professor Ogawa Tamaki, for conversations over a period of many years in which I tried out my ideas on him and profited immeasurably from his understanding and wealth of knowledge.

# FOREWORD

⚛

CHINESE LYRICISM is one of a series of Companions to Asian
Studies sponsored by the Columbia University Committee on
Oriental Studies. The series includes bibliographical guides, syllabi,
and manuals introducing different aspects of Asian civilizations to
general education and the general reader. These aids are intended to
complement the basic texts and translations appearing in the series
of Translations from the Oriental Classics and the Introduction to
Oriental Civilizations, also sponsored by the Committee.

The early phases of this project were assisted by a grant from the
Office of Education, under the National Defense Education Act, to
prepare materials for use in undergraduate general education concerning Asia. It is to the credit of the responsible officials that, in
pursuing this aim, they consulted with representatives of the
academic community, and were prepared to support the type of
program recommended to them as truly in our broadest national
interest—one which emphasized the humanistic study of Asia and
an appreciation of the basic values in other civilizations.

Burton Watson's name is already closely identified with several
projects undertaken in this program. The present work, a general
introduction to a major phase in the development of the classical
lyric poetry of China, takes a place alongside two other distinguished
works in this series: Watson's *Early Chinese Literature* and C. T.
Hsia's *Classic Chinese Novel*. It demonstrates anew Professor Watson's
superb gifts as a translator and interpreter of Chinese literature.

*Wm. Theodore de Bary*

# CONTENTS

☗

# CHINESE LYRICISM

# I

# INTRODUCTION

☗

CHINESE POETIC literature has three important forms: the *shih,* the *fu,* and the *tz'u.* The latter two, though they have enjoyed moments of great popularity, have tended to be somewhat restricted in theme and treatment, and to dominate the literary scene for only limited periods. The *shih* or lyric form, by contrast, is as old as Chinese literature itself, and has continued in use down to the present century. It is the vehicle to which the Chinese have entrusted their profoundest and most heartfelt utterances, the form that has come to be recognized as characteristic of the Chinese poetic spirit at its greatest.

In my *Early Chinese Literature* I have discussed the beginnings of the form, when it was employed in the songs of the *Book of Odes,* the

On the history of Chinese poetry, see A. R. Davis, Introduction to *The Penguin Book of Chinese Verse,* tr. by Robert Kotewell and Norman L. Smith; David Hawkes, "Chinese Poetry and the English Reader," in Raymond Dawson, ed., *The Legacy of China,* pp. 90–115; James R. Hightower, *Topics in Chinese Literature: Outlines and Bibliographies* (1950; rev. ed., 1953); James J. Y. Liu, *The Art of Chinese Poetry;* Burton Watson, *Early Chinese Literature.*

For general selections of Chinese poetry in translation, see Cyril Birch, ed., *Anthology of Chinese Literature;* Paul Demiéville, ed., *Anthologie de la Poésie Chinoise Classique;* Robert Payne, ed., *The White Pony;* Arthur Waley, *Chinese Poems,* (selected from three earlier books: *The Temple and Other Poems, One Hundred and Seventy Chinese Poems,* and *More Translations from the Chinese*).

For further information on translations, see Martha Davidson, *A List of Published Translations from the Chinese into English, French and German,* Part II, Poetry.

oldest anthology of Chinese poetry. Readers are referred to that
work for a detailed treatment of the subject, though I shall recapitu-
late here the points that bear upon the period under discussion.
After the compilation of the *Book of Odes* around 600 B.C., the *shih*
form, which employed a predominantly four-character line,[1] declined
in popularity and for a while was all but eclipsed by other poetic
forms. In the second century A.D., however, it enjoyed a revival, this
time using lines of five or seven characters in length. My discussion
begins with this sudden resurgence of the form and traces its development through the next thousand years, including the three centuries
of the T'ang dynasty, by common agreement the greatest age of
Chinese poetry. It ends sometime before the fall of the Sung dynasty
in 1279, when the Mongol invasion brought changes that were to
have a profound effect upon Chinese civilization and culture, and
when the *shih* form had clearly reached the end of its period of
greatest growth and creativity.

What follows, therefore, is an attempt to describe the poetry
written over a thousand years in a single form, with only a cursory
glance at that in the older four-character *shih* form that preceded it,
or that in the *fu* or *tz'u* forms which at times paralleled it. I have
not, however, attempted to write a systematic or comprehensive
history of the form. Instead it has been my aim to present groups of
poems, arranged, except for minor departures, in chronological
order, that seem to me to illustrate the most important formal,
stylistic, and thematic developments in its long process of growth.
The groups of poems are accompanied by whatever explicatory
material I felt would be useful to the reader, sometimes in the form
of notes to particular poems, sometimes in that of brief essays
relating to the group as a whole.

The poems, about two hundred of them, were selected because
they are of intrinsic value and interest, as well as being illustrative

[1] Ancient Chinese is essentially monosyllabic and, in the system of writing
developed some time before 1000 B.C. to record it, one character represents
one syllable; thus the length of the line could also be described in terms of
syllables or words. But in later periods there was a growing tendency toward
bisyllabic or polysyllabic compounds. In order to avoid troublesome discussions
of word boundaries, therefore, I prefer to define the length of the line in terms
of the number of characters.

of the particular points under discussion, and will, I hope, constitute an anthology of sorts—one dictated by personal preferences and my estimation of what will go best into English, but representative withal of the best styles and trends of the period. I should mention at this point, however, that, although I have tried in my discussion and illustrative material to cover the major themes and stylistic developments of the *shih*, I have not necessarily attempted to do full justice to all the major poets who worked in this medium. The reason is that I wished to avoid retranslating poems that have already been beautifully translated, or repeating background material that is available elsewhere, and thereby to make room for more poetry that is less familiar to the English reader. Thus, for example, two of the most famous poets of the period, T'ao Ch'ien and Po Chü-i, are not extensively treated because excellent studies and translations by Waley, Acker, Hightower, and others are readily available, and because the stylistic and thematic characteristics which mark their work can equally well be illustrated by the works of their contemporaries. By way of compensation, greater space has been devoted to the poets of the Six Dynasties and Sung eras, whose works have so far not received the attention they deserve. I have tried to keep attention focused upon the poems themselves rather than upon the lives of the poet. Traditional Chinese literary historians have tended to regard a man and his work as inseparable, and there are perfectly valid philosophical assumptions underlying their view. But we in the West need not be bound by such assumptions and it is time that an attempt be made, when treating the literary history of China, to keep the biographical and anecdotal element under a firmer control.

The poetry dealt with in this volume is in the language known as classical Chinese. Classical Chinese was the written, and presumably the spoken, language of ancient China, particularly that of the Han dynasty (206 B.C.–A.D. 220), and continued to be used as the standard medium of written expression long after the spoken language had evolved a rather different vocabulary and syntax. For the period under consideration here, which begins with the closing years of the Han and ends shortly before the fall of the Sung dynasty in 1279, it is difficult to say just what relationship existed between the written and the spoken language at any given time, and hence to determine whether poems written in the classical language would have been intelligible to the ear as well as to the eye, or were intended primarily for the latter alone. Certainly the poems of the early part of the period, many of them folk songs or works in a folk song idiom, must have been reasonably close to the spoken word, and even in the ninth century, the middle years of the T'ang, we hear of Po Chü-i's poems being set to music and performed as popular songs, which presumably means that they were fully intelligible to the hearer. But by Sung times the spoken language, to judge from the recorded examples we possess, had begun to diverge significantly from the classical written language, and it is doubtful whether the Sung poems presented here would have made much sense to the ear alone, at least to that of the ordinary listener. When I speak, therefore, of a colloquial or conversational tone in some of the poetry discussed, the reader must understand that I am referring in many cases to a relative phenomenon within the context of the classical written syntax and diction. For classical Chinese, though based upon and growing out of the ancient language, did not remain a uniform and unchanging medium. Both the prose and the poetic works in the language give evidence of marked stylistic growth and change, albeit less sudden and drastic than that undergone by the spoken language. Poetry in particular, presumably because of its close affinity with song, often borrowed phrases and turns of speech from the vernacular, and showed itself bolder and more experimental in its modes of expression than the prose tradition.

While these changes in diction and syntax were taking place, a similar process of change was affecting the sound system of the Chinese language. But I shall not have much to say about sound and sound changes in my discussion of Chinese poetry here. This does not mean that I regard sound as an unimportant element. On the contrary, it is, as in the poetry of all other languages, a factor of prime literary importance, one which serves subtly to underline and dramatize the meaning and at times may become so prominent that it reaches the point where, as one poet puts it, "the words ring like gongs and meaning goes out the window."[2] Chinese, as everyone

[2] Edward Field, "Ode to Fidel Castro."

knows, is not written with a phonetic alphabet, but the characters or graphs which are used to represent it in many cases contain elements that do give a clue to their pronunciation. Linguists, working on the basis of these and other data, have reconstructed the sounds of early and middle Chinese. However, these reconstructions, valuable as they are to the expert, are couched in symbols that are hardly even pronounceable by the layman, and leave him totally un-informed, needless to say, as to what esthetic or emotive values may have attached to these sounds. In my discussion of rhyme and other euphonic elements of the poems, I have therefore not attempted to employ these learned reconstructions, but have transcribed the sounds as they exist in modern standard Chinese, a distant and much-mutated descendant of the speech of T'ang and Sung times.

The case of tones, those various pitch and inflectional values associated with individual words which give modern Chinese its characteristic singsong quality, is similar. From the fifth century on, tones were recognized as an important element in Chinese prosody, and a T'ang work could speak of "the level tone, sad and peaceful," or "the entering tone, abrupt and urgent," etc.[3] The tone of the rhyme words would seem to have been especially crucial in helping to create the emotional atmosphere the poet was after. A striking example is Tu Fu's 140-line "Northern Journey," a poem describing scenes of terror, pathos, and anxiety, which employs rhyme words in the entering tone—that characterized as "abrupt and urgent"—throughout. But these T'ang tones, although four in number, were not the same as the four tones of modern Mandarin, and we can only guess at just how they were pronounced. The reader, therefore, must accept my word for it, as I accept the word of my Chinese mentors, that euphony played a very significant part in the beauty and expressiveness of these poems, and that behind the English vocables in which they make their appearance here lie worlds of lost Chinese melody. For the rest, I shall limit my comments to those elements of meaning and style that can be brought across and discussed in translation.

[3] *Yüan-ho hsin-sheng yün-p'u,* quoted in Shen-kung's "Ssu-sheng wu-yin chiu-lung fan-niu t'u-hsü," *Yü-p'ien.*

But if time has muffled and distorted the auditory effects of classical Chinese verse, what of its visual effect? Here many Western readers have been misled by Pound and other enthusiasts into thinking that Chinese characters are in fact "little pictures" that in some miraculous way convey the object or concept directly to the eye of the beholder without any need for semantic intermediaries. It is true that Chinese characters often contain, or even consist of, pictographic elements. But many of these have been distorted beyond recognition by orthographic convention, and the reader of Chinese is hardly more conscious of them than is the English reader of the individual letters that make up any given word. That visual effect plays, or ought to play, some role in a writer's choice of words is attested by a brief set of rules given by Liu Hsieh (*ca.* 465–552) in his *Wen-hsin tiao-lung* (sec. 39), a work on literary theory and practice, which warns the writer to avoid creating a series of visually monotonous or ill-matched characters.[4] But it is clear that, in Liu Hsieh's opinion, one is to concern himself about such niceties only after he has met the much more basic demands of sound and sense. Again, Westerners are often misled by the sight of Chinese poems written out in beautiful calligraphy, particularly poems that are inscribed on paintings, into supposing that there is some necessary connection between artistic and literary effect. Considered simply as pieces of abstract design, columns of Chinese characters can have great esthetic appeal (though many of the people who admire them most extravagantly might feel differently if they were aware that the characters are usually saying such things as "The gentleman walks no bypaths," or "One day no work, one day no eat!"). No one would deny that fine calligraphy enhances the attractiveness of a Chinese poem, just as fine type and expensive paper do that of a printed poem in English, but these are mere accidents as far as literary intent or value are concerned. Nearly all the poets to be discussed here lived before the invention of printing, and none of them, so far as I know, had the slightest control over how his works were to be spaced on the page, what style of calligraphy they would be written in, or other details of visual presentation. The custom of

4 See the English translation by Vincent Yu-chung Shih, *The Literary Mind and the Carving of Dragons,* p. 212.

matching up a painting and a poem is relatively late, becoming widespread only with the Sung dynasty. Sometimes the painting was done to accompany the poem, sometimes the reverse, but in either case they were seldom from the same hand. The kind of elaborate production that Blake turned out, with poem, picture, typography, and color all the work of one man, would most likely have struck the Chinese gentleman as vulgarly assertive.

When I come to discuss particular poems, I trust that the special excellences of classical Chinese—its vigor and economy, its ability to dispense with connectives, the versatility of its words—will become apparent, as well as its less admirable ambiguities. Here I should like to comment on two features of the language that often figure in discussions of its suitability as a medium for poetry. The first is the fact that nouns contain no indication of number. The writer of Chinese may, of course, if he feels it important, supply an additional word or two to make clear his intent—"many trees," "solitary peak," etc.—but more often he leaves his nouns unqualified as to number. Professor James Liu in his *Art of Chinese Poetry* (p. 40), a book to which I am much indebted, argues that, in poetry at least, this is all to the good, since the poet should be concerned "with the universal rather than the particular," and "it is of no consequence," for example, "whether 'mountain,' 'bird,' and 'valley' are singular or plural." Such an assertion of the superiority of the generalized over the particular might have gladdened a reader of English poetry in the time of Dryden or Pope. But the twentieth-century reader, influenced as he is by Imagism, by demands for real toads in his imaginary garden or declarations that there are "no ideas but in things," is hardly likely to give such ready assent. He would object, I think, that unless one can "get the picture" he will not know what mood or idea the poet is trying to convey; that it is of great consequence indeed whether "bird," for example, is singular or plural, since one bird is suggestive of loneliness, but a flock of them are more likely to seem either menacing or jolly, depending upon how one feels about birds to begin with. To be sure, English, by distinguishing so importantly between "one" and "more than one," and then leaving us in the dark as to how many more, presents almost as fuzzy a picture, but at least it is moving in the direction of visual precision. Chinese, on the other hand, as in so many nature poems of the Six Dynasties or early T'ang, offers us a landscape which is not really a landscape at all, if I may pursue the painting analogy, but rather a blank canvas (quintessence of landscape?) inscribed "tree," "bird," "mountain," "water" in the appropriate areas, upon which we are asked to execute our own realization of the scene.

A second characteristic of classical Chinese, the fact that its verbs lack any indication of tense, has likewise been extolled by Professor Liu because it "enables the poet to present the scene not from the point of view of any specific time but almost *sub specie aeternitatis*." There are cases where this is probably true: when a Chinese poet states, for example, that "the river flows on," we may surmise, from what we know of the nature of rivers and of Chinese attitudes toward them, that he in fact means "the river flowed, is flowing, and will always flow on." But there are countless other cases—the majority, surely—in which tense, though not indicated explicitly, is clearly implied by the context. This tenselessness, after all, is not confined to poetry, but is just as much a feature of Chinese prose, including historical narrative, where position and sequence in time are crucial.

But I do not wish to labor the point. My only concern here is that what are in fact mere accidents of language should not be mistakenly singled out as the source either of literary shortcomings or of some unusual felicity of expression. Countless speakers of English employ the present tense when recounting events of the past, but we do not praise them for presenting their narrative *sub specie aeternitatis*; rather we chide them for being too fond of vivid speech, or dismiss them as grammatical sloths. And if we are to claim that Chinese nouns are intrinsically more poetic than those of English because they lack number, and are hence more universal, we must by the same reasoning claim that English nouns are more poetic than those of, say, French or Italian because they lack gender, a claim that few Frenchmen or Italians are likely to allow.

Instead of saying anything further about the characteristics of classical Chinese, it may be well at this point to illustrate these characteristics through an examination of two poems written in that language. The first is an anonymous folk song from the fourth or fifth century A.D., of the type associated with a singing girl named Tzu-yeh (see p. 60 below). It belongs to a group of songs that describe scenes of the different seasons, this one pertaining to summer. The poem is in four lines of five characters each and, in the romanized form of its modern Mandarin pronunciation, looks like this:

> Shu   sheng   ching   wu   feng
> hsia   yün   po   mu   ch'i
> hsi   shou   mi   yeh   hsia
> fou   kua   ch'en   chu   li

The end rhymes *ch'i* and *li* remain consonant in modern pronunciation, though this is unhappily not true of many of the rhymes of early poetry.

The poem is simple and direct, without the allusions and ambiguities that make so many Chinese poems difficult to interpret and even more difficult to translate. A literal rendering into English character by character would go something like this:

> Heat   height   calm   no   wind
> summer   cloud   toward   evening   rise
> take   hand   dense   leafage   under
> float   melon   dunk   crimson   plum

So simple is the poem that the literal rendering is quite comprehensible and, as so often happens in translations of Chinese poetry, would at first glance almost seem preferable to a wordier and more conventional version. No particular problems are presented by the number of the nouns; one feels it is not vital to the poem's meaning whether one pictures one summer cloud or a bank of them, one crimson plum or a handful. The only real difficulty lies in the verbs "take," "float," and "dunk," which must, in the reader's mind at least, be assigned some subject, tense, and mood, e.g., "I took your hand," "Please take my hand," "You will take my hand," etc. "Melon-floating and plum-dunking," incidentally, seems to have been one of the conventional pastimes of summer and is mentioned in a letter dating from the early third century A.D. (see p. 48). Here is an English rendering of the poem that, while supplying number to the nouns and subject, tense, and mood to the verbs, attempts as far as possible to preserve the simplicity of the original:

> In the hottest time, when all is still and windless
> and summer clouds rise up at dusk,
> under the dense leaves, take my hand
> and we'll float melons on the water, dunk crimson plums.

The second poem I want to present is deceptively like the one above, a quatrain that employs the same five-character line. It is by the T'ang nature poet Wang Wei (699–759), who will be discussed at some length in Chapter IX. A transcription in modern Mandarin pronunciation gives this:

> K'ung   shan   pu   chien   jen
> tan   wen   jen   yü   hsiang
> fan   ying   ju   shen   lin
> fu   chao   ch'ing   t'ai   shang

In pidgin English:

> Empty   mountain   not   see   man
> only   hear   man   talk   sound
> return   light   enter   deep   wood
> again   shine   green   moss   on

Here questions of number in the nouns, and subject, tense, and mood in the verbs, only mildly troublesome in the case of the first poem quoted, rise up in full force to plague the translator and make him wonder if his task is not entirely hopeless. For it is obvious that Wang Wei is deliberately manipulating his nature images in such a way as to create an atmosphere of mystery and bodilessness, to achieve a degree of abstraction that will allow the symbolic levels of meaning to come through most clearly. Thus the poem, like so many of Wang Wei's, though superficially couched in the plainest language, exploits the economy and vagueness of classical Chinese to suggest a wealth of philosophical subtleties lurking beneath the surface. To see just how this works, let us examine the poem line by line.

The first line begins with the word *k'ung,* "empty" or "deserted," a word which, while indicating the stillness and remoteness of the mountains, at the same time, because of its Buddhist connotations, suggests the illusory nature of the entire phenomenal world. The verb "see," though obviously meant to be taken in the active mood, lacks any expressed subject; presumably the subject is the poet, who does not see anyone else in the hills, but since he has already characterized them as "empty," one wonders what he is doing there. In English such a degree of vagueness is all but impossible to suggest and, distasteful as it may be, one ends by resorting to a lame passive—"no one is seen"—or some other circumlocution to render the phrase.

In the second line we have the same disquieting lack of subject: who hears? the poet? you or I if we were there? some nonhuman presence? In the second line the number of the noun also becomes a problem: does one hear the sound of a number of people babbling away, or only the murmur of one man talking to himself? Finally, as in the line above, if the mountain is in fact "empty," why are there voices there?

In the last two lines of the poem the human being or beings, which in the preceding lines have been hazy and insubstantial to say the least, disappear altogether and we are left with a description of a natural phenomenon that occurs in the mountain forest at sundown. The term *fan ying* may mean "reflected light," but here it seems to mean "returned light," the sunlight which, having earlier in the day shone down on the forest from directly above, now streams in among the trees once more, this time from the side, as the sun sinks in the west. The verbs and nouns offer no particular problems here until one gets to the very last word, when a serious question of interpretation arises. The word *shang* has customarily been taken as the equivalent of a preposition, "on," or "over," referring to the late sunlight playing over or across the surface of the moss. It may, however, be taken as a verb, "to rise" (and tonal considerations suggest that this is the correct reading). If it is taken in this way, a further refinement is added to the picture of the late afternoon sun.

The line now reads, in literal rendering, *again shine green moss ascend,* and we have a picture of the sunlight retreating up the side of the mountain as the sun drops behind an obscuring peak.

This last is presumably not the kind of ambiguity that a poet would deliberately seek, and if we could somehow establish contact with Wang Wei's shade we might discover which reading he actually intended. I dwell on it here because it illustrates the kind of basic problem of interpretation that arises so often with Chinese poetry, and suggests why renderings of a particular poem, even when done by experts, may differ so surprisingly from translator to translator. The following is my own translation of the Wang Wei poem which, now that the reader has some knowledge of the original, will be seen to abound in unhappy compromises, though perhaps something of the mood of the Chinese comes across. For the possible symbolic connotations of the late sunlight, see the discussion on p. 177.

Empty hills, no one in sight,
only the sound of someone talking:
late sunlight enters the deep wood,
shining over the green moss again.

I hope, as I have said, that the poems in my selection may be regarded as the core of what follows, with the explanatory material serving to surround and set them off. Space will not always permit such elaborate analysis as in the example above. I have, however, tried to anticipate and answer the kind of question that the ordinary reader is likely to raise concerning the formal characteristics, themes, stylistic peculiarities, and general historical background of the body of poetry under discussion, though I have preferred in most cases to let these answers emerge in the course of the elucidation of particular poems or groups of poems rather than to deal with them in formal essays.

There remains one more matter for comment, that of the translations of the poems. Enough has already been said by others on the problems and special difficulties of translation from Chinese so that I need not write at length; those who wish to read further on the subject would do well to consult the excellent discussion by A. C.

Graham in the introduction to his *Poems of the Late T'ang* (Penguin Books, 1965). With regard to the particular body of poetry translated here, however, I would like to take up one or two of the questions that may occur to the reader and explain my position on them.

Since these are "old Chinese poems," dating from the second to the twelfth century, should not this oldness be somehow suggested in the translation? My answer to this is an emphatic no! Their oldness is no more than historical accident; all were unquestionably new when they were written. The *Greek Anthology* is even older and embraces a longer time span, yet no reputable modern translator that I am aware of makes any attempt to suggest this fact in his translation. The good translator, it seems to me, no matter how he may project himself back into time in order to understand the ideas and sentiments of his author, must, when it comes to getting the words over into another language, proceed as though he himself were the author, writing the work afresh today.

But since, as I have said, these poems are written in a literary idiom which is at times quite far removed from the spoken language of the time, should this fact not find reflection in some particularly elegant or old-fangled tone to the translation? My answer once more is no, though more for practical reasons than for those of principle. First of all, it is very difficult, as I have indicated, to determine just how far apart the literary and the spoken languages may have been at any given period, though this would be essential before one could decide just what degree of elegance and artificiality he ought to strive for in translation. Moreover, it would mean that, although the earliest poems, written when the literary language was close to the colloquial, might be rendered into an easy, conversational style, the English of the translations would have to grow increasingly stilted in the works of succeeding ages, until the poems of the Sung period were all but cast in the language of Spenser. Someday there may appear a translator so gifted that he can not only recreate in splendid English the full sound and sense of Chinese poetry, but convey as well the particular flavor that attaches to the literary language in each period of its long history. Meanwhile, I think it best, while recognizing the existence of an unattained ideal, to keep the demands we make upon our translators within the bounds of reason.

I myself translate into the spoken language of present-day America. It is obviously the language I know best and therefore the one in which, if I am to achieve any success at all, the chances for success seem brightest. That is, I proceed as though I were writing poetry of my own, taking as a model those contemporary American poets I most admire.

Unless otherwise noted, all the translations are my own. As stated, I have in some cases deliberately avoided lengthy treatment of certain famous poems or poets that have already been well translated into English. In a few cases, such as the "Nineteen Old Poems" of the following section, beautifully translated by Arthur Waley, I have nevertheless made my own version, since I think it is important that the reader not mistake the style and idiosyncrasies of a particular translator for some feature of the original. In what follows, therefore, although my own style may impose a certain monotony, the reader may be certain that when he does detect differences of style or tone, these are reflections of genuine differences in the Chinese.

# II

## THE "NINETEEN OLD POEMS"

## OF THE HAN

*Few things that can happen to a nation are
more important than the invention of a new form
of verse*—T. S. ELIOT

※

IF THESE WORDS of Eliot are true, then China, in the otherwise grim and uncertain years that marked the close of the Han dynasty, had reason to rejoice. The last two centuries of the dynasty's rule, known as the Latter or Eastern Han (A.D. 25–220), particularly the second century, saw the sudden flowering of what, practically speaking, was a new poetic form. It is known loosely as the *shih,* a term that dates back to the *Shih ching,* the *Book of Songs* or *Book of Odes,* an anthology compiled around 600 B.C. and containing poems from the preceding four or five centuries. But the *shih* of the *Book of Odes* were cast in a meter dominated by lines of four characters each. This four-character meter, though originally a song form that, judging from the evidence we have, enjoyed great popularity among both the aristocracy and the common people, appears suddenly, around the time of Confucius, to have lost its vigor and appeal, and there are no known examples of its use from the three succeeding

For a study of the "Nineteen Old Poems," see Jean-Pierre Diény, *Les dix-neuf poèmes anciens.*

For translations, see Payne, *The White Pony,* and Waley, *Chinese Poems.*

THE QUOTATION ABOVE IS FROM "SENECA IN ELIZABETHAN TRANSLATION."

centuries. It was revived in Han times, mainly for hymns and state pieces that drew dignity from its now archaic tone, and was employed on occasion by both major and minor poets of the period of disunity that followed the collapse of the Han. But their best efforts never succeeded in infusing it with new vitality; it remained a literary vestige, isolated from the mainstream of development by its own archaism, and for this reason no poems in the four-character form will be dealt with in this study.

The new *shih* form that rose to prominence in the years of the Han differed from the old principally in the fact that it employed a five-character or, somewhat later, a seven-character line. The earliest examples of the form, dating from around the first century B.C., suggest that it was associated with popular songs and children's ditties. It was slow to gain respectability, and did not become an important vehicle for serious literary expression until the second century A.D., when it was taken up by men of the scholar class.

The *shih* form, both the old four-character version and the newer five-character or seven-character version, is marked by a strong preponderance of end-stopped lines. The poem is constructed almost wholly of these one-line units or building blocks; only rarely, most often in the last couplet, does the poet use a run-on line. Moreover, to continue the metaphor, these blocks are fitted together with little or no grammatical mortar; parataxis rather than hypotaxis is the rule. Occasionally an "'although" or a "moreover" may be inserted, but for the most part the logical connectives must be supplied by the reader. Poems that comprise a single sentence, such as are not uncommon in English, or those in which the entire syntax is kept in suspension until the final syllables, as in Japanese, are unknown.

Because of the factors just described, there is a tendency for poems in the *shih* form to fall apart into a series of disconnected lines. Two formal devices help to overcome this tendency toward disintegration and serve to weld the lines together. One is verbal parallelism, in which the syntax of the first line of a couplet is repeated in the second line, often with the highest degree of exactitude. Numerous examples of such parallelism will be encountered in the pages that follow and further comment will accordingly be reserved for those occurrences. Here I need only note that the device has two obvious drawbacks. First, it serves only to link the two lines of a couplet and does not prevent the couplets in turn from falling apart, as often happens in mediocre poetry. In addition, it must be employed sparingly and with taste if it is not to deteriorate into vapid mannerism.

The second device used to bind the poem together is end rhyme. It is found in the earliest poetry in the language, that of the *Book of Odes,* and continues to be a constant feature of the *shih* in all succeeding centuries. Customarily it is employed at the end of each even-numbered line and thus serves to link one couplet to the next; sometimes the rhyme changes after two or three couplets, sometimes the same rhyme continues throughout the poem. (Chinese rhymes, it might be noted, are more numerous and, presumably, to the Chinese, less monotonous than those of English.) The *Wen-hsin tiao-lung,* the sixth-century work on literary theory and practice mentioned in the Introduction, recommends that the use of a single rhyme be limited to less than one hundred lines (beyond which it would become tedious), but extended to more than two lines (to avoid too busy an effect).[1]

Western readers may wonder why the Chinese were content for so many centuries to continue using this rather simple type of rhyme scheme. They surely were not unaware of other possibilities, and in fact, in the period around the end of the second century A.D. and later, experimented with one of them, the rhymed couplet. From what I have already said, however, the disadvantages of extended use of the rhymed couplet in Chinese should be obvious. The same rhyme occurring at the end of both lines of the couplet will serve only further to isolate the couplet from its neighbors. Moreover, where verbal parallelism is employed in the couplet, it will mean that the rhyme will invariably fall upon the same part of speech in both lines, thus adding to the effect of monotony which is already a danger in parallelism. Just why the more complex patterns of alternating rhymes, such as are used in Western poetry, were not favored by the Chinese, I do not know; perhaps they felt that these would distract from what were, for them, more important formal

[1] Sec. 34; see Vincent Shih, *The Literary Mind and the Carving of Dragons,* p. 189.

elements of the poems. When Chinese poets turned their attention to formal complexity, it was the possibilities of verbal, and later tonal, parallelism that interested them rather than those of more intricate or interlocking rhyme.

Only one more formal characteristic of the *shih* needs to be mentioned. The four-character *shih* of the *Book of Odes* often employ particles or even what appear to be nonsense words to fill out the line, and these were presumably pronounced rather lightly. As a result, though in written form the line consisted of four characters, it may have contained only three, or even two, strong beats. In the later five-character and seven-character *shih*, however, such particles are sparingly used. (This is one of the main characteristics that distinguish the *shih* line from similar five-character or seven-character lines in the *fu* or rhyme-prose form.) Thus the line ordinarily consists of five or seven "full words," that is, words carrying a full load of meaning and demanding a strong beat. To relieve the heaviness and monotony of such a line, a light caesura is often inserted, after the second character in the five-character line, after the fourth character in the seven-character line. Rarely, the caesura may occur after the third character of the five-character line, as in the fourteenth of the "Nineteen Old Poems":

> 1        2    3       4    5
> Out the outer gate, (I) look ahead

or the more self-consciously irregular couplet by Chang Han (258?–319?):

> 1    2      3      4       5
> Glory and youth, both departed;

> 1        2    3      4      5
> obscurity and age, closing in.   (*Tsa shih, Wen hsüan* 29)

But such irregular placing of the caesura is very unusual. Many lines contain no caesura at all, but read right through in a single breath. Where the caesura does occur, however, it normally breaks the line into a 2-3 or 4-3 pattern.

The "Nineteen Old Poems," thirteen of which will be presented in translation and discussed below, represent some of the most important and influential of the early works in the *wu-yen shih* or five-character *shih* form. Of uncertain date, they are preserved in the *Wen hsüan* or *Literary Anthology,* a compilation of the early sixth century, and may well have existed as a group from earlier times. Some have been attributed to known authors of the Han, and attempts have been made on the basis of internal evidence to show that at least some of them date back to the second or first century B.C. But these attributions and theories of dating remain tentative; my own feeling, shared by most experts who have gone more deeply into the subject than I have, is that they are in the main products of the second century A.D., and that is how I shall discuss them here.

Like most of the songs of the *Book of Odes,* which they resemble in many ways, the "Nineteen Old Poems" are anonymous; only rarely does the poet give us any indication of his occupation or place in society, and often the very sex of the speaker is in doubt. In theme, manner of expression, and diction the poems owe much to the folk songs of the Han, the so-called *yüeh-fu* or Music Bureau songs that will be discussed in Chapter IV. It is very doubtful, however, that they are actual songs of the people; rather they seem to be reworkings of earlier folk song material, executed by a member or members of the educated class. The anonymity of the author has been explained by the fact that, as mentioned earlier, the five-character *shih* form seems originally to have been associated with the lower classes, and it is presumed that a scholar of the second century A.D., while proud to append his name to some stuffy piece of arch-aism in four-character meter, would have preferred not to have it linked with anything in the new form.

Evidence of the upper-class origin of the poems, at least in their present form, is to be found not only in the references to carriages, banquets, and official careers, but in the way in which they allude to or draw upon earlier works of Chinese literature such as the *Book of Odes* or the *Ch'u Tz'u,* works which, unless we have greatly underestimated the degree to which a knowledge of such literature was diffused in Han society, would be familiar only to members of the educated class. But let us reserve further general comment for later, and turn now to an examination of the poems themselves.

The numbers refer to the order of the poems in the original set of nineteen.

1. On and on, going on and on,
   away from you to live apart,
   ten thousand li and more between us,
   each at opposite ends of the sky.
   The road I travel is steep and long;
   who knows when we meet again?
   The Hu horse leans into the north wind;
   the Yüeh bird nests in southern branches:
   day by day our parting grows more distant;
   day by day robe and belt dangle looser.
   Shifting clouds block the white sun;
   the traveler does not look to return.
   Thinking of you makes one old;
   years and months suddenly go by.
   Abandoned, I will say no more
   but pluck up strength and eat my fill.

✎ Lines 1–2: Because of the lack of indication of tense or number and the frequent omission of any expressed subject, so typical of classical Chinese, the original poems are in most cases vaguer than it is possible to be in English translation. Here it is unclear whether it is the speaker who is going away or the other party; I have translated as though it were the speaker. "To live apart," literally "living separation," the opposite of a separation caused by death, is a phrase that derives from the sixth of "The Nine Songs" in the *Ch'u Tz'u*, the line which in Hawkes's translation reads "No sorrow is greater than the parting of the living."[2] Because of this earlier usage of the phrase, it is probable that the separation here is one of husband and wife or lovers, though nothing in the poem rules out other types of separation, e.g., the separation of friends or of ruler and loyal minister.

Lines 3–4: Earlier poetry and prose had been content to express the idea of great distance by the phrase "one thousand li," but with Chinese expansion into Korea and southeast China and increased knowledge of the states of Central Asia, this no doubt came to seem inadequate. For the Han people, with their penchant for hyperbole, nothing less than "ten thousand li or more" would do. A li is approximately one third of a mile. The *Huai-nan Tzu* (sec. 4), a work compiled shortly before 122 B.C., incidentally, gives the dimensions of the

2 David Hawkes, *Ch'u Tz'u: Songs of the South*, p. 41.

"area within the four seas," that is, the civilized world, as 28,000 li east to west and 26,000 li north to south.

Lines 7–8: An example of perfect, if rather naïve, verbal parallelism. Hu, a general term for the area north of China from Korea west to Tibet, is paralleled by Yüeh, a designation for the area around the mouth of the Yangtze, a region which, in earlier centuries at least, was looked on as the southernmost limit of civilization. So the two place names serve as a concretization of the "ten thousand li or more" in the line above, translating its vague dimensions into specific geographic terms. But the lines are undoubtedly meant to have some further symbolic meaning within the context of the poem. Earlier or contemporary usages of the same or very similar expressions seem to be intended to illustrate the way in which each creature enjoys or longs for the environment it is accustomed to. Thus to the Hu horse of the Mongolian plains, the cold north wind is welcome; he "leans into it," or, if we follow a variant reading of the text, he "neighs," presumably with delight; while the Yüeh bird is most content to nest in the southern branches which it knows. But here this meaning seems inappropriate. More likely the poet is using the northern horse and the southern bird as symbols of the parted lovers, emphasizing not only the great distance that separates them but the hardship of the man's lot as he travels through the barbarian wastes, perhaps serving in one of the border wars that summoned so many of the Han men from their homes, while his wife or sweetheart waits for him like a patient bird in the sunny homeland of the south.

Lines 9–10: Thus far the poem has followed a single rhyme—the rhyme words, in modern pronunciation, come out in romanized form as *li, yai, chih, chih;* here the rhyme changes, the remaining rhyme words being *huan, fan, wan, fan.* Up to this point, the increasing distance in space and time that parts the lovers has been emphasized; here we are presented with a concrete result of this separation: the person or persons involved grow thinner and thinner through worry and longing. It is impossible to say for certain which party grows thin, the traveler or the one left behind; perhaps the statement is meant to apply to both. But commentators quote a couplet from an early *yüeh-fu* fok song:

Leaving home, day by day I go farther away,
robe and belt day by day grow more loose;

which suggests that it applies to the traveler.

Lines 11–12: *Fou-yün,* floating or shifting clouds, have a wide range of connotations in Chinese prose and poetry. They may stand for something unsubstantial, vain, or fleeting; or, conversely, for that which is free and unfettered. In conjunction with the sun they often represent evil ministers who obscure the light of the ruler. Here, however, this political connotation seems inappropriate (unless we are prepared to read the poem as the complaint of a minister who has been banished from his ruler's side). The clouds would seem rather to stand for the changeability of fortune, the variability of the weather that accompanies the journey and the passage of time, particularly the change from the bright sunny weather of the past, before the lovers were parted, to the clouds of the present and future. Some commentators, bent upon an even more precise interpretation of the symbolism, would make the clouds represent a "new love" in the life of the man, which has appeared to cloud his memories of an earlier devotion and happiness. The second line of the couplet may mean either that the traveler has given up hope of being able to return, or that he no longer possesses the will to return, depending on whether we take the clouds to be mere external obstacles that bar his way home, or see them as a more subtle and sinister force that has insinuated itself into his mind and blotted out all attachments to the past.

Lines 13–14: Here the passage of time, which has been stated in the "day by day" of lines 9 and 10 and implied in the image of the drifting clouds passing over the sun, is made the subject of the statement: thinking or longing for the absent one has the effect of actually speeding up the aging process, bringing one to premature senility. Time not only passes, but passes "suddenly," at more than normal pace. We have moved from an objective description of the circumstances of separation, and the physical effects they entail, to a subjective realm where passage of time and the aging of the body, processes that one would suppose to be invariable for all men, are in fact accelerated by the grief and longing of the individual.

Lines 15–16: Someone has been abandoned but determines to say no more— the poem, or parts of it, have been made up of the complaints of the abandoned one, who vows now to desist from speaking further. With the last line, interpretations diverge sharply because of the lack of pronouns in the original. It may be read as "I hope that *you* will pluck up strength and eat your fill"—i.e., forget about me—the noble, self-sacrificing interpretation favored by older commentators; or as "*I* will pluck up strength and eat my fill" (and to hell with you!). Since I cannot be as ambiguous as the original and still make sense in English, I have had to make my choice explicit, but the reader is of course free to differ with it if he chooses.

The problem of the over-all interpretation of the poem remains: that is, if we grant that it concerns the separation of husband and wife or lover and beloved (and not that of fond friends or subject and sovereign), then which lines apply to which party? Is the first half of the poem a description of the wandering husband or lover, and the second half the words of the abandoned wife? Or is the entire poem written from the point of view of one party, the wife *imagining* her husband traveling "on and on," or the husband *imagining* that his wife is saying "I've been abandoned!"? This we can probably never decide, nor should we try too hard to do so.

The poem is built up of a series of anguished utterances, broken by images (the Hu horse, the shifting clouds), probably metaphorical but not always necessarily so, which suggest the plight of the speakers. The beauty and power of the original derive from the fact that it avoids making explicit the speaker, his sex, or his location. The terrible fact of separation has fallen upon two people and so deranged their lives that time and place no longer retain their customary meaning. The statement of the lovers' predicament takes on urgency precisely because it is not lucidly or reasonably made, but is fraught with incoherence and ambiguity. It is important to note that, although the poem expresses sadness, and does so with great poignancy, such words as "grief," "sorrow," or "sadness" never appear. The poet does not *name* emotions, but calls them into being, a sure indication of the quality of his art.

2. Green green, river bank grasses,
   thick thick, willows in the garden;
   plump plump, that lady upstairs,
   bright bright, before the window;
   lovely lovely, her red face-powder;
   slim slim, she puts out a white hand.
   Once I was a singing-house girl,
   now the wife of a wanderer,
   a wanderer who never comes home—
   It's hard sleeping in an empty bed alone.

The poem requires little comment other than to note the way in which, as so often in Chinese poetry, the poet begins his description by viewing the scene from a distance, then moves closer and closer to pick out the details, until his attention is fixed upon a single small object, the slim white hand of the lady. The first six lines display great boldness in the use of reduplicated adjectives, six in a row. I have translated the last four lines as though they were the words of the lady, though they could as well be a continuation of the poet's voice.

3. Green green the cypress on the ridge,
   stones heaped about in mountain streams:

between heaven and earth our lives rush past
like travelers with a long road to go.
Let this measure of wine be our merriment;
value it highly, without disdain.
I race the carriage, whip the lagging horses,
roam for pleasure to Wan and Lo.
Here in Lo-yang, what surging crowds,
capped and belted ones chasing each other;
long avenues fringed with narrow alleys,
the many mansions of princes and peers.
The Two Palaces face each other from afar,
paired towers over a hundred feet tall.
Let the feast last forever, delight the heart—
then what grief or gloom can weigh us down?

◁ Lines 1–2: The cypress, along with the pine, figures often in Chinese literature as a symbol of longevity or changelessness, e.g., *Chuang Tzu*, sec. 5: "Of
those that receive life from the earth, the pine and cypress alone are best—they
stay as green as ever in winter or summer." The stones in the second line
presumably represent a similar concept, that of durability. Both the cypress and
stones serve as contrast to man and his fleeting life.

Lines 7–8: The Eastern Han had its capital at Lo-yang. The city of Wan,
southeast of Lo-yang, was renowned for its splendor and, because it was the
home of the founder of the Eastern Han, Emperor Kuang-wu, was honored
with the title of Southern Capital.

Lines 13–14: The Two Palaces are those of the emperor and of the heir
apparent situated in the northern and southern sectors of the city respectively.
The city was laid out in a grid of broad avenues from which branched numerous
smaller alleyways.

4. We hold a splendid feast today,
   a delight barely to be told in words.
   Strike the lute, raise joyful echoes,
   new notes of ghostly beauty.
   Let the talented sing fine phrases;
   he who knows music will understand.
   One in mind, we share the same wish,
   though the thought within remains unspoken:
      Man lives out his little sojourn,
      scudding by like a swirl of dust.

Why not whip up your high-stepping horses,
be first to command the road to power?
What profit to stay poor and unhonored,
floundering forever in bitterness!

Songs were a regular part of the entertainment at a Han banquet and many of the song texts from the period contain a section in which the singer speaks directly to the diners, urging them to drink and be merry. We know too that a melancholy tone was one of the most admired qualities in the music of the time, so it is not surprising to find this poem, which begins with a description of a feast, ending on a note of despair and cynicism.

5. Northwest the tall tower stands,
   its top level with floating clouds,
   patterned windows webbed in lattice,
   roofs piled three stories high.
   From above, the sound of strings and song;
   what sadness in that melody!
   Who could play a tune like this,
   who but the wife of Ch'i Liang?
   The clear *shang* mode drifts down the wind;
   halfway through, it falters and breaks,
   one plucking, two or three sighs,
   longing, a grief that lingers on—
   It is not the singer's pain I pity,
   but few are those who understand the song!
   If only we could be a pair of calling cranes,
   beating wings, soaring to the sky!

Lines 7–8: Ch'i Liang, a man of the state of Ch'i, was killed in battle in 550 B.C. According to legend, his grief-stricken wife committed suicide by throwing herself into the Tzu River. She seems to have been the subject of several early songs or stories, and is often depicted as playing a lute just before her death. In one version of the legend, her pitiful cries cause the city wall to collapse.

Lines 9–10: *Shang* is one of the five modes or keys of traditional Chinese music, that associated with autumn, hence the epithet "clear." The association with autumn also suggests sadness and decay.

As in #2, the description moves from a distant view of the tower to a more detailed inspection, then in line 5 switches from visual to aural perception. With the phrase *chih-yin,* "one who understands the song," in line 14, the poet turns from a recording of an apparently private and particular sorrow to a general statement upon the unhappy fate of man, his seeming inability to establish communication with his fellow man, to find a true friend, someone who "understands his song." In the last couplet the poet expresses the wish that he and the singer could somehow flee from the "tall tower" of life, invoking the winging birds that throughout Chinese literature are the symbol of escape and freedom.

7. Clear moon brightly shining in the night,
   crickets chirring by eastern walls;
   the jade bar points to early winter;
   crowding stars, how thick their ranks!
   White dew soaks the wild grasses,
   cycle of the seasons swiftly changing;
   autumn locusts cry among the trees;
   dark swallows, where did they go?
   Once we were students together;
   you soared on high, beating strong wings,
   no longer recalling the hand of friendship;
   you've left me behind like a forgotten footprint.
   Southern Winnow, Dipper in the north,
   Draught Ox that will not bear a yoke—
   truly, with no rock to underpin them,
   what good are empty names?

Lines 1–2: The cricket is mentioned in the *Odes* (e.g., #114) as a harbinger of the cold. Here it is called *ts'u-chih* or "hurry with the weaving!" because its song reminds the women of the house that they must get on with their weaving before winter comes.

Lines 3–4: The "jade bar" seems to refer to the handle of the Big Dipper, whose position now indicates the approach of winter.

Lines 13–14: An allusion to *Odes, #203,* the lines:

Bright shines that Draught Ox
but one yokes it to no wagon; ...
South there is the Winnow
but it can't be used to sift with;

north there is the Dipper
but no wine or sauce it ladles.

The Draught Ox, Winnow, and other constellations of Chinese astronomy
mentioned in the poem, though bearing useful-sounding names, are in fact as
worthless as the friendship of the fellow student to whom the poet addresses
his bitter reproach.

8. Frail frail, lone-growing bamboo,
   roots clasping the high hill's edge;
   to join with my lord now in marriage,
   a creeper clinging to the moss.
   Creepers have their time to grow,
   husband and wife their proper union.
   A thousand miles apart, we made our vow,
   far far—mountain slopes between us.
   Thinking of you makes one old;
   your canopied carriage, how slow its coming!
   These flowers sadden me—orchis and angelica,
   petals unfurled, shedding glory all around;
   if no one plucks them in blossom time
   they'll wilt and die with the autumn grass.
   But if in truth you will keep your promise,
   how could *I* ever be untrue?

It is not clear whether the couple in the poem are merely engaged,
or have already married and are now separated. The latter interpretation is suggested by the depth of the woman's love, which,
theoretically at least, should not exist before marriage under the
old system of arranged matches, and the fact that in the last line she
refers to herself in the original as "your humble maid servant," a
term customarily used by wives. The mention of the "canopied
carriage," however, suggests that she is still waiting for the man to
fetch her in marriage, and the flower images likewise imply virginity.

9. In the garden a strange tree grows,
   from green leaves a shower of blossoms bursting.
   I bend the limb and break off a flower,
   thinking to send it to the one I love.

Fragrance fills my breast and sleeves,
but the road is far—it will never reach you.
Why is such a gift worth the giving?
Only because I remember how long ago we parted.

10. Far far away, the Herdboy Star;
    bright bright, the Lady of the River of Heaven;
    slim slim, she lifts a pale hand,
    clack clack, plying the shuttle of her loom,
    all day long—but the pattern's never finished;
    welling tears fall like rain.
    The River of Heaven is clear and shallow;
    what a little way lies between them!
    only the span of a single brimming stream—
    They gaze and gaze and cannot speak.

The Herdboy has already appeared in #7 under the name Draught
Ox. Here the constellation, once seen as an ox, is thought to be a
young cowherd who is in love with the Weaving Lady, another
constellation on the other side of the Milky Way or River of Heaven.
According to legend, the lovers are doomed to year-long separation
except on the night of the seventh day of the seventh lunar month,
when sympathetic magpies form a bridge for them across the
stream of stars. The Herdboy constellation corresponds roughly to
Aquila, the Weaving Lady to Vega and the Lyre.

11. I turn the carriage, yoke and set off,
    far far, over never-ending roads.
    In the four directions, broad plain on plain;
    east wind shakes the hundred grasses.
    Among all I meet, nothing of the past;
    what can save us from sudden old age?
    Fullness and decay, each has its season;
    success—I hate it, so late in coming!
    Man is not made of metal or stone;
    how can he hope to live for long?
    Swiftly he follows in the wake of change;
    a shining name—let that be the prize!

13. I drive my carriage from the Upper East Gate,
    scanning the graves far north of the wall;
    silver poplars, how they whisper and sigh;
    pine and cypress flank the broad lane.
    Beneath them, the ancient dead,
    black black there in their long night,
    sunk in sleep beneath the Yellow Springs;
    a thousand years pass but they never wake.
    Times of heat and cold in unending succession,
    but the years Heaven gives us are like morning dew.
    Man's life is brief as a sojourn;
    his years lack the firmness of metal or stone.
    Ten thousand ages come and go
    but sages and wise men discover no cure.
    Some seek long life in fasts and potions;
    many end by poisoning themselves.
    Far better to drink fine wine,
    to clothe ourselves in soft white silk!

The Upper East Gate has been identified as the northernmost
of the three gates in the east wall of Lo-yang. The graves are those
situated on the hill called Pei-mang northeast of the city; see p. 39.
The Yellow Springs is the land of the dead. The reference to pois-
oning is deadly serious; many eminent men, including emperors,
brought illness or death on themselves by drinking "longevity
medicines" containing mercury and other dangerous ingredients.

15. Man's years fall short of a hundred;
    a thousand years of worry crowd his heart.
    If the day is short and you hate the long night,
    why not take the torch and go wandering?
    Seek out happiness in season;
    who can wait the year to come?
    Fools who cling too fondly to gold
    earn no more than posterity's jeers.
    Prince Ch'iao, that immortal man—
    small hope we have of matching him!

Wang-tzu Ch'iao or Prince Ch'iao, who appears in early texts simply as a man who lived a long time, later becomes an important figure in the cult of the *hsien* or immortal spirits and many legends cluster around his name. The poet-scholar Ts'ai Yung (131–92) describes a grave and shrine dedicated to him to which, in 165, the emperor sent his personal representative to perform sacrifices, so his worship must have played a role of some significance in Han times.

17. First month of winter: cold air comes,
    north winds sharp and cruel.
    I have many sorrows, I know how long the night is,
    looking up to watch the teeming ranks of stars.
    Night of the fifteenth: a bright moon full;
    twentieth night: toad and hare wane.
    A traveler came from far away,
    put a letter into my hand;
    at the top it spoke of "undying remembrance,"
    at the bottom, of "parting long endured."
    I tucked it away inside my robe;
    three years—not a word has dimmed.
    With whole heart I offer my poor love,
    fearful you may not see its worth.

Line 6: The dark and light areas on the surface of the moon were interpreted as the outlines of a toad and a hare who inhabit the moon.

Looking back at the poems as a whole, we note that they are dominated by a tone of brooding melancholy. The songs of the *Book of Odes* had often complained of hardship and sorrow, but they were for the most part complaints over specific human ills that presumably were capable of being remedied. With the poems of the *Ch'u Tz'u*, a more generalized air of grief was introduced into Chinese literature, and it is this air that pervades the "Nineteen Old Poems," expressed here for the first time in the new five-character *shih* form. We are not told who the people of the poems are nor, in most cases, what particular grievances beset them; we know only that, as men, they are all victims of the passing of time, the changeability of fortune, and the dire inevitability of death. The "cures" that may exist for these ills are only feebly offered—enjoy life, join in the race for power, strive for the immortality conferred by a "shining name"—and one possible avenue of escape that so many men of the time pinned their hopes upon, that of discovering a path to immortality through drugs and occult practices, is held up to ridicule. In the end, we must resign ourselves to the realization that existence is by definition sorrowful.

The ruling house of the Han, after a period of eclipse, regained power in 25. The capital was moved from Ch'ang-an in the west to Lo-yang in the east, and the era known as the Eastern Han began. The restoration for a while seemed to have imbued the dynasty with new life and rescued it from the maladies that had earlier laid it low. Philosophers such as Wang Ch'ung (27–92?) lauded the new era, and the scholar-poets Pan Ku (32–92) and Chang Heng (78–139) composed lengthy descriptive poems in the *fu* or rhyme-prose form in which they compared the old capital at Ch'ang-an with the new one at Lo-yang, hopefully demonstrating to their readers the superiority of the latter. But such efforts to convince men that they had never had it so good constitute in effect evidence that many felt they had. This conviction seems to have grown as the dynasty once more fell prey to the ills that had formerly debilitated it: the usurpation of power by eunuchs and the maternal relatives of the emperor, the growing autonomy of the provincial landlords, and the weakening of the central administration. Life at court was marked by intrigue and uncertainty and scholar-officials who one day enjoyed great favor might on the next face house arrest or execution. As conditions continued to worsen in the second century A.D., men of intelligence and learning came to recognize that the imperial system, for reasons they were not always sure of, was faltering badly. There was a high degree of material comfort, even luxury, at least among the ruling class, but it was constantly threatened by the uncertainties of official life and the growing lawlessness of society. The poverty of the common people, the hardships inflicted upon them by military conscription and the exactions of rapacious officials are reflected in the *yüeh-fu* songs and ballads of the period. The "Nineteen Old Poems" reflect rather the carriages and fine clothing, the mansions and entertainments of the upper classes, the affluence that meant so much because it could be so quickly snatched away. And they reflect the despair of men who, having experienced great luxury, know that it is of no solace to the soul, who look out upon a landscape that, for all its material grandeurs, is a moral and spiritual wilderness. Anonymous voices speaking to us from a shadowy past, they sound a note of sadness that is to dominate the poetry of the centuries that follow.

# III

# CHIEN-AN AND THE NEW
# REALISM

*Straight as a bowstring—die by the road;*
*crooked as a fishhook—get to be a lord.*

ぴ

THE "NINETEEN OLD POEMS" are anonymous works of uncertain
date that, against the background of a generalized landscape, set
forth the sorrows of unnamed lovers or air the grievances of men
whose identity can only be guessed at. With the next group of
poems to be discussed these clouds of anonymity part dramatically
and we are faced with works that are not only from the hand of
known writers, but also in many cases deal with actual historical
events and can often be dated by the exact year and month of composition. They are works, finally, that share a common tone of
realism, confronting the reader with the bare, often ugly facts of
life as the poet saw it, from the tedium of office work to the horrors
of war and famine and the hateful finality of death. The product of
men who for the most part flourished in the last period of Han

On Ts'ao Chih, leading poet of the Chien-an period, see Hans H. Frankel,
"Fifteen Poems by Ts'ao Chih: an Attempt at a New Approach," *Journal of the
American Oriental Society*, 84, no. 1, (Jan/March 1964); and David Roy, "The
Theme of the Neglected Wife in the Poetry of Ts'ao Chih," *Journal of Asian
Studies*, 19, no. 1 (1959). Translations of Chien-an poetry will be found in J. D.
Frodsham and Ch'eng Hsi, *An Anthology of Chinese Verse: Han Wei Chin and the
Northern and Southern Dynasties*; and Waley, *Chinese Poems*.

THE QUOTATION ABOVE IS A CHILDREN'S RHYME, 2D CENTURY A.D.

history, that known by the era name Chien-an, which lasted from 196 to 220, they include some of the finest early works in the five-character *shih* form.

Realism is a tricky word, and before proceeding to the particular group of poems at hand it may be useful to make a few general remarks about the types and degree of reality to be found in Chinese poetry as a whole. Chinese poetry, particularly that in the *shih* form, customarily shuns abstractions or overt philosophizing and seeks expression instead through a succession of images, most often drawn from the natural world. Since, as Graham has remarked, the Chinese is "the world's most sensible and temperate poetic tradition" (*Poems of the Late T'ang*, p. 89), these nature images are almost always derived from the real world, or at least are so constructed as to have an air of reality about them. There are various types of "real" landscapes to be found in Chinese poetry. First are the landscapes which, we may assume, are directly before the eyes of the poet as he writes, and from which he selects those particulars of mountain or tree, flower or bird that best evoke the mood he wishes to convey. Again, they may be landscapes of the past which the poet once witnessed and which he now summons from the storehouse of memory, usually for purposes of contrast with the present. Or they may be landscapes of the past never actually seen by him but realistically constructed in his imagination on the basis of what he has learned from history (here the line between real and imaginary begins to blur); such scenes are most common in the type of poem called *huai-ku* or "thinking of antiquity," a meditation on the great or moving events of history and the meaning they may have for the world of the present. Another type of imagined landscape that is real in the sense that it is drawn with all possible verisimilitude is that which the poet imagines to exist in some other place which he or the person he is writing for will see in the future. Landscapes of this type are most common in poems of parting, where several lines are often allotted to descriptions of the place or places which the poet, or the person who is being sent off, will presumably view on his journey or at his destination.

In contrast to all these is the landscape of pure fantasy, which does not pretend to represent anything existing or known to have existed in the real world. A realm of mythical mountains and rivers inhabited by strange birds, animals, and other creatures drawn from folk legend, Taoist, or sometimes Buddhist, lore, it appears most often in poems dealing with or presented to recluses or Taoist adepts, who presumably are able to roam to worlds that are inaccessible to the ordinary mortal. Such lands of fantasy, except when drawn by the hand of a master, tend to be rather dull affairs, furnished century after century with the same old stock of wonders. Perhaps the Chinese, living in a land that stretched from the deserts and tundra of the north to the lush southern seacoast, found such wealth and variety in the real world around them that they felt no need to invent the kind of dream world that served to divert those peoples who inhabited a more monotonous environment.

There is certainly little that is dreamlike in the landscape of the poems we will examine next, unless it is the somber air that surrounds them and at times takes on the terror of a nightmare. The first is a set of two poems by Wang Ts'an (177–217) entitled "Seven Sorrows," the "seven" of the title apparently meaning "many." They were written around A.D. 195 when the poet fled from Ch'ang-an, the so-called Western Capital of the Han, and journeyed south to the semibarbarian region of Ching in the upper Yangtze valley. The troubled conditions mentioned earlier had continued, exacerbated by the outbreak of widespread peasant revolt. Military leaders, claiming as their object the restoration of order, wrested more and more power from the civil government. In 190 the foremost of these, the dictator Tung Cho, forced the emperor to move from Lo-yang to Ch'ang-an, firing the palaces of Lo-yang in his wake. By the time these poems were written, Tung Cho had been assassinated and his rivals for power, the "wolves and tigers" of the second line, were preparing to descend upon the unhappy city, which had already been devastated by disease and starvation.

1. The Western Capital in lawless disorder,
  wolves and tigers poised to prey on it:
  I'll leave this middle realm, be gone,
  go far off to the tribes of Ching.
  Parents and kin face me in sorrow,

friends running after, pulling me back;
out the gate I see
only white bones that strew the broad plain.
A starving woman beside the road
hugs her child, then lays it in the weeds,
looks back at the sound of its wailing,
wipes her tears and goes on alone:
　　I don't even know when my own death will come—
　　how can I keep both of us alive?
Whip up the horses, leave her behind—
I cannot bear to hear such words!
South I climb the crest of Pa-ling,
turning my head to look back on Ch'ang-an.
I know what he meant—that falling spring—
sobbing racks my heart and bowels.

The phrase "that falling spring" refers to *Odes* #153, a song of sorrow and nostalgia for the capital of the Chou dynasty which, like Ch'ang-an, had fallen on evil days. It employs the refrain, "Cold the waters of that falling spring!"

2. Tribes of Ching—that's not my home;
　　how can I stay for long among them?
　　My two-hulled boat climbs the great river;
　　the sun at evening saddens my heart.
　　On mountain and ridge, a last ray of light,
　　slope and embankment in deepening gloom;
　　foxes and badgers hurry to their lairs,
　　flying birds go home to the woods they know.
　　Sharp echoes wake from the roaring torrents,
　　monkeys peer down from the cliffs and cry.
　　Strong winds flap my robes and sleeves,
　　white dew soaks the collar of my cloak.
　　I can't sleep at night alone
　　but get up, put on a robe, and play the lute;
　　strings and paulownia wood know how I feel;
　　for me they make a sorrowful sound.
　　On a journey that has no end,
　　dark thoughts are powerful and hard to bear!

These poems of Wang Ts'an are noteworthy both for their intrinsic beauty and for the important position they occupy among the earliest datable examples of five-character *shih*. Here is a powerful, deadly serious statement being made in the new poetic medium; the poet no longer adopts the anonymity of the folk song but speaks out directly in his own voice, telling of his particular grievances at a specific point in time and space. The first poem alternates between symbolic and realistic imagery; the wolves and tigers, as we have seen, are metaphors for the evil and bloodthirsty contenders for power; the kin and friends, and particularly the starving woman, are as starkly real as anything in all Chinese literature; while the "falling spring" of the final couplet takes us back to symbolism again, this time drawn from a specific source, the *Book of Odes*. In the second poem, we have a more subtle and sophisticated blending of realistic and symbolic images. The description of the river journey is in some ways similar to accounts of journeys found in poems in the *fu* form of the Han period, and no doubt Wang Ts'an, himself a writer of *fu*, drew upon the techniques developed in the older form. But the *fu* tend to be exhaustive in their descriptions, to offer copious lists of tree or bird or animal names in which, because of their very richness, the symbolism of the individual image becomes obliterated and one is left with what might be called image clusters or aggregates. The *shih*, on the other hand, as we see in this journey passage by Wang Ts'an, is highly selective; we are given only those particular details of the landscape that for some reason strike the poet as most meaningful, and which are likely to carry the greatest wealth of symbolic associations. The whole poem is at once a realistic description of the poet's journey up the Yangtze in his catamaran or "two-hulled boat," and the sights that confront him along the way; and a presentation, through such symbols as the setting sun, the flying birds who, in contrast to the poet, are returning to their home, or the crying monkeys, of the poet's mood of loneliness and deepening despair.

The next poem is by the man who, in these turbulent years, eventually emerged as the most powerful military leader in northern China, Ts'ao Ts'ao (155–220). Even allowing for the flattery of official accounts, Ts'ao Ts'ao seems to have possessed considerable

learning and a fine literary sense, and is noted for his poems in the
*yüeh-fu* or ballad style, which he himself is supposed to have set to
music. He is the only writer of the period who succeeded in infusing
the old four-character meter with any vitality, mainly because he
discarded the archaic diction customarily associated with it and
employed the ordinary poetic language of his time. The poem to be
quoted here, however, is in five-character form. Entitled " Song on
Enduring the Cold," it was probably written early in 206, when
Ts'ao Ts'ao was crossing the T'ai-hang Mountains of northern
Shansi to attack a rival.

The Han period *yüeh-fu* ballads, as well as the folk songs of the
*Book of Odes,* often described the hardships of military service, usually
from the point of view of the disgruntled common soldier. Ts'ao
Ts'ao here takes up the same theme. But he writes neither as the
leader of the campaign nor as a member of the rank and file; rather
he seems to give voice to the complaints of the entire army as it
stumbles over the bleak mountain trails. As in Wang Ts'an's river
journey, the description is at once harshly realistic and rich in
symbolic overtones, and ends, as did Wang's first poem, with
an allusion to a song in the *Book of Odes* that deals with a similar
situation, thus linking the poem to the literary heritage of the
past.

North we climb the T'ai-hang Mountains;
the going's hard on these steep heights!
Sheep Gut Slope dips and doubles,
enough to make the cartwheels crack.

Stark and stiff the forest trees,
the voice of the north wind sad;
crouching bears, black and brown, watch us pass;
tigers and leopards howl beside the trail.

Few men live in these valleys and ravines
where snow falls thick and blinding.
With a long sigh I stretch my neck;
a distant campaign gives you much to think of.

Why is my heart so downcast and sad?
All I want is to go back east,
but waters are deep and bridges broken;
halfway up, I stumble to a halt.

Dazed and uncertain, I've lost the old road,
night bearing down but nowhere to shelter;
on and on, each day farther,
men and horses starving as one.

Shouldering packs, we snatch firewood as we go,
chop ice to use in boiling our gruel—
That song of the Eastern Hills is sad,
a troubled tale that fills me with grief.

Eastern Hills: *Odes* #156, a song describing the hardships of a military campaign.

The next two poems are by Ts'ao Ts'ao's younger son Ts'ao Chih (192–232), the first major figure in the new *shih* tradition and one of the two or three greatest poets of the pre-T'ang period. Wang Ts'an's poem quoted above described Ch'ang-an, the Western Capital of the Han; this one deals with Lo-yang, the Eastern Capital. As mentioned earlier, the Lo-yang palaces had been burned by Tung Cho in 190 and the city had suffered terribly in the civil strife that ensued. The poem is the first of two entitled "Written on Parting from Mr. Ting"; the exact date of composition is uncertain.

On foot I climb Pei-mang Slope,
looking far off at Lo-yang's hills:
Lo-yang—how still and desolate,
palaces and chambers all gutted and charred,
every wall and fence row gaping and torn;
thorns and brambles reach up to the sky.
No sight of the old men who used to be;
all I meet are unknown youths.
I try to pick a foothold but no path goes through;
overgrown fields lie unplowed.

The wanderer has been so long from home
he no longer recalls the grid of streets.
The plains about—how bleak and bare,
a thousand li and no smoke of cooking fires.
Thinking of the place I used to live,
my breath chokes up and will not let me speak.

The second poem of Ts'ao Chih to be quoted is, like many Chinese poems, prefaced by an introduction which describes the circumstances under which it was composed. Ordinarily these introductions or *hsü* are added by the poet himself; in this case there is some doubt about the authorship of the *hsü*, but the facts which it records fit well with what is known from other sources. The poem is in seven sections and is often regarded as a seven-poem sequence. Most of the sections are connected by what Hawkes calls "linking interaction," a device used as early as the *Book of Odes*, in which the phrase at the end of the last line of one section is repeated in the opening line of the next section. I will quote the introduction and explain its contents before proceeding to the poem itself.

"Presented to Piao, the Prince of Pai-ma. *Huang-ch'u* 4th year (A.D. 223), 5th month: the Prince of Pai-ma, the Prince of Jen-ch'eng, and I together went to attend court at the capital on the occasion of the seasonal gathering. After we had reached Lo-yang, the Prince of Jen-ch'eng passed away. In the 7th month, the Prince of Pai-ma and I prepared to return to our territories. Presently, however, those in charge of such matters decided that in returning to our fiefs it was proper that we should stop at separate places along the road. I was vexed and grieved at this, for it meant that in the space of a few days we had to take leave of each other for a long time to come. Herein I have laid bare my feelings in farewell to the Prince, making a poem of my resentment."

The Prince of Jen-ch'eng was Ts'ao Chang, an older brother of the poet; the Prince of Pai-ma was Ts'ao Piao, a younger half brother. All three brothers had journeyed to Lo-yang to pay their respects to their eldest brother, Ts'ao P'ei, who in 220 had ascended the throne as ruler of a new dynasty, the Wei. Later report claims that the emperor poisoned Ts'ao Chang, but the plague raged in

Lo-yang at this time and he may well have died of natural causes.
Both Ts'ao Chih and Ts'ao Piao had to travel east to return to their
respective fiefs, but the emperor evidently wished them to travel
separately so they would have no opportunity to plot against him.
It is recorded that there were heavy rains in the Lo-yang area in the
summer of 223.

Audience with the emperor, Hall of Inherited Brilliance;
now to return to my old domain,
in clear dawn departing the imperial city,
at sundown past Shou-yang Hill.
The Yi and Lo are broad and deep;
I want to cross over but there's no bridge.
The bobbing boat leaps giant waves;
I hate the longness of this eastern road,
look back fondly at the city gates,
stretching my neck, within me thoughts of sorrow.

Great Valley—how vast and wild,
mountain trees thick in blue blue gloom;
endless rains turn the trail to mud,
swollen streams spill to left and right.
The road breaks midway, ruts washed out;
I veer into a new path, drive up the tall hill,
a long slope that climbs to clouds and sun,
my black horses yellowing with strain.

Yellow with strain, they still push on,
but my thoughts are tangled fast in gloom;
tangled in gloom—what do I think of?
That near and loved one far away.
At first we thought to keep each other company;
it changed—we couldn't go together.
Kites and owls screech at the carriage yoke,
jackals and wolves lurk by the way;
blue flies with their muck turn white into black,
glib talk and lies put kinsmen apart.
I want to go back but the road is cut off;
reins in hand, I halt in indecision.

Undecided, but how can I stay?
Thoughts of you will never be done.
Autumn wind brings a subtle chill,
cold cicadas cry by my side;
upland moors—how bleak and bare,
the white sun all at once lost in the west.
Homing birds head for the tall trees,
*p'ien-p'ien* go their swift wings flapping;
a lone animal seeks its mates,
grass in its jaws, no time to eat.
Moved by these creatures, my thoughts are dragged down;
I strike my heart and give a great sigh.

A great sigh—what will that do?
Heaven's decrees are set against me!
What good to think of my mother's son?
Once gone, his body returns no more,
his lonely soul on wing to old haunts,
his coffin at rest in the capital.
The living—how quickly they pass,
their bodies rotting away in death.
Man lives his single age,
gone like morning dew that dries.
The year rests between Mulberry and Elm,
a shadow, an echo, not to be pursued.
To think I am not made of metal or stone,
and in an instant—it grieves my heart.

Grieves my heart and moves my soul—
but lay it aside and say no more!
A brave man's eyes are set on the four seas;
ten thousand miles are next door for him.
Where love and bounty are not lacking,
distance will bring us closer each day.
Why must we share quilt and curtain
before we can bare our deepest concerns?
Fretting till you make yourself sick and feverish—
this is mere childish, womanish love!

Yet suddenly parted from flesh and blood,
can I help brooding in bitterness and pain?

Bitterness and pain—what are my thoughts?
The decrees of Heaven bear no trust.
Useless to seek the ranks of immortals;
Master Sung has deceived us too long!
Change and mishap are here in a moment;
who can live out his hundred years?
We part—it may be forever;
when will I clasp your hand again?
Prince, be cautious of that worthy body;
together let us live to see the white-haired years.
I wipe back the tears and take my long road;
the brush I hold bids you farewell for now.

✦ "Mulberry and Elm": constellations, here representing the closing of the
year and, by extension, of one's lifetime.

Like so many great Chinese poems, this one takes the form of a
letter in verse, a long, deeply felt message from Ts'ao Chih to his
younger brother Ts'ao Piao. The skillful handling of form and
structure and the way in which the tempo and focus of the poem are
constantly varied show with what astonishing rapidity the five-
character *shih* form matured in the hands of the poets of the late
second and early third centuries. The poem is particularly noteworthy for the way in which moods of despair and hope alternate,
a contrast to the unrelieved gloom of so many works of later
centuries.

The poem begins with two sections telling of Ts'ao Chih's
departure from the capital after his audience with the emperor.
The description, like that in the earlier journey passages we have
seen, is realistic but charged with symbolic overtones, expressing
the sorrow and uneasiness of the poet as he leaves the city where
one brother reigns and another lies dead, to return to virtual exile
in the east. The separation of the brothers, who are cut off from each
other by rank, suspicion, and death, is suggested by images of
bridgeless rivers, roads cut off, and obliterating rains. In the third
section Ts'ao Piao, the recipient of the poem, is introduced, the

"near and loved one" whom the poet longs to be with. For a few lines the poem passes over into pure metaphor, kites, owls, jackals, wolves, and blue flies all being conventional symbols for evil or slanderous men at court.

The fourth section may be taken as a continuation of the journey description; but while it is undoubtedly meant to depict the landscape along the way, it is even more highly charged with symbolism, much of it pertaining to the passing of time. This leads, in the fifth section, to thoughts of the dead brother, Ts'ao Chang, the poet recalling his funeral in the capital and musing on the evanescence of life. Having sunk into these gloomy thoughts, he attempts in the sixth section to inject a note of greater calm and resignation, but in the last section his courage once more falters before the grief which separation brings. Here, in his reflections on the brevity of life, he pauses to make specific denial of the possibility, believed in by at least some of his contemporaries, that man can gain immortal life through elixirs. We have already encountered such beliefs in the fifteenth of the "Nineteen Old Poems," where reference was made to a legendary figure called Prince Ch'iao. Here the poet alludes to another famous name in the cult of the immortals, the equally legendary Master Sung or Master of the Red Pine. The poet rallies once more at the very end as he looks forward hopefully to the time when he and his brother may be together again and "live to see the white-haired years," though he must have known that the emperor's suspicious nature, fanned by the slanders of courtiers, made such a future unlikely.

Not all the poetry of this period is both as grim and as personal as the examples quoted so far might suggest. Often, as we shall see in the next chapter, the poets, rather than speak in their own voice, adopted a persona from the folk song tradition, speaking through an anonymous soldier or a woman forsaken by her husband or lover. Other poems, though as personal and realistic as the ones already presented, are less dramatic and forbidding in theme. The next three poems I shall quote deal not with warfare and famine, but with the headaches that come with bureaucratic paperwork and the depression, uneasiness, and suffering induced by a long spell of heavy rain.

The first is by Liu Cheng (d. 217) and bears the title *tsa-shih* or "miscellaneous poem," which I have translated as "Poem without a Category." A great deal of the poetry written at this time, as well as later, was occasional in nature, composed at banquets, outings, or farewell parties, or was addressed to a particular individual and sent with, or in lieu of, a letter. The title *tsa-shih* was applied to poems which did not fit into any of these various categories of occasional poetry but which represent rather the private musings of the poet, introspective, charged with feeling, and at times couched in highly metaphorical language. Liu Cheng was an official in the service of the Ts'ao family who, at the time the poem was written, shortly before 217, were feudal rulers with their capital in the city of Yeh in Honan. The poem begins with the same kind of realistic recording that we have seen in the descriptions of Ch'ang-an and Lo-yang, and then moves for its resolution to the flight symbolism already encountered in the fifth of the "Nineteen Old Poems." Birds as symbols of freedom and escape recur constantly in ancient Chinese culture, from the monstrous *p'eng* bird of *Chuang Tzu* to the feathered immortals of Han art, and poets seem never to tire of voicing a desire to join their happy flocks.

Office work: a wearisome jumble;
ink drafts: a crosshatch of deletions and smears.
Racing the writing brush, no time to eat,
sun slanting down but never a break;
swamped and muddled in records and reports,
head spinning till it's senseless and numb—
I leave off and go west of the wall,
climb the height and let my eyes roam:
square embankments hold back the clear water,
wild ducks and geese at rest in the middle—
Where can I get a pair of whirring wings
so I can join you to bob on the waves?

The second poem, by Fu Hsien (239–94), is entitled "Ruinous Rains" and dates from a somewhat later period. It describes, in the briefest and most concrete terms, the disastrous effect that a period of excessively heavy rain can have upon the economy.

Lift your feet and you sink deeper in the mud!
On market roads, no carts go by.
Orchids and cinnamon sell for the price of garbage,
firewood and grain more precious than bright pearls.

The third poem, also about heavy rains, is by the poet-official Lu
Chi (261–303). Written around 298, it is the second of a set entitled
"Two Poems Presented to the *Shang-shu-lang* Ku Yen-hsien." Both
the poet and his fellow official Ku Yen-hsien were from Wu, the
region of the Yangtze delta, where the rains presumably had the
worst effect.

Off at dawn to service in the walled and storied palace;
rest at evening, back to the officials' lodge.
Shrill thunder blares at midnight,
shafts of swift lightning streak the darkness.
Black clouds oppress the vermilion towers,
rough winds beat on lattice windows.
Streams gush and spill from the long roof gutters,
yellow puddles swallow up the terrace stairs.
Stolid skies mesh and will not break apart,
the broad thoroughfares turn into canals.
Crops are under water in Liang and Ying;
toward Ching and Hsü the homeless peasants drift.
And what, I wonder, of our old home?
There they'll be no better off than fish!

The closing years of the Han, as we have seen, were marked by
rebellion, disorder, famine, and disease. The great empire, that had
endured with only one brief interruption for four hundred years,
fell to pieces, and no one knew how or when it could be put back
together again. As faith in the old political order, and the customs
and beliefs that had sustained it, faltered and gave way before
doubt and despondency, Chinese society seems to have been gripped
by a feeling of terror, to have undergone a massive failure of nerve.
The story is told of a Confucian scholar of the time who, walking
along the road, came upon a packet of money that someone had
dropped. He tied it to a tree where the owner might easily find it and

went on his way, but later, on returning to the spot, he found the whole tree strung with packets of money. The villagers, seeing the first packet hanging there, had supposed that the tree was sacred and were taking no chances of incurring its wrath or being left out of its protection.[1] The Confucian scholar was appalled, for to him their behavior no doubt represented yet another indication of the growing superstition of the time, another blow to the ideals of rationalism and humanism that, at least among the upper classes, had commanded allegiance during the flourishing years of the Han.

Faced with the uncertainty of life in a decaying social order, many men, particularly of the lower classes, turned to Taoist-inspired cults that promised cure of the body's ills and the advent of a happier age. Some began to investigate the teachings of the Buddhist religion, newly introduced from Central Asia, which the Chinese, through a faulty understanding of the concept of karma, mistakenly supposed to be offering them promises of immortality. Others, as we have seen, believed that immortality, or at least a considerable prolongation of the life span, was obtainable through the use of diets, medicines, and occult practices.

For the members of the educated class, however, such escapes were scarcely thinkable. On the whole, though they often expressed the wish that immortality were attainable, they seem to have remained faithful to the old Confucian rationalism, with its agnostic view of the other world. At the same time the wars and outbreaks of strife and pestilence that swept the country brought death to them as swiftly and mercilessly as it did to the most ignorant peasants, and increasingly they felt the longing for some refuge from the scourge of fate. At least some of them—the group we are concerned with here—found a solution of sorts in a concept that goes back to the earliest days of Confucianism, that of the immortality of literature. Man may be cut down in the very prime of life, but if he can leave behind him some enduring work of literature he may still emerge victor in the battle against oblivion.

Nearly all the poems presented in this group so far have been by members of the Ts'ao family or the men who served at their court.

---

[1] *San-kuo-chih,* ch. 11, commentary, biography of Ping Yüan.

Ts'ao Ts'ao and his sons Ts'ao P'ei and Ts'ao Chih were all patrons of learning and literature as well as first-rate poets themselves, and they and the group they gathered about them—particularly the so-called Seven Masters of the Chien-an period, which include Wang Ts'an and Liu Cheng quoted above—wrote some of the finest poetry in the language. And these men took greater pains with their literary endeavors, and were more careful to see that they were preserved, because they were aware that they were writing in the shadow of death. Ts'ao P'ei, in a letter to a friend written around A.D. 215, recalls in the following words the happy life he had lived a few years earlier with his literary associates: "After mulling over the secrets of the Six Classics and wandering at will through the Hundred Philosophers, we found time to squeeze in a little chess, ending with a game of *liu-po*.[2] Lofty discourse delighted our minds, plaintive strings were soothing to the ear. We galloped in haste to the northern ground, feasted with the crowd in the southern hall, floating sweet melons in the clear fountain, dunking crimson plums in its chilly waters. And when the bright sun had gone into hiding, we continued by the glow of the moon. Sharing a single carriage or driving side by side, we were off to outings at the inner gardens, our carriage wheels solemnly turning, attendants following without a sound. A fresh breeze sprang up with the night and melancholy flutes sounded their faint cry. Joy departed and grief came in its place; sorrowful were the thoughts that visited us. I turned to you and said, 'Such joys can never last!' and you and your companions all agreed."[3]

Writing to the same friend in 218, after a particularly severe outbreak of the plague that killed four of the Seven Masters of the Chien-an, Ts'ao P'ei remarks: "In the disease and contagion last year many of my kin and old friends met with disaster—Hsü Kan, Ch'en Lin, Ying Ch'ang, and Liu Cheng, all carried off at one time!... Recently I have been gathering up the writings that these men left behind and putting them all together in a single volume. Looking at the names, I know they are already entered in the registers of the dead, and yet, as I think back over the outings we used to have, I

[2] A game like backgammon played with bamboo dice and ivory pieces.
[3] *Wen hsüan* 42, "Letter to Wu Chih, Magistrate of Chao-ko in Liang."

see these men still in my mind's eye. And now they have all been changed and reduced to stinking earth!" [4]

It was this same keen awareness of the brevity and uncertainty of life that led Ts'ao P'ei to write his *Lun wen* or "Essay on Literature," the first important statement on Chinese literary theory, in which he stressed the immortality of the written word and urged men to devote themselves to the creation of literature while they still had time.

The Ts'ao family usurped the throne from the Han and founded their own dynasty, the Wei, but they were not powerful enough to control all China and the empire split up into three contending states. It was unified briefly in the latter part of the third century but broke apart again, to remain in a state of disunion for almost three centuries more. The wars and intrigues which these shifts of power involved, as well as the outbreaks of disease and famine noted above, took a terrible toll of life, particularly among the literati who were so often caught in the political crossfire. Considering the fearful number of literary men who died, or were put to death, early in their careers, it is hardly surprising that their poetry should at times seem completely gripped by thanatophobia, the morbid fear of death. This is nowhere better illustrated than in the popularity of a type of poem known as *wan-ko* or coffin-puller's song, a title that derives from the dirges sung by the men of Han times as they pulled the hearse to the graveyard. Many men tried their hand at composing poems of this type, sometimes writing from the point of view of the family and mourners accompanying the dead man, sometimes from the point of view of the dead man himself. It is said that people of the time were in the habit of singing such songs at parties and drinking bouts, presumably to keep themselves mindful of the fate that might overtake them at any moment.

Here I will quote two such poems, the first, entitled "Poem in the Form of a Coffin-puller's Song," by Miu Hsi (186–245).

In life I stroll the capital city,
in death I am cast in the midst of the plain.

[4] *Ibid*, "Letter to Wu Chih."

At dawn I step forth from the high hall,
at dusk to lodge beneath the Yellow Springs.
The white sun sinks into the Gulf of Yü,
its chariot halted, its four steeds at rest.
The Creator, for all his godly glory,
cannot restore me to wholeness again!
Body and face slowly losing shape,
teeth and hair bit by bit falling away—
since time began it has been like this for all—
who's the man could ever break away?

◁ "Gulf of Yü": the place where the charioteer of the sun goes to rest at evening.

The second, bearing the same title, is the third of a set of three such poems by the famous poet T'ao Yüan-ming (365–427), of whom I shall have more to say in Chapter V.

A plain of wild grasses, broad and tangled,
white poplars that whisper and sigh;
biting frost of the mid-ninth month:
they are taking me far away from the city.
On four sides no human dwelling,
only the ridge and rise of tall grave mounds.
For me the horses look skyward and neigh,
for me the wind takes on a mournful tone.
The dark chamber, once sealed,
for a thousand years will not see the dawn.

A thousand years it will not see the dawn;
neither worthy nor wise man can force its doors.
Those who just now saw me off
have all gone back, each to his home,
my kin perhaps with a lingering grief,
but the others are finished with their funeral songs.
And what of the one who has departed in death,
body left to merge with the round of the hill?

We have already seen this tendency to brood upon the graveyard and its folk in the thirteenth of the "Nineteen Old Poems" and Ts'ao

Chih's long poem to his brother. Here, however, the theme is presented in its most concentrated form, a kind of studied meditation upon all that is horrible and hopeless about death. The popularity of such poems no doubt owed something to the vogue for Taoism, particularly the writings of Chuang Tzu, which often linger over the ugly and grotesque side of existence in order to free the reader from his bondage to the conventional concepts of joy and sorrow, life and death, and make him see that one is just as desirable as another. But these poems lack the detachment and wry humor that rescue Chuang Tzu and other Taoist writers from morbidity. In a literary tradition noted generally for its restraint and common sense, they display a fascination with death and its attributes that, like the age itself, can best be described as gothic. In the writings of Christian or Buddhist asceticism, such persistent dwelling upon the corruptibility of the flesh serves a purpose, for it directs one's attention to realms that are incorruptible. But here there is no suggestion either that death is somehow sweet, or that it can in any way be escaped or transcended. There is only hopelessness so complete and unvaried that, if the poems were any longer, they would verge upon the intolerable.

# IV

## YÜEH-FU: FOLK AND

## PSEUDO-FOLK SONGS

*When men and women had anything they were grieved*
*or angry about, they got together and made a song,*
*the hungry man singing of a meal, the weary man*
*singing of his task*—HO HSIU

THE *Book of Odes* contains many works that appear to be genuine folk songs, or at least works in a folk song idiom, telling of the delights and tribulations of the common people. Because the anthology, the oldest in the language, was supposed to have been compiled by Confucius and comprises one of the Five Classics, considered the source of all wisdom and truth, it is not surprising that folk songs have occupied an important place in the Chinese poetic tradition.

It is said that the body of songs from which Confucius made his selection had been collected by officials dispatched by the court for that express purpose, the government believing that this was the best way to learn the temper of the people and become acquainted with their complaints. In the *Analects* (XVIII, 9) Confucius is quoted as urging his disciples to study the *Odes* because, among

On the early *yüeh-fu* poetry, see Jean-Pierre Diény, *Aux origines de la poésie classique en Chine*; further translations will be found in Frodsham, *Anthology of Chinese Verse*; Payne, *White Pony*; and Waley, *Chinese Poems*.

THE QUOTATION ABOVE, BY HO HSIU (129–82), IS FROM HIS COMMENTARY ON *Kung-yang chuan*, DUKE HSÜAN 15TH YEAR.

other things, they will "help you to express your grievances"; and many subsequent writers on the *Odes* have praised them for the way in which they voice political criticisms without becoming seditious. The scholars of later times in fact became so engrossed with this view of the *Odes* as primarily a catalogue of political complaints that they read politics into everything, turning even innocent love songs into allegories of the ruler-subject relationship. But, whatever the excesses of their zeal, they were perfectly correct in identifying at least some of the poems as attacks on misrule and injustice, and the protest song thus became established as one of the most respectable of genres.

We should not be surprised to learn, in view of this, that Emperor Wu of the Han, who reigned from 140 to 87 B.C. and was responsible for declaring Confucianism the official creed of the state, set up an office called the Yüeh-fu or Music Bureau, one of whose functions was to collect folk songs from the countryside, as had been done in antiquity, and use them to determine the mood of the populace. It is probably due to Emperor Wu's bureau, and the importance which educated men in general attached to works in the folk song form, that we possess a number of songs, known collectively by the term *yüeh-fu*, which date from Han times. Some of these early ballads use lines of irregular length, varying from two to nine characters; they often employ nonsense syllables. It is said that many of the songs of this period were written to be sung to melodies imported from Central Asia, and these nonsense syllables were presumably used as fillers to make the words fit the tune. Other songs are predominantly or entirely in five-character or seven-character lines and are thus indistinguishable, in line form at least, from the ordinary *shih*.

The folk songs of the *Odes* are, like folk songs everywhere, essentially the tale of the little man, often at the moment when he finds himself in a big mess. But, although the songs have much to say about men and women in their prime, their labors and household chores, their successes and failures in love, their loneliness and despair when war or trouble part them, the songs are curiously reticent on the subject of sickness and old age. Similarly, although marriage is the theme of many songs, children, which are its natural outcome, are barely mentioned, and never, as in later poetry, described in detail. It would appear as though some system of taboos were operating, among either the makers of the songs or their collectors, which prohibited the treatment of such themes.

No such prohibitions seem to have operated in later centuries, however, and the ailing wife, the orphan, or the gray-haired veteran who returns after years of service to his old village are among the most famous figures in the *yüeh-fu* songs of the Han. Love, as in earlier times, continues to be an important theme, sometimes that of unnamed lovers, sometimes of historical or pseudohistorical personages. By far the longest poem of the period, a ballad in five-character form entitled "The Wife of Chiao Chung-ch'ing," which tells of a young couple who are forced by the groom's mother to separate and who eventually commit suicide, is said to have been based upon an actual tragedy of that nature that occurred in the Chien-an period. Many of the songs are meant merely to amuse and entertain, pleasant accompaniment to the banquets and drinking bouts of the well to do, but others, such as those which complain of the hardships of military service or the poverty of the oppressed peasantry, are clearly intended as works of social protest in the old tradition of the *Odes*.

The language of the *yüeh-fu* ballads is on the whole direct, simple, and often very colloquial, which makes them at times extremely difficult to read. As in the *Odes,* birds, plants, insects, and other objects in the natural world are mentioned when their behavior or properties bear some portentous significance for mankind, or when they seem to form a striking parallel or contrast to man's condition. In some cases the key to their presence lies in *paronomasia,* the punning use of an object whose name is homophonous with some common word. The lotus (*lien*), for example, appears in love songs with great frequency because its name suggests the word "beloved" (*lien*), and fish, in addition to being an ancient fertility symbol, may owe something of their popularity to the fact that their name is similar in pronunciation to the word for sexual desire. Aside from these devices, however, the ballads are almost totally innocent of the allusions, similes, metaphors, or other tropes that play such an important part in the poetry of the literati. One famous exception, the striking metaphor that appears in several of the songs:

Thoughts in my heart I cannot speak:
cart wheels inside me turning;

only proves the rule.

These anonymous Han ballads, because they are for the most part
in irregular meters, and because excellent translations are easily
available in the works of Arthur Waley, Robert Payne's anthology
*The White Pony,* and elsewhere, need not be dealt with further here.
I would like instead to turn to some of the imitations of the ballads
written in regular five- or seven-character meter by known poets of
the third century. It was very common for writers of later ages to
compose imitations of the Han folk songs, though such works were
seldom intended to be sung. For the most part, what the poets
imitated were the themes of the early ballads and the simple, lively
idiom in which they were cast. Such imitations generally had two
purposes. One was to express the kind of anger and spirit of protest
that had moved the unknown authors of the original ballads and
hopefully in this way to gain the ear of the authorities. In order to
avoid criticizing the government too openly, the poets customarily
retained the original setting with its characteristic Han names and
places, though the ills they were commenting upon were clearly
contemporary. A second purpose that motivated the poets was the
desire to try their hand at a larger variety of subjects and styles than
those offered by the ordinary occasional poetry of the times, to test
their imaginative power and literary skill by setting aside their
own voice and speaking in that of, say, an old soldier, a starving
peasant, a forsaken wife, or a pampered lady of the harem. The
difficulty encountered in trying to give a fair assessment of these
later poems in *yüeh-fu* style comes from the fact that it is often hard
to determine which of these two purposes was uppermost in the
poet's mind; to decide to what extent he was using the ballad form
to make some important statement of personal belief or feeling, and
to what extent he saw it merely as an opportunity to display his
inventiveness and verbal dexterity.

The first of the ballad imitations I would like to discuss is by Ch'en
Lin, one of the Seven Masters of the Chien-an period, whose death
in the terrible plague epidemic of A.D. 217 we have seen lamented in

Ts'ao P'ei's letter on p. 48. The poem takes its title, "Song: I Watered My Horse at the Long Wall Caves," from the opening line, and uses a mixture of five-character and seven-character lines that skillfully suggests, without actually copying, the metrical irregularity of the old ballads. The subject, the hardships of military service, we have already encountered in Ts'ao Ts'ao's poem in *yüeh-fu* style on p. 38; here the conscript has been assigned to work on the Long Wall or Great Wall on the northern border. Like so many of the ballads, it is highly dramatic and elliptical in form, consisting of exchanges between the soldier, the boss of the labor gang to which he is assigned, and his wife back home, interspersed by brief passages of narrative. We possess one other early poem which takes up the same general theme and bears the same title, which is sometimes listed as an anonymous work and sometimes attributed to the poet Ts'ai Yung (133–92). Its treatment, however, is quite different, focusing almost entirely on the wife, and it lacks the power and starkness of Ch'en Lin's poem. Whether Ch'en wrote his poem as a gesture of protest it is difficult to say. Certainly he lived in an age of almost incessant warfare and, as a courtier in the service of the Ts'ao family, he may have hoped in this way to draw the attention of his patrons to the terrible hardship which military and *corvée* labor service inflicted on the common people, though, as we have seen, Ts'ao Ts'ao was as keenly aware of these hardships as anyone could be. The poem is all the more powerful in that it offers no solution to the ills it describes and refuses even to reveal to us what the final fate of its suffering protagonists may have been.

> I watered my horse at the Long Wall caves,
> water so cold it hurt his bones;
> I went and spoke to the Long Wall boss:
>     "We're soldiers from T'ai-yüan—will you keep us here forever?"
>     "Public works go according to schedule—
>     swing your hammer, pitch your voice in with the rest!"
> A man'd be better off to die in battle
> than eat his heart out building the Long Wall!
> The Long Wall—how it winds and winds,
> winds and winds three thousand li;

here on the border, so many strong boys;
in the houses back home, so many widows and wives.
I sent a letter to my wife:
   "Better remarry than wait any longer—
   serve your new mother-in-law with care
   and sometimes remember the husband you once had."
In answer her letter came to the border:
   "What nonsense do you write me now?
   Now when you're in the thick of danger,
   how could I rest by another man's side!"
[HE] If you bear a son, don't bring him up!
   But a daughter—feed her good dried meat.
   Only *you* can't see, here by the Long Wall,
   the bones of the dead men heaped about!
[SHE] I bound up my hair and went to serve you;
   constant constant was the care of my heart;
   too well I know your borderland troubles;
   and I—can I go on like this much longer?

The next poem, in five-character form, entitled "The Forsaken
Wife," is attributed to Ts'ao Chih, two of whose poems have been
quoted in Chapter III. Some editors treat it as an ordinary *shih*
rather than a *yüeh-fu*, and its sophistication of diction and complex
symbolism are certainly far removed from the simple Han ballads,
but its theme, that of the neglected wife, places it squarely within
the *yüeh-fu* tradition. This is a theme frequently encountered in Ts'ao
Chih's poetry and Chinese critics, accustomed to allegorical interpretation, have taken it as symbolic of the strained relations that
existed between Ts'ao Chih and his eldest brother, Ts'ao P'ei, who
reigned as Emperor Wen of the Wei. Such an interpretation may
add a note of poignancy to the reading of the poem, but it is in no
way necessary to its understanding.

The pomegranate grows in the garden front,
pale green leaves that tremble and turn,
vermilion flowers, flame on flame,
a shimmering glory of light and hue;

light that flares like the ten-colored turquoise,
fit for holy creatures to sport with.
Birds fly down and gather there;
beating their wings, they make sad cries.
Sad cries—what are they for?
Vermilion blossoms bear no fruit.
I beat my breast and sigh long sighs;
the childless one will be sent home.
She with children is a moon that sails the sky;
the childless one, a falling star.
Sky and moon have end and beginning,
but the falling star sinks in spiritless death.
She whose sojourn fails of its rightful goal
falls among tiles and stone.
Dark thoughts well up;
I sigh till the dawn cocks crow,
toss from side to side, sleepless,
rise and wander in the courtyard outside.
I pause and turn to my room again;
chamber curtains swish and sigh;
I lift them and bind my girdle tighter,
stroke the strings of a white wood lute;
fierce and pleading, the tone lingers on,
soft and subtle, plaintive and clear.
I will dry my tears and sigh again;
how could I turn my back on the gods?
The star Chao-yao waits for frost and dew;
why should spring and summer alone be fertile?
Late harvests gather good fruit—
if my lord will only wait with trusting heart!

ㄐ "Chao-yao": first star in the handle of the Big Dipper; when the handle
points west-southwest, it signals the beginning of autumn.

The third of the *yüeh-fu* imitations, by a third-century writer
named Tso Yen-nien, is as forceful and compact as any of the anonymous folk songs of the Han. It is entitled "Call to Arms."

How bitter for these border men!
One year, three calls to arms;
three sons sent to Tun-huang,
two sons in Lung-hsi now;
five sons gone to distant battle,
five wives, every one with child.

The next group of poems to be discussed comprises folk songs
dating roughly from the fourth and fifth century, when south
China was ruled by a succession of native dynasties and the north
was in the hands of foreign invaders. War, appropriately enough,
is one of the major themes, the other being that unfailing preoccupation of man, whether in time of calm or chaos, love.

Many of the folk songs in the *Book of Odes,* though long misin-
terpreted, are in fact songs of love and courtship. Because the
liaisons they described seemed in many cases to be premarital,
condemned by the rules of Confucian morality, the scholar-exegetes
of later times felt compelled to distort or gloss over their meaning
by the use of allegorical interpretations or other lexical sleight of
hand. The *yüeh-fu* ballads of the Han likewise dealt with love but,
in keeping with an age dominated by Confucianism, it was almost
always that of the properly married.

In the period of disunity that followed the Han, however, love songs
like those of the *Book of Odes* appeared again. Perhaps, as traditional
scholars would no doubt claim, their appearance indicates a decline
of public morality due to the temporary waning of Confucian
influence; perhaps it only means that literate men at this time felt
daring enough to record what had existed all along but had earlier
been passed over in silence. Whatever the reason, the impatient
lovers who in the time of the *Odes* had slipped out to a rendezvous
by the city gate or climbed over walls and crept into midnight
chambers once more make their entrance on the poetic scene.

The love songs are brief and usually quite direct. Like the Japanese
*kouta,* which they closely resemble, they rely for their effect upon
simple nature imagery, often indicative of the particular season,
puns and word plays, and an engaging air of sauciness and candor.
Here, for example, is one of extreme simplicity which comes from

northern China and bears a title, " *Ti-ch'ü* Song words," the meaning
of which is uncertain. It is unusual in that it uses a four-character line.

Oh oh—ah ah—
thoughts of you will never end!
Your left arm I used for a pillow,
and when you turned on your side, I turned with you.

The songs I will quote below all use the regular five-character line
and are mostly four lines in length. The first four belong to a category known as " Tzu-yeh Songs." Tzu-yeh was supposed to have
been a professional singing girl of the Eastern Chin dynasty, in the
fourth century, and in the songs that bear her name, one of which
has already been quoted in the Introduction, she speaks with
disarming frankness of the joy of her lover's embraces, complains
of his infidelity, or stations herself boldly before the window,
declaring:

This flimsy skirt so easily blown about—
if it opens a little, I'll blame the spring wind.

The first two songs are in the form of an exchange between a
young man and his love.

1. Out the southern gate at sundown
   I look and see you passing by,
   your lovely face and intricate hairdo,
   fragrant perfume that even now fills the road!

2. The fragrance comes from the scent I wear,
   a lovely face I wouldn't dare claim.
   Heaven's not deaf to a body's pleas—
   that's why it has brought me to you!

3. Cool breezes—I sleep by the open window
   where the light of the setting moon shines in.
   At midnight there are no voices,
   but within my gauze curtains, a pair of smiles.

4. When ice on the pond is three feet thick
   and white snow stretches a thousand miles,

my heart will still be like the pine and cypress,
but your heart—what will it be?

The next song, which bears the title "Ch'ing-yang Ford,"
describes the fulling of cloth, a process by which cloth is pounded
on a stone to spread the fibers and make them soft and shiny. In it,
a young girl indulges in fanciful description while pounding cloth
to make a new set of clothes for her lover. In addition to the obvious
sexual connotations, there would appear to be a pun in the last line:
the phrase "gently pounding," *ch'ing-tao*, suggests a phrase of
similar pronunciation that may mean either "to long for" or "to
fall over backward," either of which meanings might be appropriate to the singer.

Greenest jade for a clothes-pounding stone,
a golden lotus pestle set with seven jewels:
lift it high, slowly slowly bring it down,
gently pounding for you alone.

A pun is involved as well in the next song, entitled "Stone Castle
Music." The *huang-po* or *Phellodendron amurense*, used in medicine and
noted for its bitter taste, is commonly planted in hedges. The word
*li* or "hedge" is almost identical in written form with the word *li*,
"separation" or "parting"—hence the dual meaning: bitter
hedge/bitter parting.

They say my love is going far away;
I've come to see him off at Fang Hill Stop.
Wind blowing over the *huang-po* bushes—
how I hate to hear that bitter parting sound!

Fish figure prominently in the next song, entitled "The Goddess
Chiao." The shrine of the goddess, a popular deity who watched
over matters pertaining to the ear and hearing, was apparently
situated on or at the side of the bridge.

Crowds of shuffling feet pass over the bridge
where river waters flow west to east;
above, the immortal goddess dwells;
below are fishes, westward swimming.

When they go, they never go alone,
but three by three or two by two.

With this compare the *kouta* from the *Kanginshū,* a collection of
Japanese folk and popular songs compiled in 1518:

Even the killifish under the bridge
   decline to sleep alone—
      cruising upstream, cruising down.

The next song, entitled "Picking Rushes," requires no comment.

At dawn setting out from a cassia and orchid shore,
noontime resting beneath mulberry and elm;
picking rushes along with you,
one whole day gets me less than an armful!

Most of the love songs quoted so far have come from the southern
dynasties. The last example, from the north, bears the title "Song of
the Breaking of the Willow Branch," a type of song originally sung
at partings when willow branches were broken off and given as
gifts; here the title merely indicates the tune and has no particular
relevance. The song employs the type of nature imagery so common
in the *Odes,* in which the opening image, taken from the natural
world, parallels or contrasts with the human situation described in
the succeeding lines. Here the jujube tree stands in antithesis to the
rapidly maturing daughter, and its name, *tsao,* suggests the word
*tsao* or "soon," an admonition to the mother to delay no longer.

Before the gate stands the jujube tree,
year after year never growing old;
but mother, unless you give your daughter away,
how can you ever hold a grandson in your arms?

The next four folk songs deal not with love but with war and, not
surprisingly, come mostly from the north, where the fighting was
most frequent. The first, entitled *Ch'i-yü-ko* (meaning uncertain),
though listed as southern in origin, was written to be sung to the
semibarbarian music of the north.

Man—pitiful insect,
out the gate with fears of death in his breast,
a corpse fallen in narrow valleys,
white bones that no one gathers up.

The following two, a pair entitled "The Other Side of the Valley,"
use a seven-character line.

1. I am in the castle, my younger brother is beyond,
   no string to my bow, no tips to my arrows;
   rations all run out, how can I live?
   Come and save me! Come and save me!

2. I am taken captive to suffer hardship and shame,
   bones bare, strength gone, food never enough!
   My younger brother is an official, his horses eat grain—
   why is he too stingy to come and ransom me?

The last, "Song of the Breaking of the Willow," is written from the
point of view of a non-Chinese prisoner in the north, and is perhaps
actually a translation from some foreign language. The "River"
is the Yellow River; "man of Han" is a term for the Chinese. One
interpretation would make it the song of a captive "daughter"
rather than a "son."

Far off I see the River at Meng Ford,
willows thick and leafy there.
I am the son of a captive family
and cannot understand the Han man's song.

The songs quoted above are the work of unknown commoners,
or aristocrats who preferred not to disclose their names. In the
same simple, direct vein is the following "Song of the Thoroughfare" by Hsieh Shang (308–57), a high-ranking official and military
leader. It is said that he composed it while perched in the upper
story of a gate overlooking the market place and main thoroughfare
of the city, singing it to the accompaniment of his *p'i-pa* or guitar.
Innocent of all frills or rhetorical embellishment, it nevertheless
captures that magical quality of true song, the ability to infuse the

plainest words with a momentousness they would never possess in ordinary context:

The second and third month of sunny spring,
willows green and peach trees red:
carriages, horses—hard to make out—
noises that fall through the yellow dust.

"Hard to make out" translates the phrase *pu hsiang shih,* literally "[one] doesn't know [one]," which, by its ambiguity, may mean that the occupants of the milling carriages do not know or recognize one another in this crowded and dusty market place; that the singer in his gate tower does not recognize the people in the carriages below him; or that the people in the carriages do not recognize the singer. With a touch of vivid green and red and a cloud of obscuring yellow, the poet catches up all the press and clamor of a Chinese city in spring.

While these brief, eloquent songs were taking shape, the poets of the literati continued to fashion lengthier variations on the old *yüeh-fu* ballad themes. As might be expected, these imitations, having increasingly lost over the centuries the freshness and spontaneity of their models, sought to compensate for the loss by means of ingenious variations of diction and treatment or greater intricacy and polish. Inevitably, their derivative nature tends to a considerable degree to limit their appeal, though they are not without an interest and charm of their own. Some of them continue to describe the harsh lot of the soldier or the poor man, though such works, coming largely from the hands of men who had had little experience of either soldiering or poverty, are somewhat lacking in conviction. Others, more successful, deal with mildly erotic themes and accord more closely with the elegant, rather effete tone typical of the other types of poetic literature of the time. The two examples I will quote here are of this type, poems that are noteworthy for their rich imagery and subtle handling of language rather than for any great depth of feeling. They are also, as will be apparent, devoid of any outright note of protest, though it is not impossible that one or two satiric barbs, difficult to identify at this far remove, are hidden beneath their satiny surface.

The first, by Hsieh Hui-lien (397–433) and entitled "Fulling Clothes," is usually classified as a *tsa-shih*, but I have chosen to treat it as a *yüeh-fu* because of the obvious folk song derivation of its themes and the fact that the poet speaks through the persona of a young lady. We have already encountered the process of *tao-i* or the fulling of cloth for clothing in the folk song entitled "Ch'ing-yang Ford" on p. 61, and noted the erotic connotations that sometimes accompany its appearance in poetry. Here it is given a very much more elaborate treatment. Because it was customarily done in the fall, when the women were preparing cloth to make new clothes for winter, the poet begins with a rather extended evocation of an autumn evening. When we first catch sight of the women who are to do the pounding, we find them donning makeup and jewelry, hardly appropriate attire for an evening of strenuous labor. Apparently they are highborn ladies, or a lady and her maids, who live in a complex of adjoining rooms or mansions, and are perhaps hoping to dispel their ennui by trying their hand at physical toil. The poet seems to hint that their beauty is made peculiarly exciting by the unaccustomed sweat that breaks out on their flushed and powdered faces. The poem ends with one of the women describing the gift she has prepared to send to her loved one, again a theme drawn from the old Han *yüeh-fu*. The simple, uncrowded style of this closing section contrasts interestingly—some might say strangely— with the dense and polished elegance of the rest of the poem.

> The stars Heng and Chi never halt their courses,
> the sun runs swiftly as though pursued.
> White dew wets the garden chrysanthemums,
> fall winds strip the ash tree in the court.
> Whirr whirr go the wings of the grasshopper;
> shrill shrill the cold crickets' cry:
> twilight dusk enfolds the empty curtains,
> the night moon enters white into chambers
> where lovely women put on their robes,
> jeweled and powdered, calling to each other.
> Hairpinned in jade, they come from northern rooms;
> with a clinking of gold, they walk the southern stairs.

Where eaves are high comes the echo of fulling mallets,
where columns are tall, the sad sound of their pounding.
A faint fragrance rises from their sleeves,
light sweat stains each side of the brow:
    My cloth of glossy silk is done;
    my lord is wandering and does not return.
    I cut it with scissors drawn from this sheath,
    sew it to make a robe he'll wear ten thousand miles.
    With my own hands I lay it in the box,
    fix the seal that waits for you to break.
    Waist and belt I made to the old measure,
    uncertain if they will fit you now or not.

The last poem, by Pao Chao (414–66), is entitled "In Imitation of
'The King of Huai-nan'" and is in seven-character form with occasional five-character lines. It deals with Liu An (d. 123 B.C.), the king
of Huai-nan, a prince of the Han royal family whose name is associated
in popular lore with the cult of the immortals.[1] It is an imitation of an
earlier poem on the subject; in some versions, it is broken into two
poems, the first ending with line nine.

The King of Huai-nan,
craving long life,
tried elixirs and breath control, studied the Classic of the Immor-
    tals;
of lapis lazuli his bowls, of ivory his plates;
in golden caldrons with spoons of jade mixing magic cinnabar,
mixing magic cinnabar,
sporting in purple rooms,
purple rooms where bright-robed ladies toyed with earrings of
    pearl,
sang like the *luan* bird, danced like phoenixes—how they broke
    my lord's heart!
Nine gates to the vermilion city, each with nine small portals;

[1] For a discussion of the theme of the *hsien* in poetry, see E. H. Schafer, "Mineral
Imagery in the Paradise Poems of Kuan-hsiu," *ASIA MAJOR*, 10, 1 (1963),
73–102.

I want to chase the bright moon, to enter my lord's bosom,
enter my lord's bosom,
twine myself at his sash.
I hate my lord, I curse my lord, I wait for my lord's love.
May it be firm as a builded city, may it be keen as swords;
may I flourish with him, wane with him, and never be cut off!

Pao Chao is considered to be the finest writer of poems in *yüeh-fu*
style of the late Six Dynasties period, but even his works at times
seem to struggle against the dead weight of the centuries. Anyone
surveying the poetic scene at the end of the fifth or sixth century
would probably have predicted that the last ounce of literary interest
and invention had been wrung from the old ballad themes and that
they were destined for extinction. As so often happens in literary
history, he would have been dead wrong. It only needed men with a
sincere feeling for the experiences that had originally inspired the
ballads, men who were troubled and angry and needed some appropriate verse form in which to frame their protest, for the *yüeh-fu*
to spring to life again. These men we will meet when we come to
the subject of T'ang poetry.

# V

# THE POETRY OF

# RECLUSION

*Why only the music of strings and flutes?*
*Mountains and waters have clear notes of their own.*

—TSO SSU

☩

IN CHAPTER III we have noted the striking tone of realism and
concreteness that characterized much of the poetry of the Chien-an
period. In the hands of Wang Ts'an, Liu Cheng, and the members of
the Ts'ao family, the new five-character *shih* form was used to depict
an army on the march, a bureaucrat's littered desk, or a starving
woman abandoning her baby by the roadside. We read poems that
voiced the particular griefs and complaints of particular men,
often at a particular time and place. We encountered imagery that,
whatever symbolic associations it might arouse, was first of all a
description of the actual scene before the eyes of the poet.

For studies and translations of T'ao Ch'ien, see J. R. Hightower, "T'ao Ch'ien's
'Drinking Wine' Poems," in *Wen-lin: Studies in the Chinese Humanities*; William
Acker, *T'ao the Hermit*; and Lily Chang and Marjorie Sinclair, *The Poems of T'ao
Ch'ien*. On Hsieh Ling-yün, see J. D. Frodsham, *The Murmuring Stream: The Life
and Works of Hsieh Ling-yün*, 2 vols; and Richard B. Mather, "The Landscape
Buddhism of the Fifth Century Poet Hsieh Ling-yün," *Journal of Asian Studies*,
18, 1 (Nov., 1958). Further translations of the poetry of reclusion will be found
in C. J. Ch'en and Michael Bullock, *Poems of Solitude*; Frodsham, *Anthology of
Chinese Verse*; Payne *The White Pony*; and Waley, *Chinese Poems*.
THE QUOTATION ABOVE, BY TSO SSU (FL. A.D. 300), IS FROM "INVITATION TO
HIDING."

Such realism may appear often in the arts, customarily, as Huizinga has noted, in reaction against excessive stylization of thought
and image. "Once such a realism has developed," he writes, "it
usually dissolves again quickly, after having given new life to
precisely the tendencies it seemed in opposition to. A new symbolism, a new ideography, typology, or style frequently derives its
strength from the firmness in which it is rooted in a preceding
realism." [1] The excessive stylization which the Chien-an poets were
reacting against was no doubt that prevailing in the *fu* and four-
character *shih* forms during the closing centuries of the Han. The
new style that in time grew out of their realism is to be seen in the
work of Juan Chi (210–63), the first important poet in the period
following the Chien-an.

Juan Chi is best known for his long series of poems entitled
*Yung-huai-shih*, "Singing of Thoughts." The series as we now have
it contains 85 poems, 82 in five-character form, the rest in four-
character; 17 are included in *chüan* 23 of the *Wen hsüan*, from which
the examples quoted here are taken. Though undoubtedly composed
at different times, the poems seem to be intended as a single set or
opus.

Like the "Nineteen Old Poems" and many of the works of the
Chien-an period, the poems are essentially expressions of sorrow and
loneliness. But whereas in the earlier poetry the sorrow had most
often been presented as the emotion of a particular person and
occasioned by definite, and possibly remediable causes, in Juan
Chi's work it is universalized, made ubiquitous and inescapable.
Man, by being subject to change—which in Juan Chi almost
always seems to be change for the worse—is inevitably doomed
to despair.

The tendency toward a generalized or abstract statement of
feeling results in a shift in the character of the imagery. The poet,
we sense, is no longer interested in describing the natural world as
it exists in reality, but only in extracting from it elements that will
serve as symbols for his ideas and emotions. He openly admits
as much when, on occasion, he places side by side the statement of
an idea first in direct, then in symbolic form, as in the couplet:

[1] "Renaissance and Realism," in *Men and Ideas: Essays of Johan Huizinga*, tr.
by James S. Holmes and Hans van Marle, p. 309.

Evil slanders cause friends to be estranged;
drifting clouds turn midday to darkness.

Most often the images from nature have to do with the passing of time and the cycle of the seasons, those processes of change which, while sweeping man forward to his death, mock him with their own endlessness. Birds play a role of particular importance as symbols of freedom and longed-for escape, being mentioned 56 times in the 85 poems of the series.

Juan Chi's pessimism surpasses anything voiced in earlier poetry. In his emphasis upon man's hostility and ill will toward his fellow creatures, upon the stupidity which he displays in his pursuit of pleasure and gain, in short, upon the essential evilness of man, at least as we know him now, he expresses, in extreme form, a position common in Taoist thought, and it is important to note that Taoism enjoyed great vogue among the intellectuals of Juan's time. But he seems to reflect only the cynical aspects of the Taoist view, and in his moroseness remains unmoved by its wit and humor or its promises of freedom. At times he seems to think that, through the practice of hygienic arts, it may be possible to attain immortality, or at least to prolong life, but elsewhere he expresses doubt on the subject. He rejects outright the other escapes from sorrow suggested in earlier poetry, such as sensual enjoyment or the hope of lasting fame. He also appears to reject one consolation much prized by Chinese poets of later ages, that of wine. Although there are many anecdotes concerning Juan Chi's fondness for the bottle, including one that tells how he stayed drunk for two whole months in order to avoid being drawn into a marriage alliance he considered dangerous and distasteful, wine finds no place in the philosophy of life expressed in his poetry and is mentioned only once in the entire *Yung-huai* series.

But let us turn to some of the poems themselves; the numbers refer to their order in the *Wen hsüan*.

3. Beautiful trees make paths beneath themselves:
   peach and plum in the eastern garden.
   Autumn winds toss the drifting bean leaves;
   now all things begin to wither and fall.

Brightest blossoms have their fading,
the high hall is grown over with briar and thorn.
Leave it—spur the horses and go,
climb the foot of the Western Hill.
Hard enough to keep one body whole;
harder when you long for wife and child.
    Chill frost will clothe the grassy meadow,
    the year will darken and then be gone.

"Western Hill": retreat of the hermits Po Yi and Shu Ch'i.

8. Years ago, when I was young,
heedless, rash, I loved strings and a song.
West I wandered to Hsien-yang,
passing time with the Chaos and Lis.
Pleasures had not been fully tasted
when all at once the white sun slipped away.
I raced the horses, came home again,
turning my eyes over the three rivers.
My hundred taels of yellow gold gone,
every day I grumble at the cost of things.
Like the man who faced north when he meant to go south,
I've lost the road—where do I go now?

"Hsien-yang": old name for Ch'ang-an, the capital of the Han dynasty.
The Chao and Li families, related to the imperial family of the Western Han,
represent the height of luxurious living.

The following poem is based on the story of Shao P'ing, marquis
of Tung-ling under the Ch'in dynasty, who, after the overthrow of
the Ch'in and the founding of the Han, was content to make a
living growing melons outside the east gate of Ch'ang-an. His
melons were known as "Tung-ling melons" and were prized for
their excellent flavor. The image in line seven of the torch that
consumes itself, symbol of man's self-destructive search for gain,
derives from *Chuang Tzu,* sec. 4.

9. Tung-ling melons—men say that long ago,
    close beyond the city's Green Gate,
    they grew by fieldsides, rambling left and right,

mother vine and child linked and laced together,
five-colored fruit that shone in the morning sun,
rich buyers from four directions crowding round—
   The grease-filled torch burns itself out,
   abundant wealth will harm and harry you!
   The body can get by in coarsest cloth;
   lavish stipends—what use are they?

11. Long ago, at fourteen or fifteen,
high in purpose, I loved the Classics,
dressed in coarse brown, a gem in my heart,
hoping some day to be like Yen and Min.
I threw open the window, looked out on the four fields,
climbed the hills and let my hopeful eyes wander:
   Grave mounds cover the heights,
   ten thousand ages all brought to one!
   A thousand autumns, ten thousand years from now,
   what will be left of a "glorious name"?
   At last I understand Master Hsien Men;
   I can laugh out loud at what I used to be!

◄ "Yen and Min": Yen Yüan and Min Tzu-ch'ien, poor but eminently virtuous
disciples of Confucius.
   "Master Hsien Men": a *hsien* or immortal spirit of ancient times.

13. This summer's burning heat,
in its last weeks now, beginning to fade;
green leaves drooping on fragrant trees,
cool clouds splayed across the sky:
the four seasons one by one take leave,
sun and moon trail each other in turn.
I wander weeping through empty halls;
there is no one who knows me!
I long for a friend to be glad with forever,
never to know the pain of parting.

16. In North Ward they do many strange dances,
clandestine music on the banks of the P'u.
The careless wanderer, bold and unwitting,
bobs and sinks, dips and follows with the age;

by shortcuts and byways he goes,
driving himself on to excess and ruin.
I may never see the immortal Prince Ch'iao
riding the clouds, flying up to Teng-lin;
but still I have his "art of long life";
with this let me console my heart.

✣ "North Ward": the dances and music referred to in the first two lines are the evil and licentious entertainments of lost dynasties of antiquity.

"Prince Ch'iao": an immortal spirit of ancient times who has already appeared on p. 29.

Two themes of great importance to later poetry, themes that are often curiously linked, are touched upon in the Juan Chi poems quoted above, reclusion and friendship. The former appears in the first poem, in the allusion to the Western Hill where the hermits Po Yi and Shu Ch'i had lived and died in ancient times, and the hint that the poet intends to abandon his family and become a recluse himself. Po Yi and Shu Ch'i, brothers who chose to starve to death in the wilderness rather than acknowledge allegiance to a ruler whom they regarded as a usurper, were praised by Confucius and honored by his followers as paragons of virtue. For Confucians, reclusion was essentially a form of political protest, to be carried out when one felt that conditions in the government were so unsavory that there was no longer any hope of reform and conscience forbade one to hold public office or remain longer in the everyday world. Naturally any new regime coming to power did all it could to attract to its service those men who had withdrawn to the hills under its predecessor, and as a result a period of retirement often served in fact to forward one's political career.

For the Taoists, the hermit is a man who has retired from society for purely selfish motives, that is, to remove himself from the corrupting influence of civilization and further his own chances for safety and survival. But, in the *Chuang Tzu* at least, it is made clear that there are numerous ways to withdraw from society, and that the man who is too infatuated with the recluse ideal and too fastidious in guarding his own purity may be as much the slave of convention as the crassest worldling. The real recluse, Chuang Tzu

implies, is the man who "buries himself among the people" (sec.
25), who creates his own wilderness wherever he may be through
the loftiness and detachment of his mind.

Juan Chi lived in a time of political intrigue and instability and
his *Yung-huai* poems are often read as laments for the waning
fortunes of the Ts'ao family and condemnations of its unscrupulous
enemies. He was the leader of the famous group of scholar-poets
known as the Seven Sages of the Bamboo Grove who, deeply
influenced by Taoism, held aloof from the court and spent their time
drinking, debating philosophy, and making music in a forest
retreat. But how much their woodland outings, their drunkenness
and their general defiance of convention were inspired by Taoist
ideals and how much they were a gesture of political protest is
difficult to determine.

Certainly, in these troubled times, it was safer to stay away from
government affairs, as the large number of eminent men of the
period who died in the frequent coups would indicate. And yet,
for an educated young man of good family (and the society of the
time was dominated by a small number of powerful aristocratic
clans), government service offered the only opportunity for a real
career. The life of the farmer, the artisan, and most certainly the
merchant, was too far below him to be seriously considered, and the
Buddhist clergy, though it might attract him, required a rejection of
family ties that was hard for a wellborn Chinese to accept. He was
thus torn between his desire for a full and meaningful role in society,
which meant a career in public office, and a longing for the much
safer, though potentially more lonely and frustrating, life of the
recluse.

The tensions involved in the pursuit of the eremitic life and the
ambiguities that often surround the motives of the men who adopt
it are reflected in the poetry on the theme. In Han times a poet at the
court of Liu An, the king of Huai-nan, had written a poem entitled
*Chao-yin-shih* or "Invitation to a Gentleman in Hiding," [2] in which,
addressing a gentleman of talent who had retreated to the mountains, he urged him to return to society, expressing the typical Han
view of the wilderness as a forbidding and terror-filled place. In the

[2] Translated in Hawkes, *Ch'u Tz'u: The Songs of the South*, p. 119.

third and fourth centuries a type of poem became popular which, although it borrowed part of the old title, *Chao-yin*, expressed the opposite view, becoming now an "invitation *to* hiding." Customarily it described either a visit by the poet to some carefree recluse, or the poet's own longing to go into retirement. The epigraph with which this chapter opens is taken from one such "Invitation to Hiding" by the Chin poet Tso Ssu.

The following poem is the earliest known example of yet another type known as *Fan-chao-yin* or poem "in refutation of the Invitation to Hiding." By an otherwise unknown writer named Wang K'ang-chü of the fourth century, it argues *against* the eremitic idea.

Little hiders hide in the hills and groves,
big hiders hide in the city market.
Po Yi burrowed in on Shou-yang Mountain,
Lao Tan lay low as Clerk of the Pillar.
Long ago, that time of perfect peace—
it too had its Nest-dwelling Man.
Today in a bright and glorious age,
are we without our forest gentry?
You would free your soul beyond the blue clouds,
bury your traces in the deepest hills;
but partridges cry before the break of dawn,
mournful winds come with nightfall;
icy frost scars your ruddy face,
cold fountains hurt your jade-white feet.
All-round talent the mass of men trust;
one-sided wisdom has only itself to lean on.
Do with what's given you and gain heavenly harmony;
twist your nature and you lose the highest truth.
Come back! And what is there to hope for?
To live and die the same as other things!

The poem, whose purpose is to ridicule the hermits of the wilderness and call on them to return to society, begins by reminding them that the true man of understanding can be aloof from the world while remaining in it. In contrast to Po Yi, who felt compelled to bury himself in the mountains, the writer places Lao Tan, or Lao

Tzu, the great patriarch of the Taoist faith, who, according to legend, served as librarian at the Chou court with the title of Clerk of the Pillar. Next he denies that the existence of the recluse is any reflection upon the quality of government. Even during the "time of perfect peace" long ago when the sage Yao held the throne, there was a malcontent named Ch'ao-fu or Nest Father who perversely retired to the wilderness and lived up in a tree like a nesting bird; and the writer's own age, though likewise one of peace and order, has its similar disaffected minority. The poet then gives a brief description of the hardships which the recluse must face. Cold fountains and crying partridges may not strike one as particularly vexatious, but perhaps the point here is not so much the real ruggedness of the forest life as it is the delicate nature of the gentlemen who go off to endure it. In conclusion Wang returns once more to the point made so often by the Taoists that any kind of purposeful striving, be it for worldly gain or unworldly detachment, results in a twisting or violation of the inborn nature, and is to be condemned.

Wang K'ang-chü's poem attacks all that is foolish and offensive in the recluse ideal, its arrogance in passing judgment upon the age, its narrow-mindedness and air of self-approving sanctity. The next poem will illustrate its better side. It is by the man who from early times has been hailed as the father of eremitic poetry, T'ao Ch'ien or T'ao Yüan-ming (365–427). T'ao is one of the greatest pre-T'ang poets and to do justice to his work would require far more space than I can spare. Here I wish merely to discuss how he fits into the tradition of eremitic poetry.

First, it is important to note that T'ao did not come from a particularly powerful or distinguished family, and his career in public office was relatively brief and inconsequential. His retirement to private life, therefore, did not represent any great sacrifice on his part, nor was it a significant blow to the prestige of the dynasty he had served. Moreover, the type of withdrawal he chose did not entail the drastic rejection of family and friends and the flight to remote regions insisted upon by more extreme ascetics. He merely retired to a farming village in his native region near Mount Lu south of the Yangtze in present-day Kiangsi. He did not feel impelled to make any more forced or ostentatious withdrawal because, as he explains in one of his most famous poems, "A heart that is distant creates a wilderness round it." [3] His reclusion thus belongs to the highest type, that of the mind and the spirit. And because it was free of the faddism and hypocrisy, the ambiguity of motive that so often accompany such moves, it serves perfectly to illustrate the tensions called into being by the eremitic life.

The following poem by T'ao Yüan-ming touches upon the principal themes of his poetry as a whole: quietude and rustic simplicity, the joys of wine and family life, and a vague longing for the past. It is the first of two poems entitled "Matching a Poem by Secretary Kuo."

Thick thick the woods before my hall,
in midsummer storing up clear shade;
southwinds come in season,
gusts flapping open the breast of my robe.
Done with friends, I pass the time in idle studies,
out of bed, fondling books and lute;
garden vegetables with flavor to spare,
last year's grain that goes a little farther—
there's a limit to what you need;
more than enough would be no cause for joy.
I pound grain to make good wine,
ferment and ladle it myself.
The little boys play by my side,
learning words they can't pronounce—
true happiness lies in these,
official hatpins all but forgotten.
Far far off I watch the white clouds,
my longing for the past deeper than words.

The poem opens with a typical evocation of the benignancy of nature and the quiet joy which the poet found in his country retreat. Next T'ao cites the particular pastimes that make life in retirement enjoyable: "idle studies," which commentators suggest refers to the study of Taoist, as opposed to Confucian, writings, and the lute, which from earliest times has been one of the most frequently

[3] "Drinking Wine," #5, tr. by Arthur Waley.

mentioned sources of consolation for the Chinese gentleman. That the poet should be so delighted to be "done with friends" seems rather strange, in view of what I shall have to say later concerning the subject of friendship, and the fact that the poem is written to "match" or "harmonize with"—that is, follow the same rhymes as—one by his friend Kuo; but presumably he means here the kind of irksome friendships one becomes entangled in when he enters the official world. He then turns to the subject of food, which appears so often in poems on the recluse ideal. It is frequently the hermit's boast that he can live on the meagerest fare, even that he requires no sustenance at all, being so rarefied in spirit as to be able to sustain himself on dew alone. Here T'ao, scorning all such boasts and affectations, tells us simply that he has enough to eat. Living in the countryside in a time of drought, famine, and peasant uprisings, he knew that this was something to be grateful for indeed.

Next among his joys he names wine, a subject recurring with such frequency in his poetry that it is inseparably associated with his name. Wine, or what he referred to as "the thing in the cup," gave him consolation and helped inspire his writing, and in one of the poems "in the form of a coffin-puller's song" which he wrote for his own funeral, he declared his only regret was that he had not been able to get enough of it while he was alive. At times he had to depend on what friends and neighbors might bring him; here he has the satisfaction of brewing his own.

T'ao then mentions the delight which he takes in his sons—he had five of them—who are elsewhere made the principal theme of his poems. I have noted the strange silence of the early poets of the *Book of Odes* on the subject of children, as though to mention them might arouse the envy of the gods and place their lives in jeopardy. The poet Tso Ssu, who flourished around A.D. 300, wrote a long poem full of fatherly pride on the subject of his two daughters. Unfortunately it is not suitable for translation because of the faulty condition of the text. From this period on, children become increasingly common in poetry, and we will see them described frequently and at great length in the works of the T'ang and Sung.

T'ao Yüan-ming, having declared himself in possession of the things that bring "true happiness," and asserted that he has all but forgotten "official hatpins," the ornate pins used by bureaucrats and men of wealth to hold on their caps, which he had once aspired to, in the closing lines of the poem turns suddenly to the image of white clouds far away in the sky. We will come upon these white clouds often in the poetry of the recluse. They are associated first of all with the mountains that are in many cases the home of the recluse, for the Chinese believed that the rocky peaks and caverns of the mountains literally gave birth to the clouds that so frequently surround them. Moreover, clouds, because of their whiteness and utter freedom of movement, serve as an apt symbol of the purity and detachment of the mind of the hermit. But here T'ao speaks of the clouds as "far far off," and we realize that, with characteristic realism and modesty, he is admitting that he himself is still far from attaining the kind of perfect peace and transcendence represented by the clouds. For all his honest delight in the quiet life of the countryside, his family, his books, and his wine, T'ao could never conquer his sense of loneliness and frustration at being denied by fate and the evil state of the times the career in government, the place in society to which birth, learning, and inborn talent entitled him. For all his efforts to cultivate a Taoist indifference to the world and its values, he remained at heart a Confucian, with a Confucian's sense of service and moral duty to mankind. This is the reason, I think, that his poem, which set out to catalogue the happinesses that the poet enjoys, ends with an unfulfilled longing, a longing for antiquity, the age of the sage-rulers so often extolled by Confucius and his followers, when true worth was invariably recognized and men like T'ao were not obliged to live out their lives in rustic obscurity.

T'ao Yüan-ming is customarily described by Chinese critics as the first great poet of *t'ien-yüan*, the "fields and gardens," because so much of his work deals with life on his small farm in Kiangsi. As such, he is distinguished from another recluse-poet of the time, Hsieh Ling-yün (385–433), dubbed the father of *shan-shui* or "mountain and water" poetry.

Mountains from earliest times have been sacred in China, looked on as the abode of nature deities and immortal spirits, places to be sacrificed to from afar or ascended in search of magical powers or life-prolonging herbs. Taoist literature is full of tales of mountain-dwelling sages, and when Buddhism was introduced to China, it added its sanctity by founding monastic centers at Mount Lu and other famous mountain sites. When the members of the ruling class were pushed out of north China by foreign invaders in the early years of the fourth century and forced to flee south to set up a new capital at present-day Nanking, they were particularly impressed by the beautiful mountainous scenery of Chekiang and the lower Yangtze valley.

Hsieh Ling-yün was born in K'uai-chi (sometimes romanized Kuei-chi) in Chekiang, the son of one of the powerful aristocratic families that had been obliged to move south. Though he held office at various times, much of his life was spent in retirement at his estates in the south, and his most important poetic works deal with the joy he found there. Poems in the *fu* form had often included passages of landscape description, particularly those pieces that dealt with musical instruments, which commonly began with a spirited sketch of the wild mountain forests where the wood or bamboo from which the instrument was fashioned grew. In addition to describing the great sights and forces of the natural world, the *fu* also hinted that there were moral and philosophical lessons to be read in nature, in the purity of the snow, the everlastingness of the river, or the divine mystery of the sea. What Hsieh did was to take the kind of lush, diffuse description of nature found in such *fu* (and in his own great work in that form, the "*Fu* on Dwelling in the Mountains"), extract its essence, and mold it to fit the *shih* form. The result is a type of landscape poetry that is at once vivid, closely observed, and charged with symbolic meaning.

These qualities will be illustrated, I hope, in the following example, entitled "Written on the Lake, Returning from the Retreat at Stone Cliff." There is some doubt about the nature of the place referred to as "the retreat," though it would seem to have been a small lodge in the hills used for the practice of religious austerities. Hsieh was a devout Buddhist and the author of a work on Buddhist philosophy.

The weather changeable at dusk and dawn,
mountain waters shot through with clear light,

a clear light that makes men joyful:
the wanderer, lulled, forgets to go home.
Out of the valley, the sun still high;
boarding the boat, the light fading now,
forest and ravine clothed in sombering color,
clouds of sunset wrapped in evening mist;
lotus and caltrop, their leaves one by one shining;
reeds and cattails propped against each other—
push through, hurry down the trail to the south,
returning contented to bed behind the eastern door.
Thoughts at ease, outside things weigh lightly;
mind relaxed, nothing going wrong.
A word to you gentlemen "nourishers of life"—
try using this method for a while!

As will be seen, the descriptive parts of the poem have largely to
do with atmosphere and light. This is true of a great deal of Six
Dynasties nature poetry; the poets seem always to be looking up at
the sky. It was apparently these features of the southern landscape
that most intrigued the Chinese, particularly the mists that filtered
and colored the light, that wreathed the mountains and gave them
their air of mystery and breathing vitality. One should also note the
studiedly realistic time sequence of the poem, from an hour when
"the sun [is] still high," to bedtime. Chinese poetry often achieves
its most poignant effects of timelessness and universality precisely
through this device of confronting the reader with a segment of
carefully clocked time. The closing lines of the poem repeat the old
lesson of the importance of inner harmony. The "nourishers of
life," a phrase taken from the *Lao Tzu*, sec. 50, presumably refers
to men who are attempting to lengthen their lives through external
means, forgetting that nothing can comfort the body when the mind
and spirit are not at ease.

Hsieh spoke often of what he called *shang*, "appreciation" or
"recognition," which he described as one of the finest of emotions.
He emphasized the need for man to take an active part in recognizing
and appreciating the beauties of nature for, as he says at the conclusion of one poem, "Should these scenes go unheeded, who will

report their Truth?" ("The Scene as I Crossed the Lake from South
Mountain to North Mountain"). Apparently, Hsieh felt that he had
stumbled upon a whole new world of beauty and truth that other
men had ignored or been ignorant of, and he was filled with the
excitement of his discovery. We have already noted the frequent
association that occurs in Taoist literature between mountain
retreats and the enlightened man, which might have encouraged
Hsieh to think that the craggy and remote scenery of his native
Chekiang, in addition to being extremely beautiful, embodied some
special kind or degree of truth not to be found in tamer landscapes.
It has also been suggested that, as a devout Buddhist, he looked
upon the appreciative viewing of such landscapes as a kind of
religious contemplation of Reality.[4] What Hsieh must have known,
however, is that both Taoism and Buddhism, while on a practical
level approving the freedom from human distraction that a mountain retreat customarily affords, on a philosophical level condemned
any attachment to place that would see the landscape of the far-off
hills as intrinsically more beautiful or valuable than the landscape near
the city, or that would see beauty or value at all in the landscape.
As the poet Chiang Yen (444–505), writing half a century after
Hsieh, put it, the finest type of recluse is one who "takes the purple
heavens to be his hut, the encircling sea to be his pond, roaring with
laughter in his nakedness, walking along singing with his hair
hanging down."[5] It is only pettier men who insist upon hiding in
caves and mountain fastnesses, or retreating to the isolation of a
farm, says Chiang Yen.

We have noted earlier the question so often raised when a Chinese
went into retirement, particularly one of prominent family and good
education who had held, or was qualified to hold, public office.
Was he thereby expressing some disapproval of the government or
one of its factions? Did he retire in the expectation that the government would soon be imploring him to return to public life, perhaps
on more advantageous terms than before? Was he withdrawing out
of motives of fear or laziness, or because the life on his country

[4] See J. D. Frodsham, *The Murmuring Stream: The Life and Works of Hsieh Ling-
yün*, I, 100.
[5] Letter in Reply to Yüan Shu-ming, *Chiang Wen-t'ung chi*, ch. 5.

estate was in fact more genial and pleasure-filled than that in the capital? Or did he know of some secret herb or medicine to be gotten only in the mountains; had he hopes of establishing contact at last with the elusive immortals?

All these questions are raised by Hsieh Ling-yün's retirement from public life and the poetry he wrote while in seclusion. His poetry also, as we have seen, raises the question of how a man can profess to be so cool and indifferent toward the world and yet become so much the captive of natural beauty. These anomalies run throughout the eremitic tradition and the poetry that surrounds it, the conventionality that men fall into when they try to flout convention, the fastidiousness and contempt that so often characterize those who claim to be indifferent to the world. Hsieh Ling-yün had a passionate appreciation of the wild beauties of nature, and yet it would be dishonest not to mention that he spent great sums of money on the landscaping and upkeep of his country estate. His poetry is full of the shifting lights and colors, the wonders and unsung splendors of the southern lakes and mountains, but it is not the poetry of a man who has attained, or at least is speaking from, the highest level of Taoist or Buddhist enlightenment—which is why it remains poetry rather than becoming philosophical doggerel. Had Hsieh been a better philosopher he might, like so many of the "Taoist poets" of the age just before his, have written much poorer poetry.

In the chapter on the T'ang we will encounter more poetry of the eremitic tradition, poetry written by or about mountain recluses that displays the same characteristics that have been discussed here, and raises the same questions of sincerity and depth of purpose. It would be presumptuous to try to decide which are the "true" recluses or the "true" eremitic poems. I would like here merely to quote the closing lines from a poem entitled "The Hermit of Mount Lu" by Tu Hsün-ho (846–904) of the T'ang, which seem to me significant:

Old trees strangled in twining creepers,
spring pool muddied by passing deer:
far far removed, you do nothing at all,
as though you were not lodged between heaven and earth!

We would suppose that the recluse addressed in the poem came to Mount Lu because he felt some affinity with the old trees and the pool of clear water, because he saw them either as beautiful in themselves or as symbolic of the longevity and spiritual purity he hoped to achieve. Yet now he sits indifferent while the trees are choked by parasitic vines and the waters of the pool are roiled. Readers who have visited the Shisendō in Kyoto may recall the bamboo device, operated by water from a tiny stream, which the recluse Ishikawa Jōzan (1583–1672) rigged in order to frighten the deer away from his garden. In doing so, Ishikawa showed himself, one feels, a resourceful but not very thoroughgoing member of the hermit tribe. The real hermit is one who can ignore the deer entirely.

## FRIENDSHIP

Hsieh Ling-yün made no attempt to conceal the fact that he was not completely happy in his mountain retirement. He expressed regret that he had no like-minded friend, so that "together we might climb the ladders of blue cloud" ("Climbing the Highest Point of Stone Gate"). Repeatedly he voiced his longing for a *shang-hsin* or "companion of the heart," a sympathetic friend with whom he might share the beauty and wonder that he found in nature. I have mentioned that the theme of friendship was an important element in the poetry of Juan Chi, as seen in the closing line of the poem on p. 72:

I long for a friend to be glad with forever,
never to know the pain of parting.

It is also a theme that appears with great frequency in the poetry of the recluse. The Chinese recluse almost never speaks of wife and family. If he has brought them with him into retirement, he would rather not mention the fact; and if he has deliberately cut himself off from them, he would be loath to admit that he missed their company. But, though he may break away from all other bonds of society, the Chinese gentleman can seldom bring himself to sever the bond of friendship. The longing for true friendship is the last tie that binds him to the world.

Hsieh Ling-yün found such fellowship in the company of his younger cousin Hsieh Hui-lien (397–433), also a poet. The following poem, entitled "Replying to a Poem from My Cousin Hui-lien," was written in 430 when he was living in retirement at K'uai-chi and had received news, in the form of a poem, that Hui-lien was on his way to visit. The poem, like that of Ts'ao Chih to his younger brother, is a letter in verse, and uses the same device of repetition to link the beginning of a stanza to the end of the one that precedes it. Also, like Ts'ao Chih's poem, it moves backward in time to remembrances of the past and forward to anticipation of future happiness.

Brought to bed by sickness, cut off from men,
I hid myself among cloudy peaks.
Cliffs and valleys filled the eye and ear;
the ones I loved—their faces, their voices far away;
gone the hope of finding a heart's companion,
long regretting I must always be alone,
near the end of the road, I met my honored cousin:
frowns faded, hearts were opened up.

After we had opened our hearts,
my sole contentment was in you.
Across the valleys you searched out my room;
I opened my books, told you all I knew.
At evening I thought how the dawn moon would pale;
mornings I fretted that the sun would set too soon.
We walked together, never tiring;
we met—and now we're parted again.

Parted, taking leave at the western river;
I turned my shadow back to hills of the east.
When we parted it was sorrowful enough;
since then the pain never seems to end.
One thought—to wait for joyful news;
then came your poem about a "river-crossing,"
about your trials with wind and wave,
of every aspect of the beaches and shoals;

beaches and shoals where you linger so long,
wind and wave delaying your journey.
Wrapped in your memories of the bright capital far away,
how could I expect you to recall these empty valleys?
And though you favor me with this message,
it serves only to trouble my thoughts.
If—if you would come back as you said,
together we could enjoy the late spring.

Late spring—there would still be time!
more time for pleasure if you came the month before,
when the mountain peach unfurls its crimson petals
and meadow ferns are sheathed in purple.
Already the chatter of birds delights me,
but still there's gloom in my out-of-the-way home.
In dreams I wait your boat returning,
coming to free me from meanness and care.

Hsieh Ling-yün's poem above describes friendship in terms of two particular men who met at a certain time and place in the past, and hope to meet again. The following poem, by Pao Chao, treats the same theme in nameless and oblique manner. It belongs to a genre known as *ni-ku* or "imitations of antiquity." The practice of writing such imitations was said to have been initiated by Lu Chi and was enthusiastically taken up by lesser poets who, lacking in ideas of their own, could use it as an excuse to rework the masterpieces of the past. It was particularly popular in the fourth and fifth centuries, when poetic invention flagged. We have already noted such imitations in the *yüeh-fu* tradition; the *ni-ku* are reworkings of those *ku-shih* or "old poems," such as the "Nineteen Old Poems," that do not fall in the *yüeh-fu* category. This poem by Pao Chao, with its typical combination of concrete images and undefined sentiment, is one of the few works in the genre that strike me as artistically convincing.

Many the strange mountains of Shu and Han;
looking up, I see them level with the clouds,
shaded scarps piled with summer snow,
sunny ravines where autumn flowers fall.

Morning after morning I watch the clouds go home,
evening on evening, hear the monkeys wail,
a melancholy man, sorrow always with me;
a lonely traveler, easily cast down.
From my room I look forth, wine jar by my side,
plying the dipper, thinking back on life—
It is the nature of the stone to be firm:
do not forsake the friendship we once had!

The next poem, once more, like Hsieh Ling-yün's poem above, a letter to a friend in verse form, deals not with the voluntary seclusion of the hermit, but with that imposed by duty in a remote post in the provinces. Entitled "In a Provincial Capital Sick in Bed: Presented to the *Shang-shu* Shen," it was written in 495 by the poet Hsieh Hsüan-hui (464–99) when he was serving in Hsüan-ch'eng (in present day Anhwei) as governor of the province. It is addressed to his friend, the poet-official Shen Yüeh, whom we shall meet again in Chapter VI.

The governor of Huai-yang, arm and leg to the ruler,
served his term from a bed of ease;
and this post of mine, far in the southern hills?
Hardly different from a hermit's life!
Incessant rains—busy season for farmers:
straw hats gather in fallow fields to the east.
Daytime my state chambers are always closed,
few law suits to hear on the grass-grown terrace.
Soft mats refresh me in summer rooms,
light fans stir a cooling breeze.
Tasty bream I am urged to try,
helping myself to the best strained wine.
Summer plums—crimson fruit chilled in water;
autumn lotus root—tender threads to pluck;
but our happy days, when will they come?
Nightly I meet you in my dreams.
I sit whistling while time piles up,
a year already since I came here to govern;

I could never do it with strings and song—
patting the armrest, I chuckle to myself in scorn.

⟨glyph⟩ "Governor of Huai-yang": Chi An (d. 112 B.C.), an official of the Han who
was highly regarded by the emperor. When he tried to decline the post of
governor of Huai-yang on grounds of illness, the emperor assured him that he
could carry out his duties while resting in bed.

"With strings and song": reference to *Analects* XVII, 4, the story of how
Confucius' disciple Tzu-yu governed a city by teaching the people to sing and
play stringed instruments.

The next poem does not deal overtly with the subject of friendship,
but rather with the brevity and loneliness of life that make friendship
a thing of so great value. The middle section of the poem, in which
the poet contemplates the ruins of past glory, illustrates one of the
perennial themes of Chinese poetry. It is not surprising that Chinese
poets, living in a land of great antiquity which had witnessed the
rise and fall of countless rulers and ruling houses, should often have
dwelt on this theme. In time it came to be recognized as a distinct
genre known as *huai-ku*, "thinking of antiquity" or "longing for
the past," a phrase we have already met in T'ao Yüan-ming's poem
on p. 77. This poem, by Wang Seng-ta (423–58), is entitled "To
Match the Prince of Lang-yeh's Poem 'In the Old Style.'"

In youth I loved the adventurous race;
an official, I traveled river bed and pass.
I have walked in the footprints of far-off times,
I can tell tales of glory and decay:
majestic Chou is now a thicket and a marsh,
stately Han—grave mounds with fences!
The very sites of summer palaces have vanished long ago;
mausoleum gardens—who can find them now?
Midautumn: north border winds are rising;
a lone tumbleweed rolls from its frost-bound roots.
The white sun grows lusterless,
yellow sands spread darkness ten thousand miles:
down the bright lane, no carriage that does not follow the rut;
on the somber road, who but ghosts go there?
Sages, wise men—they too have departed—
Hold life close—have no regret!

The last two poems belong to a category we shall encounter frequently, works written when taking leave of a friend. In the first, the poet, who refers to himself as "the traveler," is setting out on a journey. In the second, he is seeing off a friend.

Ho Sun (d. 518), "At Parting"

The traveler's heart has a hundred thoughts already,
his lonely journey piling mile on endless mile.
The river darkens, rain about to fall;
waves turn white as the wind comes up.

Yin Shih (early 7th century), "Parting from the Courtier Sung"

I, a wanderer north of Tu-ling,
see you off, bound east of the Han River;
one remains, the other takes leave;
both alike are wind-driven weeds.
Autumn heads whitened with frost and snow,
aging faces that wait for wine to glow again:
parting is a time for thoughts,
when the raven's cry comes on the night wind.

# VI

# THE POETRY OF

# LOVE

※

THE SONGS of the *Book of Odes* have much to say about lovers and their fortunes, their good times and bad. However, because the songs are brief, elliptical affairs, often in dramatic form, we may catch a glimpse of the lovers performing various actions or hear them telling of their feelings, but seldom are we given any extended description of how they look. We are told that they wield certain tools or instruments, or wear certain types of clothing or jewelry, but such bits of information are meant primarily to apprise us of the person's wealth or position in society rather than to offer description for its own sake. A rare exception is the passage in #57 which extolls the beauty of a highborn lady in a series of famous similes:

hand like the supple reed-shoot,
skin like congealed lard,
neck like the tree grub,
teeth like melon seeds,
cicada-browed, moth-eyebrowed, . . .

For translations of some of the poetry discussed in this chapter see Frodsham, *Anthology of Chinese Verse* and Waley, *Chinese Poems.* Discussions of early Chinese definitions of poetry are found in Shih-hsiang Chen, "In Search of the Beginnings of Chinese Literary Criticism," *Semitic and Oriental Studies,* (1951), pp. 45–63; and Tse-tsung Chow, "The Early History of the Chinese Word *Shih* (Poetry)," *Wen-lin: Studies in the Chinese Humanities,* pp. 151–209.

These similes, which must have sounded a good deal more enchant-
ing to the ancient Chinese than they do to us, happily dropped
almost entirely out of use at an early date, leaving only the metaphor
of the mothlike eyebrows to become a cliché of later love poetry.

In Chapter IV I have discussed the *yüeh-fu* songs that are the
successors to these love songs of the *Book of Odes,* particularly the
compact and lively "Tzu-yeh songs." If the reader will turn back
to them, he will see that, as in the case of the *Odes,* the focus is
almost always on speech and action, with the barest attention to
description. But there is another kind of poetry concerned with love
and beauty from Six Dynasties times that, far from skimping on
descriptive detail, often has the presentation of such detail as its
principal reason for being. It is this poetry that I wish to discuss
next.

Much of this poetry is preserved in an anthology called the
*Yü-t'ai hsin-yung* (New songs from the Jade Terrace) compiled by
Hsü Ling (507–83). Its ten sections are devoted almost entirely to
poems about love, ranging from anonymous ballads of the Han to
works of the compiler's time. Much space is given to poems in the
so-called *kung-t'i* or "palace style," favored by Hsü Ling's patron,
Crown Prince Hsiao Kang, who is known to history as Emperor
Chien-wen of the Liang dynasty. These deal mainly with ladies of
the palace, particularly those who, out of favor with their lord,
are languishing in neglect, the pathos of their plight and implied
sexual frustration being calculated to arouse in the reader a mild
erotic tingle. The "Jade Terrace" of the title is probably meant to
suggest the apartments of such palace beauties, though it may mean
a mirror stand of jade such as women use in their toilet; and, since
the Chinese are fond of elegant euphemisms for parts of the body,
it may even have some more esoteric connotation.

Viewing the anthology as a whole, we see that it is made up largely
of poems by men, although a few women are represented, the Six
Dynasties being a time when women of the upper class seem to
have been relatively well educated. Many of the poems are devoted
to descriptions of women, real or imaginary, who range in social
station from palace ladies and wives of officials to peasant women
and *ch'ang-chia-nü* or "singing house girls." Nearly all the women

described are unhappy because of separation or abandonment, the
theme of unsatisfied desire dominating the entire anthology. A few
pieces deal, in a mild and matter-of-fact way, with homosexual love
between men. The dress and appearance of the young men, who
seem in most cases to be courtiers or page boys, are described in
the same flowery language used for women, suggesting that men
were thought desirable in so far as they resembled women, or that
the same ideals of beauty were applied to both sexes.

Other poems in the collection describe not the desirable women
or men themselves, but the palaces or objects associated with them,
the dining halls and bedchambers where they pass their time, the
musical instruments, lamps, or mirror stands that come into their
hands, or the elegantly tinted stationery upon which they write
their love notes. Poems of this type, with their hint of fetishism,
belong to a category very popular in late Six Dynasties times known
as *t'i-yung* or "assigned-topic poems." The name derives from the
fact that they were often written at social gatherings when the
guests undertook to describe in verse some designated object—a
musical instrument or other man-made article associated with the
banquet or a flower or tree in the garden—as a pleasant test of
literary skill.

It may be interesting at this point to try in very general terms to
sketch the ideal of feminine beauty that emerges from this collection
of over 600 poems. The beautiful lady of the Jade Terrace may be
summed up as follows:

Social background: perhaps a professional entertainer, perhaps
a daughter of the aristocracy. Birth and upbringing seem of trifling
importance beside the question of physical allure.

Age: quite young. Most often she is described as "fifteen or
sixteen," or "broken melon age," meaning sixteen (not for the
reason the reader might surmise, but because the character for
"melon" can be broken down into duplicates of the character for
"eight"). One poem makes her "something over ten."

Appearance: hair elaborately done up and held in place with
heavy jeweled hairpins. In addition, she carries a considerable freight
of earrings, bracelets, and girdle pendants, all of gold, jade, or

some other precious substance. She wears a variety of fragrant and diaphanous garments that trail and flap about seductively. Her waist is slim, her hands delicately white; but of her breasts and buttocks, those parts of the anatomy so prominent in Indian love poetry, we hear not a word.

Makeup: mascara on her "moth eyebrows"; lipstick; rouge and powder on her cheeks; a faint semicircle of yellow pigment on her forehead; on her face perhaps a black beauty spot painted here or there. The application of all this is an elaborate and time-consuming process which the lady is often too dispirited to complete. With makeup only half executed, she is thought to be more charming than ever.

Activities: in her more energetic moments, she may sing, dance, play the *ch'in* or horizontal lute, pound cloth in the fulling process already noted, or perhaps weave, usually a pattern of grapes or mandarin ducks, the latter symbolic of conjugal joy. But more often she appears listless, scarcely able to sustain the burden of her own robes and adornments, morosely watching the moon, the flowers, the winging of the birds, which remind her of the relentless winging of time. She weeps often and copiously, wetting her clothing and whatever else happens to be in the way. Her whole existence is meaningless and void without the company of the man she pines for—or so the men who wrote so tirelessly of her would have us believe.

As this summary no doubt suggests, most of the love poems in the *Yü-t'ai hsin-yung*, particularly the "palace style" pieces from the later centuries, consist of variations on certain stereotyped themes, notably that of the neglected wife or palace lady. Some were command performances, written at banquets or other gatherings at the bidding of noble patrons; others were literary exercises produced for the delectation of the poet and his friends. Only occasionally do we come across a piece that seems to be about real people or a real experience, a living flower among all these brittle artifacts. It is impossible to say, of course, whether in fact it *is* founded upon real experience, and indeed the question of the reality of the experience that inspired it is, as far as critical evaluation is concerned,

undoubtedly irrelevant. What is important is the tone of sincerity
that breathes life into the work and gives it an air of urgency.
As for the set pieces with their adroit but faintly weary juggling
of clichés, they lie dead upon the page, and one wonders if, even
at the time of composition, they could have commanded any real
interest.

Dull or mediocre poetry, since it exists in every language, hardly
needs illustration. The poems from the *Yü-t'ai hsin-yung* which I
have chosen to quote here are all works that for one reason or
another strike me as moving and important. The first, in *yüeh-fu*
style, could as well have been included in Chapter IV, but its theme
and early date make it crucial to the discussion here. Entitled "Song
of Regret," it is attributed to a concubine of Emperor Ch'eng
(reigned 32–7 B.C.) of the Han. A member of the Pan family and
great-aunt of the historian Pan Ku, she is known by her court
title *Chieh-yü* or Lady in attendance, her personal name being lost
to history. She is said to have composed the song when, having
ceased to enjoy favor with the emperor, she was sent to live in the
palace of the empress dowager. There is no reason to doubt the
existence of Lady Pan, but the poem in all likelihood is of later date,
probably the second century A.D. It represents the earliest known
treatment in five-character *shih* form of the theme of the neglected
palace lady and as such has had enormous influence on later hand-
lings of the theme. It treats the subject of lost love through the
image of a "paired-joy" fan, a fan made of two silk faces sewn
together to form a symbol of happy union, such as might be carried
in the front folds of a Chinese robe and drawn out for use when
desired.

> To begin I cut fine silk of Ch'i,
> white and pure as frost or snow,
> shape it to make a paired-joy fan,
> round, round as the luminous moon,
> to go in and out of my lord's breast;
> when lifted, to stir him a gentle breeze.
> But always I dread the coming of autumn,
> cold winds that scatter the burning heat,

when it will be laid away in the hamper,
love and favor cut off midway.

The next poem is by Hsü Kan (171–218), one of the Seven Masters
of the Chien-an period. In some texts it is entitled "Poem without a
Category," in others it is treated as part of a longer poem entitled
"The Wife's Thoughts." It opens with the suggestion that one
might employ a cloud as bearer of love messages, a conceit found
earlier in the *Ssu-mei-jen* or "Thinking of a Fair One" of the *Ch'u
Tz'u* (Hawkes, p. 72), and one which may be familiar to readers
through its use in Kalidasa's poem "The Cloud Messenger." But
whereas the protagonist of the Indian poem ends by declaring
optimistically that the cloud will surely carry out the mission, the
Chinese poet, with characteristic common sense, discards the idea
as unworkable.

Clouds that drift so far and free
I'd ask to bear my message,
but their whirling shapes accept no charge;
wandering, halting, I long in vain.
Those who part all meet once more;
you alone send no word of return.
Since you went away,
my shining mirror darkens with neglect.
Thoughts of you are like the flowing river—
when will they ever end?

Lu Yün (262–303), author of the next poem, is the younger
brother of Lu Chi, whose work has been quoted on p. 46. His
poem, entitled "For Yen Yen-hsien To Give to His Wife," was
written for a presumably less articulate friend, a practice which,
judging from poem titles such as this, was fairly common in Six
Dynasties times.

I on the sunny side of Three Rivers,
you in the gloom south of Five Lakes,
mountains and seas vast between us,
farther apart than bird and fish—
my eyes envision your lovely form,

my ears still ring with your soft sweet voice.
I lie down alone, full of far-off thoughts;
waking, I stroke the collar of my empty robe.
Beautiful one, sharer of my longing,
who but you will ever hold my heart?

The two poems that follow are by P'an Yüeh (d. A.D. 300). The
first is the second of two poems entitled "Thinking of My Wife."
The second, "Lamenting the Dead," is the first of three poems
written in memory of the poet's wife, who died around A.D. 298.
It became the model for later works on the theme of the deceased
wife; see p. 210.

Alone in my sorrow, where do my thoughts go?
Man's life is like the morning dew.
Wandering in distant provinces,
fondly, tenderly I call up the past.
Your love follows me even here;
my heart too turns back in longing.
Though our bodies are parted and cannot touch,
our spirits join at journey's midpoint.
Have you never seen the hilltop pine,
how even in winter it keeps the same hue?
Have you never seen the knoll and valley cypresses,
in year-end cold, guarding their constant green?
Don't say it is my wish that parts us;
far away, my love grows stronger still.

"Lamenting the Dead"
Before I know it, winter and spring depart,
cold and heat suddenly trading places,
and she has gone to the deepest springs;
heaped earth forever seals her apart.
My secret longings I cannot fulfill;
what good would it do to linger there?
Swearing allegiance to the sovereign's command,
I turn my heart back to former tasks.
But seeing the house, I think of her;

entering its rooms, I recall the past.
Curtains and screens hold no shadow of her,
her writings the only trace that remains,
the drifting scent that never quite fades,
her things left forgotten, hung on the wall.
Dazed by longing, I think she is here,
then come to myself with a twinge of pain—
   We were a pair of birds winging to the wood,
     mated, then suddenly one morning alone;
   a pair of fish swimming the stream,
     eye to eye, then parted midway—
Spring wind filters in through the cracks,
morning rain drips down from the eaves;
lying at rest, when will I forget?
Each day I sink into deeper sorrow.
Perhaps a time will come when it will fade
and I, like Chuang Tzu, can pound the tub.

爱 "Secret longings": the poet hints that he is tempted to join his wife by
committing suicide at her grave.
   "Like Chuang Tzu": when Chuang Tzu first lost his wife, he grieved for
her like other men, but in time he became reconciled and spent his days singing
and pounding on a tub. *Chuang Tzu* sec. 18.

The next poem is the second in a series called "Five Poems on the
Joy of Union" by Yang Fang (4th century). It abounds in images and
phrases such as "a concord of cocoons" which, while often im-
precise in meaning, ring with felicitous connotations.

The loadstone beckons to the long needle,
the burning glass calls down fire and smoke;
*kung* and *shang* blend their voices;
hearts alike draw closer still.
My love binds me to you,
shadow in pursuit of form;
we sleep side by side beneath close-woven quilts,
stuffed with wadding from a concord of cocoons.
In heat our waving fans are two wings that touch,
in cold the felt mat seats us shoulder to shoulder.

You laugh and suddenly I am laughing too;
you grieve and all my joy has vanished.
Coming, I match my steps with yours;
going, we share the very same dust;
equals of the *ch'iung-ch'iung* beasts,
in no act forsaking one another.
My only wish is that we never part,
that we unite our bodies in a single form,
in life partners of a common chamber,
in death two people in one coffin.
Lady Hsü proclaimed her love the truest;
our love surpasses words.

♫ "*Kung* and *shang*": the first two notes of the musical scale.
"*Ch'iung-ch'iung* beast": a fabulous creature, inseparable companion of the
equally fabulous *chü-hsü* beast, hence a symbol of fidelity.
"Lady Hsü": Hsü Shu, wife of an official of the Eastern Han named Ch'in
Chia; the *Yü-t'ai- hsin-yung* contains love poems attributed to the devoted couple.

The landscape poet Hsieh Ling-yün is the author of the next
two poems, entitled "An Exchange of Poems by Tung-yang
Stream." Though cast in a naïve folk idiom, they exemplify the wit
and sophistication typical of much Six Dynasties love poetry. Note
how the woman picks up the elaborately romantic tone of the man's
poem and mocks him with it. We are left completely in the dark as
to what the upshot of the exchange may have been.

1. How fetching! somebody's wife,
   washing her white feet beside the stream;
   a bright moon among the clouds,
   far away, too far away to reach!

2. How fetching! somebody's husband,
   riding a white skiff down the stream.
   May I ask what your intentions are,
   now that the moon has gone behind the clouds?

In Six Dynasties poetry love, particularly in its shadier manifestations, is treated with a freedom that is not found in the literature of

more Confucian-dominated eras.[1] Nevertheless, the Chinese poet, even in this time of relative frankness, does not permit himself the kind of open description of physical detail common to the erotic poetry of other cultures, but confines his attention mainly to clothing and articles of furniture. The following poems, three in a set called "Six Poems on Remembering," are about as close as the poet ever comes to a depiction of the act of love. The original set, by Shen Yüeh (441–513), describes the loved one at various moments of the day. The following three picture her as she arrives, takes her seat, and sleeps. The poems, otherwise in five-character lines like most of the poems we have been discussing, are unusual in employing a three-character opening line.

1. I think of when she comes—
    shining, shining, up the garden stairs,
    impatient, impatient to end our parting.
    Tireless, tireless, we talk of love,
    gaze at each other but never get our fill,
    look at one another till hunger is forgotten.

2. I think of when she sits—
    prim, prim before the gauze curtain,
    sometimes singing four or five songs,
    sometimes plucking two or three strings.
    When she laughs, there's no one like her;
    when she sulks, she's more lovely than before.

3. I think of when she sleeps—
    struggling to stay awake when others have retired,
    undoing her sheer gown without waiting to be urged,
    resting on the pillow till caresses find her.
    Fearful that the one by her side is watching,
    she blushes under the candle's glow.

---

[1] By literature I mean, here and elsewhere, the works written, or at least recorded and transmitted, by the educated class. What kind of love poetry, bawdy or otherwise, may have existed among the unlettered masses we will unfortunately never know.

The remainder of the love poems I shall quote need no further comment than that supplied in the headings.

Shen Yüeh: "Out early one morning, I met an old acquaintance: I composed this in the carriage to present to her."

> A touch of red left on your lip,
> traces of powder clinging here and there:
> where did you spend the night last night,
> that at dawn you brush through the dew, returning?

Shen Yüeh: "Written for my neighbor; he waited for a loved one who never came." (In the first two lines the anxious lover vainly imagines the arrival of his beloved.)

> Her shadow races with slanting moonbeams,
> her fragrance is borne on the distant breeze.
> She said yes when she really meant no.
> You'd like to laugh—but cry instead.

Wu Chün (469–520): "Song of Spring." (A man in government service in the capital longs for his wife or sweetheart; the way in which the gate and terrace are described identifies the location as the imperial palace.)

> Spring—where has it come from,
> brushing the waters, surprising the plum?
> Clouds bar the green-fretted gate,
> wind sweeps the terrace that lies open to the dew.
> A thousand miles keep me from my fair one,
> her gauze curtains drawn and never parted.
> No way to share a word with you,
> in vain I face the cup that wakes these memories.

Hsü Chün-ch'ien (6th century): "Sitting Up with My Wife on New Year's Eve." (It was the custom at New Year's to place a daddy longlegs, whose name, *hsi-tzu*, is a homophone for "happiness," in the wine, and to hide wild plums in the dumplings.)

> So many delights the excitement has no end,
> so much joy the cup is never still:
> pluck a daddy longlegs out of the wine,

find a wild plum inside the dumpling!
The blinds swing open and wind lifts the curtain;
the candle burns low, its wick turned to ash.
No wonder the pins weigh heavy in your hair—
we've waited up so long for dawn light to come!

Hsü Chün-ch'ien; "Beginning of Spring—A Stroll with My Wife."

Hairdo and ornaments all the latest fashion,
your outfit strictly in the newest style;
the grass still short enough to poke through sandals,
the plums so fragrant their perfume rubs off!
Trees slant down to pluck at your brocade shawl,
breezes sidle up and get under your crimson kerchief—
Fill the cups with orchid blossom wine!
These are sights to make the spirit sing.

✤ "Orchid blossom wine": wine on which blossoms have been floated.

Liu Ling-hsien (6th century), the wife of Hsü Fei: "Inscribed on a Plantain Leaf To Show to a Certain Person."

Tears at evening?—not infrequent;
crying out in dreams—much too often!
All this my nightly pillow is aware of;
other than it, there's none that knows.

## LATE SIX DYNASTIES POETRY

*Seeds in a dry pod, tick, tick, tick*—EDGAR LEE MASTERS

With this section we come to the end of the first major phase in the development of the five-character and seven-character *shih* form. We have seen the form grow rapidly and dramatically in the late years of the Eastern Han, and the Three Kingdoms period that followed. We have watched it settle down to a sober maturity during the Chin, and then gradually sink into lifeless imitation in the ensuing centuries. We have also noted how an early realism gave way to stylization and extensive use of symbolism as the poets withdrew their gaze from the world about them and turned increasingly to worlds of their own imagining. These worlds, to be sure, were constructed out of elements from the realm of experience, not mere fictions of the mind. But the elements were fitted together and juxtaposed in ways that would be impossible in real life.

Two devices of great importance in Chinese poetry figure prominently in this process of assembling and fitting together the elements of a poem: allusion and parallelism. Richard Aldington, writing of the Latin poetry of the Renaissance, speaks of a time "when the subtle flavors of innumerable reminiscences of earlier writers were deliberately enjoyed, when every line and phrase was drenched in older poetry." [2] Chinese poetry, especially that of Six Dynasties times, is similarly "drenched in older poetry," the device of allusion being used both to give textured compression to the language and to endow the poem with greater richness of association, greater depth in time. Needless to say, the device is open to abuse. The poet who employs allusions that are too familiar runs the risk of sounding banal; one who is too recherché merely invites bafflement. It is generally agreed that, at least by our modern standards of taste, the Six Dynasties poets overworked the device. Reading their compositions, one wearies after a time of so much borrowing and elaboration of earlier elements, of so much indirection, and longs for the man with something daring and new to say.

Ideally, allusion serves to imbue a poem with rich, nostalgic recollections of the past. Parallelism for its part provides a neat rack upon which to rearrange the elements drawn from the experiential world, to impose on them a symmetry they lack in the chaos of reality. Thus, to cite an example much admired in the writer's time, and still, I think, highly admirable, in a *yüeh-fu* style poem on the theme of the young woman sorrowing for her distant love (*Hsi-hsi-yen*) by Hsüeh Tao-heng (540–609), we find this couplet:

> Dark windows where spider webs dangle;
> empty rafters, swallow dust drifting down;

The verbal parallelism is perfect without appearing to be excessively forced or mechanical. In thought the two lines seem at first glance

---

[2] *The Portable Oscar Wilde*, p. 12.

to be almost identical: dark windows and empty rafters both convey the gloom and loneliness of the room where the woman waits, spider webs and swallow dust suggest the sad neglect into which the room—and, by implication, its occupant—have fallen. If we look more closely, however, we see that there is also an element of contrast. The musty spiders, we may surmise, are still there in their webs; but the swallows, symbols of happiness and prosperity, have departed, leaving only their old nests of mud to crumble and send dust drifting down into the room. Both lines are made up of what appear to be closely observed details, as though the poet had inspected the room with care and reported exactly what he found. At the same time they awake echoes from the past, being suggested no doubt by the couplet in the first of ten "Poems Without a Category" by Chang Hsieh (d. A.D. 307?):

> Green moss clings to the empty wall;
> spiders web the four corners of the house.

The spiders in turn date back to the *Book of Odes, #156*, "spiders are in the doorway," while the swallows likewise have a long history of occurrences in early poetry and prose.

Handled with skill and imagination, the device of parallelism is capable of conveying a kind of profound verbal, even philosophical, wit. But in Six Dynasties times its use is seldom as subtle as even the example cited above, which is still a far cry from what the device was to become in the hands of the T'ang masters, and more often the reader is merely bored or irritated by the mechanical way in which it clanks along. This is particularly true of those parallelisms that are built about some stock formula such as "looking up, I see . . .; gazing down, I note . . .".

Another device used to ornament, and often, it seems to me, to disfigure, poetry in the *shih* form during these centuries is that of elegant variation. The taste for stylization and artifice that encouraged the use of allusion and verbal parallelism also led to a demand for diction that was more elevated or refined than the ordinary speech of the day, for what the Chinese call *ya-yü*, "classic words." A greater richness of language might have resulted, but unfortunately the effect was mainly to encourage pedantry and obfuscation.

Six Dynasties society was dominated by aristocratic tastes and it is only natural that poetry as well, written by a small, highly educated elite, should reflect the common background of learning and sensibility shared by the members of the group. Very possibly those elements that strike us as pedantic and abstruse in the poetic diction of these men did not seem so at all to their contemporaries. The fact remains, however, that the tendency is to set aside the ordinary or concrete name for a thing in favor of some circumlocution involving a literary reference. Thus, for example, everyday phenomena of the natural world such as mountains or wind will be designated by the names of the trigrams or hexagrams which, in the *I Ching* or *Book of Changes*, are said to symbolize them; or such a simple thing as the human heart will be referred to as "not-a-stone" because *Odes* #26 contains the line, "My heart is not a stone to be rolled about." Similarly, adjectives will be used less to describe than to convey an aura of rarity or approbation. Deftness and refinement of language rather than precision is the ideal.

In the works of the best poets, such as Juan Chi, T'ao Yüan-ming, or Hsieh Ling-yün, such devices as allusion, parallelism, and elegant variation are employed with restraint and discretion, and for the most part do not get in the way of the ideas. But when one turns to the works of lesser men, one realizes that interest has shifted almost completely from the question of what to say to that of how to say it, and that poetry as a result has grown increasingly mannered and stereotyped. Even a first-rate writer such as Pao Chao, for example, will begin a poem describing a journey with these lines:

> The fountain's source crowns the peaceful stream,
> to the river's end cleansing the faraway waves;
> morning light clothes the tribe of waters,
> dawn air breathes through forest corners;

in which verbal cleverness, interesting as it may be, has clearly taken precedence over clarity and precision.[3]

[3] "Returning to the Capital, When I Reached Three Mountains I Looked Far Off at Stone City." Following other versions of the text, the first line of the quotation should read: "The fountain's source rests at the crown of the stream,"

We have already noted the *ni-ku* or imitations of earlier poems which came into vogue in the fourth century and opened the way for floods of mediocre verse by men who lacked inspiration to devise themes of their own. Other writers, similarly uninspired, confined their efforts to occasional poems on the subjects assigned them at social gatherings or, as though cognizant of Dryden's advice, were content to retire to "some peaceful province of acrostic land."

Hsieh Ling-yün, the great landscape poet of the early fifth century, clambered up mountains and penetrated dense forests in order to view the scenery he loved so well and in which he claimed to descry the principles of truth. But poets of the years following him, though they continued to write of the beauties of nature, were more likely to be viewing them in the parks and suburbs of the capital, even perhaps in their own private gardens. A taste for nature's grandeurs spurred interest in landscape gardening and resulted in a craze for miniature mountains and rivers created by skillful artisans within the confines of an urban estate. It seems hardly a coincidence that landscape poetry, in both the *fu* and *shih* forms, underwent a similar process of miniaturization. Poems became briefer and tidier and, rather than attempting to treat the reader to vast, panoramic views, as earlier works had done, were content to focus on a single object—a tree, a flower, a stone, or a tiny insect. It is as though all majesty had vanished from the landscape, all wonder and excitement from the viewer's soul, leaving behind a stock of quaint little images to be endlessly rearranged.

Late Six Dynasties poetry, stilted and effete in style, is rendered even more trying by its almost uniformly dolorous tone. We have noted the air of somberness that hangs over so much of the early poetry in the *shih* form, the depictions of death and desolation, the morbid preoccupation with the graveyard, the symbolism that keeps haling us back to the themes of time and evanescence. Certainly the poets, at least those of the third and fourth centuries, had much to be doleful about, living in a land repeatedly ravaged by foreign

---

which makes much better sense. In fairness to the Six Dynasties poets one should remember that what appear to be instances of strained or peculiar diction may at times be merely the result of faulty transmission of the text.

invasion, civil strife, and popular uprising, where plague and famine waited to carry off those that human rapacity may have spared. It is true that philosophy and religion, though acknowledging the existence of sorrow, in no sense condoned a preoccupation with it. Confucius had declared flatly that the truly good man is never unhappy (*Analects* XIV, 30), though he confessed that he himself had not yet reached that goal; and Yang Hsiung (53 B.C.–A.D. 18), one of the leading Confucian philosophers of the Han, reaffirmed that the sage, by definition, as it were, has no worries "because he understands Fate" (*Fa yen* sec. 3). Taoism, likewise, displays only scorn for those who allow themselves to become immersed in melancholy, and its own wise men are conventionally pictured as jovial and carefree. Of the so-called Three Religions, only Buddhism seems to place deliberate emphasis upon the pity, sordidness, and horror of human existence, and this is done only as a preliminary step, to waken the individual to the problem of suffering and set his feet on the path to salvation.

Why, then, did the Chinese intellectuals of this period, who usually professed to adhere to one or another of these faiths, permit themselves to become so despondent, even maudlin, in their poetry? One answer no doubt lies in what they conceived a poem, particularly one in *shih* form, to be. *Shih yen chih* states an ancient definition of poetry enshrined in the Confucian Classics (*Tso chuan*, Duke Hsiang, 27th year, and elsewhere). Like so many early Chinese definitions, this one is essentially a pun: *shih* (poetry) expresses *chih*. *Chih*, troublesomely broad in meaning, may be variously interpreted as "purpose," "will," "thought," or "feeling." Early scholars, who had in mind the poems of the *Book of Odes,* emphasized the purposive aspects, insisting that poetry should embody moral and political aims and values. From the end of the Han, however, there was a gradual shift away from the moralistic interpretation in favor of one that stressed the emotional nature of poetry, and this was the view that held favor in the period under discussion. In other words, men believed that the purpose of poetry was to provide an outlet for those emotions that could not be wholly stilled or redirected by philosophy or religion, and which one would hesitate to express in other types of writing where coolness and objectivity were the goal.

And because these emotions proved most often to be melancholy ones, sadness and poetry, particularly lyric poetry in the *shih* form, came to be all but inextricably linked. As Pao Chao, in a poem entitled "Answering a Visitor," puts it:

When joy comes, I dip the wine alone;
when care arrives, I forthwith write a poem.

"A clean, honest, unsentimental melancholy," says a Russian poet, "for all its air of helplessness, urges us forward, creating with its fragile hands the greatest spiritual treasures of mankind."[4] Yevtushenko, from whom the quotation is taken, representing a people whose literature is customarily thought of as predominantly gloomy, speaks with authority. The case of late Six Dynasties poetry, however, suggests that melancholy, as well as urging one forward, can also bog one down, though this may well be because it is not of the honest and unsentimental variety described above. Perhaps it is wrong to single out the air of hopelessness that marks the poetry of this period and hold it culpable for all the stylistic weakness and banality that prevailed. Perhaps, on the contrary, it is the badness of style that makes the poetry sound so hopeless. The fact remains that Chinese poetry in the *shih* form had by the end of the sixth century reached such a level of triviality and repetitiousness, both in language and sentiment, that it seemed beyond recovery. Take, for example, this poem by Yü Shih-chi (d. 618) entitled "Entering the Barrier":

Clouds of Lung, low and unbroken,
the Yellow River, sobbing as it flows;
mountains of the Barrier—how many miles of road
joined one to the other in countless lengths of sorrow!

The poem is far from representing the worst products of the period. In fact, it was selected for inclusion in the *Ku-shih-yüan* (Fountain of ancient poetry) by the eminent poet and critic Shen Te-ch'ien (1673-1769), who was certainly not one to be taken in by bathetic mediocrity. The poet, it should be noted, does not say

4 Yevgeny Yevtushenko, *A Precocious Autobiography,* tr. by Andrew R. Mac-Andrew, p. 72.

why his journey should be so sad. The geography of the poem indicates that the "Barrier" referred to is the northern border of China, in which case the poet is actually entering his homeland. One wonders, therefore, what hyperboles he has held in reserve should he some day wish to describe a journey in the opposite direction. The truth, of course, is that he mentions no reason for his sorrow because, by his time, all travel, in whatever direction, was by definition assumed to be sorrowful. Custom decreed that each step of the journey should occasion a teardrop in the eye— no other reaction was thinkable. It is this trite conventionality underlying it that vitiates the grief of Yü Shih-chi's statement and prevents the poem, for all its skill of expression, from moving us. Convention, when it departs too far or too long from the norms of human experience, ends by isolating its adherents, and even rendering them ridiculous.

# VII

## INNOVATIONS OF

## THE T'ANG

꣠

THE STRIFE and disorder that had wracked China for so long were brought to an end by the Sui dynasty, which in 589 managed to unite north and south under a single rule and which was succeeded in 618 by the more long-lived T'ang. But such milestones of political history are of little significance when one is tracing the course of literary development. The decades of the Sui and early T'ang, though of vital importance in the growth of Chinese social and political institutions, represent in poetry a mere continuation of late Six Dynasties genres and styles. It was not until the eighth century that, with the appearance of a group of talented and original poets, a distinctive new style was born, the style we think of when we speak of T'ang-shih or T'ang poetry.

Literary historians customarily divide the T'ang into four periods which, although marked by no hard and fast boundaries, are convenient for purposes of discussion. The first, when poetry continued in the ornate and mannered style described in the

The T'ang-shih san-pai-shou or Three Hundred Poems of the T'ang, the best-known anthology of T'ang poetry, has been translated by Witter Bynner and Kang-hu Kiang under the title The Jade Mountain. Articles of interest pertaining to T'ang nature imagery are A. R. Davis, "The Double Ninth Festival in Chinese Poetry," Wen-lin Studies in the Chinese Humanities, pp. 45–64; and John C. H. Wu, "The Four Seasons of T'ang Poetry," T'ien Hsia Monthly, Apr., May, Aug., Nov., 1938; Feb., Aug., 1939.

preceding chapter, is known as Ch'u-T'ang or Early T'ang. This is followed in the early eighth century by what is generally conceded to be the most brilliant era in T'ang poetry, perhaps in all of Chinese poetry, called Sheng-T'ang, or High T'ang. The period of Tu Fu, Li Po, and other renowned poets whom I shall discuss in the next chapter, it corresponds largely to the reign of the famous Emperor Hsüan-tsung (713–55), though it is customarily extended until about 765. The remaining years of the dynasty are designated Chung-T'ang or Middle T'ang, roughly 765 to 835; and Wan-T'ang or Late T'ang, from 835 to the fall of the dynasty in 907. The reasons for such periodization will become clearer later on when we examine the question of stylistic development.

Compared to the eras treated in the preceding chapters, the T'ang saw a great increase in the number of men writing poetry, and the number of poems written, or at least preserved for posterity. The *Ch'üan-T'ang-shih* (Complete T'ang poetry), compiled in the eighteenth century on the basis of earlier collections, contains over 48,000 poems by 2,200 writers. Moreover, the number of poems attributed to a single poet surpasses anything known in earlier times, Po Chü-i and Tu Fu, the two most prolific poets, being credited with about 2,800 and 1,400 poems respectively.

The T'ang is also noteworthy for the formal innovations and refinements which took place during its three-century span. The seven-character *shih* form, for example, which had been employed sporadically from the end of the second century (see p. 16), was popularized and brought to maturity. In addition, the T'ang saw the development and refinement of a whole group of new poetic forms known collectively as *chin-t'i-shih* or "modern style poetry."

In the introduction to this volume we have already noted the end rhymes, internal rhymes, and alliterations that contribute so richly to the euphonic effectiveness of Chinese poetry. In addition, the tone of a particular word was, or at some point became, an important factor in the over-all poetic effect, though we do not know enough about the role of tones in early Chinese to say just when this state of affairs began. Outside of vague references to "sound" and "harmony," the earliest clear statements we have on the function of tones in poetic composition date from the fifth century and are associated with the name of Shen Yüeh (441–513), whose works have been quoted in Chapter VI. Shen is credited with having defined the so-called *pa-ping* (eight faults), which describe eight undesirable euphonic effects to be avoided in poetry. The exact nature of these faults is not always clear and in any case need not concern us here. Four have to do with rhyme and four with tone, and the net result is to warn the writer away from any unintentional repetitions of tone or rhyme. A careful writer of English knows that he must avoid unintentional rhymes, whether in prose or poetry, as these will distract the reader and lead him to search for some added emphasis or formal adornment where none exists. The same is presumably true of tones when one is writing in a tonal language. Shen Yüeh's solution is to avoid using several words in succession that have the same tone, and, in the second line of a couplet, to avoid arranging the words in such a way that they repeat the same succession of tones as that found in the first line. In dealing with tonal effects, the four tones are divided into two groups, the *p'ing* or level tone category, and the *tse* or deflected tone category, which includes the remaining three tones. The application of Shen Yüeh's suggestions thus produces a kind of mirror-image parallelism in the two lines of each couplet, words in important positions in the upper line that are in the level tone being matched in the lower line by words that are in one of the deflected tones, and vice versa.

Not everyone accepted Shen Yüeh's dicta, and some people claimed not even to understand what he was talking about. But a sufficient number of poets began to apply them, or at least the general euphonic principles upon which they are based, so that in time they led to the development of new verse forms marked by careful attention to tonal pattern and known as "modern style poetry." Of these, the two most important are the *lü-shih* or "regulated verse," and the *chüeh-chü* or "broken-off lines."

The rules for these verse forms were not strictly codified until the seventh century, and were often violated to some degree. Those for regulated verse require that it be eight lines in length, using either a five-character or seven-character line. The type of tonal parallelism described above, in which the second line of a couplet represents a mirror image of the first line, is demanded in all couplets. In addition, the two middle couplets must observe strict verbal parallelism, of a type that forbids repetition of any word within the couplet; in the other couplets, verbal parallelism is optional. The same rhyme is used throughout and all rhyme words must be of the same tone. In Six Dynasties times, rhymes in various tones were permitted, but from the T'ang on, the rhymes had to belong to the level tone.

Rules for the *chüeh-chü* are less strict. Tonal parallelism is required but not strict verbal parallelism. Five-character, seven-character, and, rarely, six-character lines are used, the number of lines being restricted to four. The *chüeh-chü* is thus the briefest important Chinese verse form, though briefer forms have at times been used, such as four-character four-line verse or even three-character four-line verse. The last, representing a total of twelve syllables, is five syllables shorter than the Japanese haiku and almost certainly the world's shortest poetic form.

From here on, when quoting poetry, I will note the line length and form of each poem so that the reader may know when he is reading works in these new forms. The verbal parallelisms required in the *lü-shih* will, I trust, be immediately apparent in translation, though tonal parallelisms, of course, cannot be reproduced in English. With the development of these "modern style" forms, the earlier types of poetry, which were unrestricted in length and did not demand verbal or tonal parallelism, came to be referred to as *ku-shih* or "old poetry." These old forms continued to be used, particularly for ballad-like poems in *yüeh-fu* style, and many examples will be included in my selection, partly because they tend to translate better than the compressed and intricate "modern style" poems. It is interesting to note that poets of the T'ang, when they wrote in the old forms, often deliberately violated the euphonic rules laid down for "modern style" verse, varied the rhyme scheme in unusual fashion, or went out of their way to avoid verbal parallelism, as though reacting against the strictures of the newer forms and glorifying in the freedom from technical niceties.

If the T'ang saw innovations in poetic form, it proved on the whole much less inventive in matters of theme and expression. In later chapters I shall discuss some of the major poets of the period, men whose works are important and distinctive enough to be treated individually. Here I should like to present a selection of 26 poems by lesser-known men that I hope will give the reader an idea of what sort of themes were most often treated in T'ang poetry, and how. The poems range in date from the seventh to the tenth century, though the great majority belong to the High, Middle, and Late T'ang periods.

Many of the poems of the T'ang are in *yüeh-fu* style, in which the poet describes or speaks in the voice of a hunter, a rich idler of the capital, a peasant girl, or a soldier on border duty. As in earlier times, these ballads or ballad-type poems of the *yüeh-fu* tradition were written sometimes as mere literary exercises, sometimes to provide lyrics for popular songs, and sometimes to voice serious social criticism or satire. Other poems pertain to the subject of friendship, occasional pieces composed when taking leave of a friend or sent in lieu of a letter. There are poems which combine the friendship theme with that of the recluse, usually describing a visit to a hermit friend who turned out not to be at home. This last type is common enough to constitute a kind of subcategory within the larger body of eremitic poetry; the conventional wording of the title, "Looking for so-and-so but failing to find him," apparently carried deep philosophical connotations that intrigued the T'ang people.

There are a certain number of love poems, though this category is of less importance than in earlier centuries. T'ang men wrote voluminously on the subject of love, but almost always indirectly, through the personae of the *yüeh-fu* tradition. Occasionally they would allude to some romantic escapade of their own, usually with a singing girl or professional entertainer, but they were more reticent on the subject of their wives than had been their predecessors in Six Dynasties times. Exceptions such as Tu Fu may be found, but for the most part we learn of a man's affection for his wife only if he has occasion to write a lament on her death, when presumably the disclosure will no longer embarrass anyone.

Finally, there are the poems dealing with the palace lady or
*kung-jen*, another subject carried over from earlier poetry and one
which showed no diminution in popularity. In fact, so important
is this theme in T'ang poetry that it may be well to examine it here
in some detail. Why, we may ask, were the poets so fascinated
with the figure of the palace lady? What did she symbolize for
them?

Selected from among the most beautiful and desirable women of
the empire, the palace ladies usually entered service when quite
young. In most cases they were presented by their parents, who
hoped thereby to gain wealth and distinction, though occasionally
they were selected by the emperor after having caught his eye at
some outing or state function. Potentially they were capable of
rising to a position of the highest honor. History was full of tales
of women like Lady Li, or the dancing girls Flying Swallow and
her sister, favorites of Han emperors who had done just that,
and the men of the T'ang were witnesses to the most memorable
example of all, that of the beautiful Yang Kuei-fei, favorite of
Emperor Hsüan-tsung.

But there were literally thousands of women in the harems of
the T'ang rulers, and it is obvious that most of them were destined
to endure loneliness and neglect. Virtual prisoners in the palace,
seeing no one but eunuchs and ladies in waiting, they lived in
apartments opening onto small gardens where a few trees blos-
somed and shed their petals, isolated yet not so far removed that
they could escape the sound of music and laughter, borne on the
wind from other parts of the palace, telling them that elsewhere
there were revels in progress. When their beauty had faded and all
hope of the ruler's favor was gone, the women might, for one reason
or another, be sent home, though usually they continued to reside
in the palace until death. Indeed, the figure of the white-haired
palace lady who still wears elaborate coiffure and makeup and
retains her coquettish airs is often the butt of satire. On their death,
the women were buried in a special plot, the *kung-jen-hsieh* or
Graveyard of Palace Women, outside the walls of Ch'ang-an, a
place said to have been haunted on stormy nights by sounds of
singing and weeping.

All hope of happiness for the palace lady, therefore, hung upon the chance that she might attract and hold the ruler's favor, the further chance that she might bear him a child, and that it might be a boy. Otherwise she was doomed to a life of despair, deprived of all the normal consolations of family, friends, and freedom of movement. The T'ang men wrote of her because her plight sincerely moved them, and because, being themselves candidates for public office and hopeful of recognition for their talents, it was in some ways so like their own. Perhaps this is also why they pictured her as full of despondency, but never the least bit irate or vengeful. She might go on endlessly lamenting her fate, but it was unthinkable that she should ever raise a hand to change it.

The Early T'ang, as we have noted, saw a continuation of the poetic style of the late Six Dynasties and Sui. Most of the verse was either occasional, composed at social gatherings on assigned topics and rhymes, or reworkings of conventional themes, especially those of the *yüeh-fu* tradition. It was on the whole signally lacking in originality and conviction. Ch'en Tzu-ang (661–702) is customarily credited with having begun the creation of a new style, restoring to the *shih* form some of the vigor, directness, and intense personal feeling that had for so long been lacking, and it is therefore appropriate that our selection should open with him. The following famous poem, though usually classified as a seven-character *ku-shih* or old style poem, is actually composed of two lines of five characters each, followed by two lines of six.

Ch'en Tzu-ang (661–702), "Song on Climbing Yu-chou Terrace," *ku-shih*.

> Behind me I do not see the ancient men,
> before me I do not see the ones to come.
> Thinking of the endlessness of heaven and earth,
> alone in despair, my tears fall down.

Chang Chiu-ling (678–740), "Watching the Moon with Thoughts of Far Away," five-character *lü-shih*. A love poem of great subtlety and indirection; the moonlight and dew of the third couplet have mild erotic overtones. The "good times" are probably future meetings rather than those of the past.

Bright moon born of the sea,
at sky's farthest edges we share it now.
A man of heart, hating the long night,
till the end of evening wakeful, remembering:
I put out the lamp, marvel at the moonlight's fullness,
brush my cloak, learning the dampness of dew.
No way to send my gift, this handful of moonbeams,
I go back to bed, dreaming of good times.

Ch'iu Wei (694–789?), "Visiting a Recluse on West Mountain and
Not Finding Him in," 5-character *ku-shih*.

At the topmost peak, one thatch hut,
straight up for thirty li:
knock on the gate—there is no houseboy;
peer into the room—nothing but a desk;
if he hasn't rigged an awning on the firewood cart,
then he must be fishing in the autumn stream.
One this way, one that—we missed each other,
my admiration for you left untold.
But the color of the grasses under new rain,
the voice of the pines in an evening window—
these are the promised hidden wonders,
enough to open wide the ear and heart.
Though my plan for host and guest came to nothing,
somehow I've grasped the meaning of purity.
And now the mood is over, I'm off down the mountain—
what need to wait around for you?

+Я "Purity": *ch'ing-ching*, a translation of the Sanskrit *śuddha*, a Buddhist term
designating a state of perfect spiritual purity.

Wang Ch'ang-ling (698–755?), "Castleside Song," 5- and 7-charac-
ter *ku-shih*, *yüeh-fu*.

Fall winds wail in mulberry branches;
grasses whiten, the fox and rabbit frisk.
In Han-tan he's been drinking—before the wine wears off,
over broad plains north of the castle he flies his black falcon,
in the empty camp site shoots two pouncing tigers dead,
then turns home by crescent moon, bowcase slung at his belt.

Ts'ui Hao (704–54), "Songs of Ch'ang-kan," 5-character *chüeh-chü*,
*yüeh-fu*. Ch'ang-kan is on the Yangtze near Nanking. The poems,
an exchange between a woman and a traveling merchant, have been
interpreted as the attempts of a prostitute in the river town to
attract a customer, though they may just as well be the innocent
queries of a girl who thinks she recognizes someone from her
home town.

> [SHE] Tell me, where is your home?
>   I live at Sloping Banks myself—
>   Stop the boat, let me ask a minute—
>   who knows but maybe we're from the same town!
> [HE] My home looks over the Nine River waters;
>   up and down the Nine Rivers I go.
>   True, I came from Ch'ang-kan like you,
>   but I was a boy then—we never met.

Liu Chang-ch'ing (709–85), "Rejoicing that the Zen Master Pao
Has Arrived from Dragon Mountain," 5-character *lü-shih*.

> What day did you come down from that former place,
> spring grasses ready to turn green and fair?
> Still it faces the mountain moon,
> but who listens now to its rock-bound stream?
> Monkey cries tell you night is fading;
> blossoms that open show you the fleeting years.
> With metal staff you quietly come and go,
> mindless—for everywhere is Zen.

Ch'u Kuang-hsi (707–59?), "The Streets of Ch'ang-an," 5-character
*chüeh-chü*, *yüeh-fu*. A satire on the rich young noblemen of the
capital.

> Cracking whips, off to the wine shop,
> in flashy clothes heading for the whorehouse door;
> a million cash spent in an hour—
> expressionless, they never speak a word.

The Buddhist Priest Chiao-jan (730–99), "Looking for Lu Hung-
chien but Failing To Find Him," 5-character *lü-shih*. Usually it is

the layman who goes off to the country to visit the priest; here the situation is reversed.

> You've moved to a house backing the outer wall;
> I reach it by wild paths through mulberry and hemp.
> Along the fence chrysanthemums newly set out
> have yet to bloom, though autumn's here.
> I pound the gate but no dog barks.
> About to go, I ask at the house next door;
> they tell me you're up in the hills,
> never come home till the sun is low.

Wei Ying-wu (b. 736), "To Send to Li Tan and Yüan Hsi," 7-character *lü-shih*. The poet held an official post and hence felt responsible for the existence of "vagrants in the city."

> Last year among the flowers I saw you off;
> today the buds unfolding make it a year.
> The world's ways—dim and distant, hard to foretell;
> spring griefs—dull and dark; I sleep alone,
> body full of aches and ills, remembering fields of home.
> Vagrants in the city—I'm ashamed to draw my pay.
> I hear you may be coming to visit—
> from west tower, how many rounding moons must I wait?

Wei Ying-wu, "West Creek at Ch'u-chou," 7-character *chüeh-chü*.

> These I love: hidden plants that grow by the river's edge;
> above, yellow warblers in the deep trees singing;
> spring tides robed in rain, swifter by evening;
> the ferry landing deserted where a boat swings by itself.

The poem has been interpreted as a political allegory: hidden plants = gentlemen in retirement; yellow warblers = petty men in high places; spring tides, etc. = worsening political conditions; ferry landing, etc. = the ruler uncomprehending, though the remedy (a boat) lies close at hand. One would be inclined to dismiss this as nonsense were it not for the disturbing fact that there does not seem to have been any such place as West Creek (Hsi-chien) at Ch'u-chou.

Wei Ying-wu, "Sent to the Taoist Holy Man of Ch'üan-chiao

Mountain," 5-character *ku-shih*. "White stones" are said to be the
food of recluses.

This morning it was cold in my office study
and suddenly I thought of you, living in the mountains,
in valley bottoms bundling thorns for kindling,
coming home to cook white stones.
I wanted to take a gourdful of wine
to cheer you far off in evening wind and rain,
but falling leaves have filled the empty hills;
where could I find a trace of you?

Ssu-k'ung Shu (740–90?), "The Rebellion Over, I See Off a Friend
Who Is Returning North," 5-character *lü-shih*. The rebellion was
that led by An Lu-shan (see p. 149).

A world in turmoil—we came south together;
clear times—you return north alone.
In a strange country your hair turned white;
in your old land you'll see the blue hills,
by dawn moon passing ruined forts,
under crowding stars to rest by old frontiers,
cold birds and withered grasses
everywhere companion to your grieving eyes.

Yü Hu (b. 745), "Thoughts South of the Yangtze," 7-character
*chüeh-chü. yüeh-fu*. A young girl prays to the god of the river and
asks for a sign that her wandering lover is safe.

By the riverbank idly I pick white-budded reeds;
with the other girls, make offering to the river god.
So many people around, I don't dare speak out loud;
in my heart I ask news of my wanderer, toss a questioning coin.

Wang Chien (d. 830?), "Words of the Newly Wed Wife," 5-char-
acter *chüeh-chü*.

The third day I went into the kitchen,
washed my hands and made the soup.
Not yet sure of my mother-in-law's tastes,
I sent some first for sister-in-law to try.

Wang Chien, "Palace Song," 7-character *chüeh-chü.*

> I search the treetops, low-hung branches, for a trace of pink:
> one petal drifting west, one petal east.
> Peach blossoms thought only of fruit to come;
> it would be wrong to rail at the dawn-watch wind.

Paraphrase: My beauty has faded like the peach flowers and I am left alone. But I myself chose to become a lady of the palace because I hoped to bear the ruler a child and win favor. It would not be right to lay the blame for my plight upon my lord, whose attentions are naturally as changeable as the dawn wind.

Yüan Chen (779–831), "Airing Painful Memories," 7-character *lü-shih.* Thoughts of the poet's dead wife. Tao-yün, daughter of the rich and powerful Hsieh family in Six Dynasties times, was noted for her wit and intelligence; Ch'ien Lou was a worthy but impoverished scholar of antiquity.

> Lord Hsieh's youngest, his favorite child,
> married to Ch'ien Lou and a hundred cares!
> She saw I had no clothes and went digging through her wicker
>       trunks;
> I wheedled her into buying wine—off came her golden hairpins!
> Garden greens filled our tray—we were thankful for lanky
>       beanstalks;
> fallen leaves eked out the firewood—how we eyed the old ash tree!
> Today my pay comes to more than a hundred thousand—
>       and all I can offer are fasts and services for your soul!

Yü Wu-ling (b. 810), "Offering Wine," 5-character *chüeh-chü.*

> I offer you the golden flagon;
> do not disdain its brimming gift.
> Wind and rain await the opening flower,
> and partings make up too much of our life.

Li Tung (9th century), "For the Monk San-tsang on His Return to the Western Regions," 7-character *chüeh-chü.* The monk was a native of India.

> A hundred thousand li of journey, how many dangers?

Desert dragons, when you wag your tongue, will hear and be
      humbled.
The day you reach India's five lands, your hair will be white—
The moon sets on Ch'ang-an and its midnight bells.

Ch'en Tao (9th century), "Song of Lung-hsi," 7-character *chüeh-chü*,
*yüeh-fu*. Lung-hsi was a western outpost in Kansu; like so many of
the *yüeh-fu*, the poem, though it comments on contemporary affairs,
is set back in time, the "nomads" being identified as the Hsiung-nu,
a foreign people who harassed China in Han times. The Uncertain
River was so called because it frequently shifted its course; here the
poet skillfully plays upon the philosophical implications of the
name.

They swore to wipe out the nomads,
            no thought for themselves,
five thousand in sable and brocade,
            gone to barbarian dust.
Pity them—these bones by the shores
            of the Uncertain River—
to those who dream in spring chambers,
            they are still men!

Tu Mu (803–52), "Sent in Parting," 7-character *chüeh-chü*; the second
of two poems sent to a girl in Yang-chou.

Great love may seem like none at all:
wine before us, we only know that smiles won't come.
The tallow candle has a heart—it grieves at parting,
in our place drips tears until the break of day.

Wei Chuang (836–910), "Late Rising on Spring Days," 7-character
*chüeh-chü*.

Too much to drink these days, late getting up each morning.
I lie and watch the southern hills, revising old poems;
open doors and the sun is high, spring hushed and lonely.
Singing birds—three or four voices—fly up to the blossoming
      bough.

Han Wu (844–923), "Already Cool," 7-character *chüeh-chü*. In the
apartments of a palace lady who is presumably about to take an

afternoon nap. Note how her presence and actions are merely suggested by a description of the objects that surround her. The "broken sprigs" are probably sprigs of some flowering tree, though they may have symbolic significance; "dragon's beard" is a type of rush used for making sleeping mats.

> Beyond jade-green railings, embroidered blinds let down;
> ape-scarlet screens painted with broken sprigs;
> eight-foot mat of dragon's beard, square brocaded bedspread;
> the weather already cool but not yet cold.

Tu Hsün-ho (846–904), "Traveler's Thoughts," 7-character *chüeh-chü.*

> Ring of the moon, starshine, swept away as I watch;
> hue of the hilltops, river sounds, wrap me in unseen sorrow.
> Midnight by lampshine—ten years of memory
> join with the sudden rain to pelt my heart.

Chin Ch'ang-hsü (10th century), "Spring Grievance," 5-character *chüeh-chü.* Liao-hsi is an outpost on the northeast border where the singer's lover is stationed.

> Shoo the orioles, drive them away,
> don't let them sing in the branches!
> When they sing they scare off my dreams,
> and I will never get to Liao-hsi!

The Recluse T'ai-shang (T'ang), "In Reply to Questions," 5-character *chüeh-chü.*

> I happened to come to the foot of a pine tree,
> lay down and slept on pillows of stone.
> There are no calendars here in the mountain;
> the cold passes, but I don't know what year it is.


## NATURE IMAGERY IN T'ANG POETRY

Nature imagery plays an important part in Chinese poetry from the time of the *Book of Odes* on. Since many of the songs in the *Odes* have to do with hunting or farm chores, the nature images pertain, understandably enough, to the beasts and plants involved in these pursuits, or to the other tasks such as sericulture or the gathering of wild food plants that occupied the people of ancient China. Other objects in nature are mentioned in the songs because they serve as season indicators, the appearance of a particular insect or weather phenomenon giving notice to the farmer of the onset of winter or summer. Still others appear in the songs because of some omenistic significance, as the black cat or the groundhog might figure in American folk literature. Finally, there are those nature images that seem to be symbolic, creatures of the natural world that are cited because they represent either an analogy or a contrast to the speaker's condition. But these "symbolic" images are difficult to identify and interpret, and many of them may in fact be present in the poems because of some magical or punning significance that we are unaware of.

These nature images customarily occur in the opening line or lines of a stanza, followed by a description of the human events or emotions to which they presumably form a parallel of some kind. Scholars of the Han, employing an older terminology of uncertain meaning, referred to this device as a *hsing*. The word means literally "to begin," or "to lift up," and they intended it to denote a broaching of the subject or an offering of an analogy. The exact relationship between the images drawn from nature in the opening lines, and those that pertain to human affairs in the lines that follow, is left unexplained, perhaps for deliberate literary effect. As Hawkes remarks, in this way "the stark juxtaposition of images challenges the mind and compels it to take their relationship more seriously." [1] Thus, for example, #132 opens with this powerful but enigmatic exclamation:

Swift that falcon,
dark that northern wood.
I have not seen my lord yet;
my sad heart, how it pines!

In the *Odes,* particularly in the *Kuo-feng* or folk song section, there is a pronounced preference for specific imagery. Dozens of

[1] David Hawkes, "Chinese Poetry and the English Reader," in *The Legacy of China,* ed. by Raymond Dawson, p. 112.

particular species of trees, plants, birds, or insects are named, but almost never do we encounter a general term such as "trees" or "birds." One feels that, at this stage in the development of Chinese culture, there is still a magic that attaches to the use of the particular names of things, a potency that would be lost if one were to hail them in more abstract language.

The nature images of the *Odes* seem to be drawn from the ordinary sights and sounds of the north China plain; there are few that strike one as rare or fantastic. With the next collection of early poetry, the *Ch'u Tz'u* or *Songs of the South*, from the semibarbarian region of the Yangtze valley, the situation is rather different. The anthology contains shaman songs addressed to deities of the clouds, the mountains, and the rivers, and is deeply imbued with a temperament far more given to the ecstatic and the transcendental than that which informed the *Odes*. Thus, where poets of the *Odes* saw significance in the common flowers and plants of the north, the *Ch'u Tz'u* poets delighted in rare species such as those that are endowed with unusual scents or can prolong life or induce trance; or else they conjured up imaginary birds, beasts, or reptiles that, while resembling those of real life, possessed a greater power or purity. As in the *Odes,* the imagery is for the most part very concrete, though there are signs of a tendency toward the use of more generalized terms.

In the second century B.C. Confucianism was declared the orthodox doctrine of the state, and Confucian attitudes came to dominate the Chinese view of literature. Confucianism as a philosophy is concerned basically with man and the problems of human society. On the whole, it takes notice of the workings of the natural world only insofar as they affect man's activities. Man must comprehend the movements of the heavenly bodies so that he can devise an accurate calendar by which to regulate his agricultural tasks and religious ceremonies. He must learn to understand and predict the weather and to make the best use of water, soil, and other natural resources. But, at least in the more rational-minded wing of Confucianism, he need not, in fact should not, concern himself any further with nature and its secrets. The only exception, and that a very special one, was the necessity to watch for weird or unusual occurrences in the natural world that bear portentous significance for the future of mankind. The cause of such occurrences was believed to be the actions of the ruler and his ministers which, if particularly good, would call forth auspicious omens such as the five-colored clouds mentioned by Tu Fu in the poem on p. 162, and, if particularly bad, would result in the appearance of freakish creatures, spells of unseasonable weather, or natural disasters. These appearances were explained either religiously, as signs from an approving or wrathful Heaven, or mechanistically, as inevitable reflections in the cosmic sphere of human wrongdoing and disharmony. In other words, it seemed as reasonable to a Confucian to believe that a benevolent emperor on the throne could produce a lovely, parti-colored cloud in the sky as it does to us to believe that quantities of automobiles in the streets can produce an evil-smelling one.

When these Confucian scholars came to interpret the poems of the *Odes* and the *Ch'u Tz'u*, they naturally looked for the kind of ideas that they considered important—that is, moral and political ones— and if they did not find them in the surface meaning of the text, they claimed to discover them in deeper, allegorical levels of meaning. The nature imagery they treated in the same fashion, interpreting it as a set of symbols for human values or activities. What basis in truth such interpretations may have had it is difficult to say. But it is important to note that, as a result of these interpretations, the nature images of the old poetry did in fact come to be used as symbols in the works of later writers.

The attitude of Taoist thinkers toward nature was somewhat more complex. They delighted in ridiculing the Confucian view of man's importance, pointing out all the irony and absurdity of the human condition and insisting that, far from being the crowning glory of creation, man is in fact, to repeat one of their analogies, as mean and cramped as a crab louse in a pair of underpants. They counseled man to look to the natural world not for mere reflections or symbols of his own ways, but for lessons on how to live better, urging him to learn caution from the wary field mouse or contentment from the turtle dragging his tail in the mud. In addition, Taoist literature and popular lore revels in the mystery and wonder of

nature, particularly the wild retreats where the *hsien* or holy men of
the mountains practice their austerities and in time, it is averred,
attain immortality, riding off to the heavens on the back of a white
crane.

There was never any attempt to write pure Confucian poetry
(thank Heaven!), and a craze for Taoist poetry in the early fourth
century A.D. passed quickly, seemingly because the results were,
from a literary point of view, disappointingly barren and bookish.
Most poets of the centuries discussed so far continued to employ
the combinations of nature and human imagery that we have seen
in the earliest poetry, without insisting that either one or the
other should be the focus of attention. We have already examined in
some detail the nature imagery of the "Nineteen Old Poems"
and the works of the Chien-an poets, noting that it is sometimes
realistic, sometimes patently symbolic, but most often a combination
of the two. Rarely, we find a direct imitation of the *hsing* device
used in the *Odes,* as in the opening lines of the eighth of the "Songs
of History" by Tso Ssu (fl. A.D. 300):

> Flutter, flutter, bird in a cage,
> raised wings beating against the four corners;
> lost, lost, scholar of hard-luck alley,
> in an empty room sitting, clasping my shadow.

The images, juxtaposed without comment in the fashion of the
*Odes,* embody both an analogy and a contrast. The bird and the
luckless scholar are equally prisoners of fate, and it is the similarity
of their desperation that first strikes us. But we soon become aware
that, while the bird is all mindless resistance, flapping wildly from
one corner of the cage to another, the scholar sits huddled in stillness. He knows better than to imitate the vain struggles of the bird,
yet this very capacity to comprehend the true nature of his situation
makes him a more hopeless and pathetic figure.

The images in Tso Ssu's poem, in addition to being more subtly
paired than in their prototypes of the *Book of Odes,* differ in another
respect. A singer of the *Odes* would almost certainly have given us
the name of the particular species of bird in the cage; Tso Ssu is
content with the general term. The tendency toward abstraction in

nature imagery that we noted in the *Ch'u Tz'u* had continued until, in the poetry in the *shih* form of the centuries we have been discussing, general terms came to outnumber specific ones. This does not mean that the specific names drop out of Chinese poetry entirely. They continue to flourish in poems in the *fu* form, where extended catalogues of birds, trees, beasts, etc. abound. And they remain relatively common in the poems in *yüeh-fu* style which, because of their folk idiom, retain something of the old fondness for concrete names. The ordinary *shih*, by way of contrast, seem to prefer the employment of more general or abstract terms and then, if the occasion seems to demand it, to sharpen the focus of the image by the addition of a qualifying adjective or phrase. Interest shifts, for example, from the particular species of bird to the bird's shape, hue, or behavior; the bird as seen not by the canny farmer or woodsman, but by the gentleman of letters, ornithologically uninformed and preoccupied with his own thoughts.

To further illustrate what I mean by this, and to suggest some of the effects of such a practice, I should like here to present a brief analysis of the nature imagery in a sample of T'ang poetry. My remarks will be based largely upon a study of the nature imagery contained in the eighteenth-century anthology, *T'ang-shih san-pai-shou* or Three Hundred Poems of the T'ang which, in spite of its title, contains 317 poems, 90 in *ku-shih* form and 227 in *lü-shih* or *chüeh-chü* form. I have chosen this anthology as the basis of my study because it contains poems in both old and modern poetry forms; because it is representative of all the important periods of T'ang poetry (with the exception of the Early T'ang which, as we have seen, is stylistically a continuation of the preceding era); and because it includes many of the most famous and admired works of the T'ang. Counting images is a tedious job, and many questions arise as to just how it should be done; my statistics, therefore, are intended to suggest no more than the approximate frequency with which any given image or type of image may occur. Other samples or other methods of counting might well produce somewhat different proportions, but I believe my figures are basically sound; certainly they confirm the general impressions one receives from reading a large amount of T'ang poetry, and much of what I have to say will accordingly come as no surprise to anyone who has done so.

The first thing to be noted about nature imagery in the T'ang *shih* is that it functions largely on a medial level, shunning the highly abstract on the one hand, and the highly specific on the other. Almost never does one encounter a term or concept as broad, for example, as the English "nature" or "natural world," or even our words "scenery" or "landscape." Though the T'ang poet may speak at times of "heaven and earth" (*t'ien-ti* or *ch'ien-k'un*), he usually prefers to employ a more modest synecdoche such as "mountains and rivers" to stand for the world of nature. On the other hand, he does not descend to the very specific level as often as one might suppose at first glance and, when he does, it is usually in one of several rather conventional ways.

One of these, which stands as an exception to the statement made above concerning a medial level of abstraction, is the frequent use of place names. In a country as old as China, place names naturally come to have rich historical or legendary associations and their mere mention in literature is sufficient to call up scenes of departed glory, fierce battles, the excitement of a bustling city, or the loneliness of the frontier. The poets of China, like their Japanese counterparts, are fond of working place names into their poems, both for the air of crisp reality they lend—this happened not "some place" or "any place" but at a place called Such-and-such—and for the dramatic or nostalgic overtones that such names carry. Also, because the ancient religions of both China and Japan embraced the worship of mountain and water deities, the mere recital of place names often constituted a kind of litany of gods, a fact which even the poets of later and more sophisticated ages never quite forgot.

One of the most effective examples of the use of place names is in Tu Fu's poem entitled "On Hearing that the Government Armies Have Retaken Ho-nan and Ho-pei." In the poem, Tu Fu, a refugee in the far west, expresses his joy at the news that the region of central China where the capitals, as well as the poet's own home, are situated has been recovered from the rebel armies. In the last two lines he describes the itinerary of the journey home which he plans to make with his family:

Straight away from Pa Gorge, through Wu Gorge,
then down to Hsiang-yang, on to Lo-yang!

An imaginary journey sketched out in four place names that come
tumbling from the poet's brush, it conveys with great power the
excitement and anticipation of the moment.

Very different in mood is the following poem by Li Po, a seven-
character *chüeh-chü* which weaves five place names into its brief
four lines. Entitled "Song of the Moon of O-mei Mountain," it
describes a journey down the Yangtze through the Three Gorges
(which include the Wu Gorge of Tu Fu's poem), where the banks of
the river are so high that the poet cannot see the autumn moon.

Moon of O-mei Mountain, autumn's crescent,
your image on the P'ing-ch'iang River flowing:
by night I leave Green Valley for Three Gorges,
thinking of you unseen, descending to Yü-chou.

Beyond appreciating their concreteness, it is naturally difficult
for a foreigner to assess the emotional effect which such place names
may have for the Chinese reader, just as it would be difficult for
someone not a native of the northeastern section of the United
States to grasp the poignancy of a title such as *The Happy Journey
to Trenton and Camden*. I will only note, before leaving the subject,
that I have not included place names in my count of nature images;
had I done so, the frequency of mountain, river, and lake images
would have been even higher than it is.

The lack of species names is not noticeable in many of the categories of images I have counted. There is, after all, only one moon
and one sun, and, unless we are meteorologists, we tend to think
of wind, clouds, rain, or snow as entities that are not subject to
further division. Moreover, these images are frequently qualified
in Chinese poetry, though I have not taken account of these quali-
fications in my analysis. Thus we have a move toward greater
specification in images such as "dawn wind," "setting sun,"
"spring rain," or "white snow," though it is questionable whether
"white snow" is in fact any more specific than "snow," since one
would hardly visualize any other kind unless instructed to do so.

It is when we turn to categories such as trees, plants, flowers, or birds that the relative lack of specification is most noticeable. In the 317 poems examined, I have counted 51 mentions of "trees" in general, and 26 of "forest." But the modern reader will probably be curious to know what kind of trees, since he is likely to feel, rightly or wrongly, that the more concrete the imagery, the better the poetry. When it comes to names of particular trees, however, the T'ang poet is highly selective. The sample shows that the most frequently mentioned varieties are the willow (*liu* or *yang*, 29 instances), and the pine (24). Granted that these were everyday objects in the Chinese landscape, why, we may ask, have these two trees been singled out for such frequent notice? The answer, I believe, lies in their symbolic or metaphorical connotations. The pine is associated with mountain retreats, hence quietude, purity; it is a standard image in poems dealing with Buddhist monks or recluses, as may be seen in the poem on p. 116. In addition, because of its evergreen nature it has from ancient times in China been a symbol of longevity, of the enduring or unchanging aspects of nature as opposed to the ephemeral. The willow, planted along the banks of rivers or canals, was a common sight in T'ang towns and villages, and its bright new spring leaves and flying catkins figure prominently in Chinese poetry. But, as we have seen on p. 62, it is also associated by custom with partings, when willow branches were plucked and given to the journeyer, and this association accounts for a large proportion of the mentions of the willow in T'ang poetry.

When we turn to other trees we find that the frequency of occurrence drops sharply. The bamboo, another tree associated with rustic retreats, appears 12 times; the peach 10 times, mainly because its flowers function as a symbol of rapidly fading beauty and because of its association with the legendary utopia described in T'ao Yüan-ming's famous "Peach Blossom Spring"; the mulberry (7) because of its importance in sericulture; and the cypress (6) because it was customarily planted in graveyards. A few other trees such as the maple (6), cassia (5), pear (5), and plum (4) appear on occasion, but the *wu-t'ung* or Chinese parasol tree and the *mei* or flowering plum, which figure so frequently in the poetry of later centuries, are all but absent. Thirteen other trees receive one or two mentions, usually by way of literary allusion or because of some special property or geographical association. Thus, for example, in a poem on south China the poet might mention palm trees, though the palm had none of the romantic associations that it has for us; on the contrary, its presence was more likely calculated to make the refined T'ang reader shudder at the strangeness of the southern landscape.[2]

An examination of wild plant images reveals the same phenomenon. "Plants" (*ts'ao*) in general are mentioned 42 times, but the only ones mentioned by name with any frequency are the *p'eng* (8), a species of wild raspberry that breaks from its roots and rolls about like the tumbleweed, thus serving as an apt symbol for enforced wandering; and moss (6), a fixture in descriptions of mountain retreats.

The case of flowers is even more striking, particularly in comparison to English poetry, which at times gives the impression of being essentially a recital of flower names. "Flowers" in general are mentioned 87 times, but it would appear that in many, if not most, cases the reference is to the blossoms of flowering trees such as the peach, pear, or plum. The single flower most frequently mentioned is the *fu-yung* (9), an autumn-blooming mallow, but the name may also refer to lotus blossoms, which appear 4 times under a less ambiguous name. Orchids (*lan*) are mentioned 3 times because of their symbolism of purity and unrecognized worth, and chrysanthemums 3 times, mainly because T'ao Yüan-ming had mentioned them earlier in a poem that everyone knew by heart. This all but exhausts the list of flower names and suggests that, if one were to construct a T'ang poetry garden as people in the West construct Shakespeare gardens, it would be a paltry affair indeed. Here, however, the sample may be somewhat misleading, since it includes few poems of the type known as *yung-wu* or "poetic descriptions of an object." Such poems usually celebrate the beauty of a particular species of tree or flower, though seldom in ways that make for much literary interest. We know, for example, that the T'ang people were very fond of the *mu-tan* or woody peony and often made it the subject of *yung-wu* type poems. But, probably because the flower

[2] For T'ang attitudes toward the flora and fauna of the south, see Edward H. Schafer, *The Vermilion Bird: T'ang Images of the South,* esp. pp. 173–76.

lacked any pronounced symbolic associations, it did not find its way into other types of poetry.

The category of birds follows the same pattern. "Birds" in general appear 31 times; 25 specific varieties are mentioned, headed by the wild goose (23), associated in legend with letter-bearing and symbolizing communication, or more often the sad lack of it, between distant friends and loved ones. The phoenix (13) and the *luan* (5), two birds that exist only in imagination or the fanciful depictions of painters and sculptors, follow the wild goose in frequency. They are followed by the crane (6), a bird linked in popular lore with the recluse and the immortal; the male and female mandarin duck (5), symbol of conjugal love; and the *hung* (5), a kind of wild swan also associated with the recluse ideal. More common birds such as the oriole (5), the swallow (5), the gull (4), and the egret (4) appear from time to time, as well as a considerable number of other species. On the whole, the T'ang poets seem to have taken a greater interest in birds than they did in flowers or other varieties of wild life, perhaps because, as I shall explain later, they apparently spent more time looking up at the sky than down at the ground.

Animal images are relatively scarce if one omits the horse which, along with the boat, provided the most common means of transportation, at least for the upper classes. The most frequently mentioned is the monkey (11), mainly because of its melancholy cry. It is followed by the tiger (6), a standard fixture in military poems; and the wolf (4) and jackal (2), symbols of evil men. Eight other wild beasts receive notice, two of them apparently fictitious, a very skimpy list considering what the wild life of T'ang China must have been. Varieties of fish and reptiles are barely mentioned at all, with the exception of the ubiquitous dragon.

The insect world fares somewhat better. The cicada (5) and the moth (5) appear most often. The cry of the former signals the approach of cold weather; the latter appears usually in the moth-eyebrow epithet and perhaps should not be counted as a nature image at all. The silkworm (4), firefly (4), and butterfly (2) follow in popularity, the last introduced usually through allusion to Chuang Tzu's famous dream.

All of this means that the Chinese nature poet is sketching out a more or less generalized landscape—mountains, rivers, trees, birds —rather than describing in detail; and when he does decide to add a touch of the specific, his choice of detail is dictated less by what we may suppose was actually before his eyes than by the conventions of literary allusion and symbolism. This is partly due to what I have referred to earlier as the poetic division of labor between the *fu* and the *shih*. Whereas it was the function of the *fu* to give exhaustive lists of the trees, plants, fish, etc. that made up the scene being described, the aim of the *shih* was more often to evoke a mood or convey an emotion. Moreover, because the *shih* was usually relatively brief, it simply did not allow room for lengthy and detailed description. The *shih* poet, therefore, if he would present a landscape, had perforce to sketch it in bold and generalized strokes, adding only those details that would most cogently convey the mood he was seeking to express. If he chose to name species of trees or plants that lacked traditional metaphorical associations, then, no matter how interesting the images might be in themselves, they would function only on the level of concrete description, or at best as private symbols whose significance the reader could only guess at, and the poem, at least by popular standards, would accordingly be weak in symbolic overtones. One often wishes that the T'ang poets had ventured to use such images anyway, rather than always settling for the same old pine tree or wild goose. However, in a body of poetry as convention-minded as that of the T'ang, this is perhaps too much to expect. The best poets did occasionally dare to use a new image, and in this way they expanded and enriched the tradition. But the lesser ones, as in any age or language, were content merely to manipulate the stock of images bequeathed them by the past.

We have looked at the nature images of T'ang poetry from the point of view of their level of abstraction. Now let us see what types of images are found in the sample and in what proportions. Dividing the images into two large categories of animate and inanimate, we find 1,201 images of the latter type, as opposed to 625 of the former. Thus it is the lifeless, enduring objects of nature, its skies, mountains, and waters, rather than its trees, flowers, birds, and beasts that most often find their way into T'ang poetry. As this fact suggests, the poet is usually using the phenomena of nature for purposes of contrast with his own impermanent existence. When he employs images of animate beings, on the other hand, they serve partly to symbolize his own frail condition and partly to contrast with it; that is, the pine tree, though ultimately doomed, lives longer than the poet, the bird is freer, the flower more pure.

Analyzing the inanimate images, we find that 654 of them refer to the sky, the weather, or heavenly bodies; while 547 refer to water, mountains, and other land formations, which is why I remarked earlier that the poets seem to have spent more than half their time looking up in the air.

Of the heavenly bodies, the moon or moonlight is most popular (96), followed by the sky (76), the sun (72), the stars (13), and a few specific constellations or phenomena such as the Big Dipper (4) or the Milky Way (8).

Wind is the most frequent weather image (115), followed by clouds (89), rain (52), snow (32), mist (29), dew (23), frost (13), haze (7), and fog (6). One has the impression that the T'ang poets stayed in bed on clear days.

Of land formations, mountain ranges are most favored, accounting for a total of 150 images; and, as I have said, the count does not include place names which, if added, would greatly increase the number of mountain images. In fact, the word "mountain" (*shan*), along with the word "wind" (*feng*), is the most frequent nature image, appearing 115 times; other words refer to particular types of mountains or to the parts of mountains. Stones (23), stream valleys (10), ravines (11), and other precipitous land formations occur frequently, but plains and open meadows are barely mentioned, and islands, so important in the literature of many other countries, are all but ignored. Again it is obvious from this that the T'ang poets did not describe just any landscape that appeared before their eyes, but only those that struck them as particularly suggestive or appealing.

Weather images form the largest single category of images (380), perhaps because the weather, with its changeability and appearance of deliberate benignity or ill will, can function more effectively as a symbol of the poet's mood than more stable and less dramatic aspects of nature. Images relating to bodies of water follow (303). "Rivers" (81) and "waters" (79) are mentioned most often, followed by waves (29), springs (18), lakes (9), ponds (8), and other watery phenomena. The sea appears with relative frequency (36), but almost always simply as a vague terminal point—the place rivers flow to—rather than as an object to be observed and described, much less ventured out upon.

The exact symbolic significance of the various natural phenomena which I have tabulated here varies considerably with context, though one may be certain that they are intended in almost all cases to have some kind of metaphorical or symbolic connotation. Thus drifting clouds may at one time suggest freedom or leisure, at another fickleness or ephemerality, and at still another evil influences that blot out the light of the sun. Rivers connote unending motion and life, often through allusion to the passage in the Confucian *Analects* IX, 16: "The Master was standing by a river and said, 'The water flows on and on like this, never stopping day or night.'" Again, because rivers were such an important avenue of transport, they have the connotations we associate with road images, something that binds together people and places. Finally, there is the purity of the water itself, its soft, yielding quality, and its power to confer life and fertility on the land, as well as to erode, kill, and lay waste. Therefore, when the reader encounters river images or other images from the natural world in T'ang poetry, he must decide on the basis of context just which, among a variety of symbolic associations, the poet intended them to have.

One more curious fact about the nature imagery of T'ang poetry remains to be mentioned, a fact that further indicates just how selective the T'ang poets are in their use of images. A count of overt references to the four seasons in the sample reveals that spring is mentioned 76 times and autumn 59 times, as opposed to 3 mentions of winter and 2 of summer. From this it is obvious that the poets were not primarily interested in nature itself or the full richness and variety of its phenomena; had they been, they would hardly have ignored the natural world for six months out of the year. They were interested only in those aspects or phenomena of nature that held some special significance for them or that reflected their own thoughts and feelings.

The results of this brief inquiry, as I said at the outset, will surely come as no surprise to sensitive readers who are already familiar with Chinese poetry, particularly that which makes heavy use of nature imagery. I hope, however, that they may supply statistical evidence for what were heretofore mere impressions. I hope, also, that they may give pause to those writers who, heedless of how fatuous and misleading analogies among the arts can be, persist in likening T'ang poems to paintings. To be sure, the Chinese poet uses images just as does the painter, but so do all poets, imageless poetry being on the whole rare in any culture. Beyond that fact, however, the similarity ceases. The level of abstraction which we have noted as one of the most characteristic features of T'ang landscape poetry, for example, could not possibly be matched in the nonverbal arts. No Chinese painter could paint "mountains" or "trees" without first deciding whether to make them steep or gentle, tall or short; that is, without being at the outset far more specific in his representation than the poet need be. From early times the Chinese have compared the formal aspects of literature with the patterns of brocade or architectural decoration, with the ordered harmonies of music, or, characteristically, with the blend of flavors in good cooking. But it is my impression that, at least in the periods under discussion in this volume, they have been rather wary of making analogies between the representational aspects of literature and the visual arts.[3]

Finally, I hope that these remarks on nature imagery in Chinese

[3] Readers will no doubt be tempted to cite by way of refutation Su Tung-p'o's famous remark concerning the T'ang poet and painter, Wang Wei: "In his poems there are paintings, in his paintings, poems." But, as Waley long ago pointed out, the remark occurs in a passage in which Su is discussing a painting and the accompanying poem, both attributed to Wang Wei. Some critics, he says, would question the authenticity of the poem, but he himself is inclined to accept it. His remark, therefore, when taken in context, is probably not intended as a general pronouncement but refers to the particular painting and poem and could better be translated: "There is something of the painting in the poem, and something of the poem in the painting." Arthur Waley, *An Introduction to the Study of Chinese Painting* (first published 1923; Grove Press reprint, 1958), p. 144.

poetry may be of interest because of the rather striking parallels they suggest with the history of English poetry. The same progression from specific to generalized imagery which I have described, for example, has been noted in English poetry, in the movement from Shakespeare's myriad flowers and plants, through the relative abstractions of Milton, to the deliberately generalized landscape of a work like Pope's *Windsor Forest*.[4] Even the father of English landscape poetry turns out to have been something of a T'ang poet, if we accept the view of the critic who wrote: "Wordsworth frequently gives us descriptions of natural scenes, sometimes, though not usually, with considerable detail of a kind, but never with personal, individual detail. . . . He often speaks of the night sky, but one has to search very carefully among his poems for mention of a star by name."[5]

[4] See Laurence Binyon, *Landscape in English Art and Poetry*, p. 62.
[5] Herbert Dingle, *Science and Literary Criticism*, p. 112.

# VIII

# THE HIGH T'ANG

⚛

IN SIX DYNASTIES times the writing of poetry had been confined largely to members of the court or sons and daughters of the higher aristocracy. Under the T'ang, with its greatly expanded bureaucracy recruited, partly through the examination system, from a broader range of social groups, poetry writing became more widespread. Even more than in earlier eras, it was part of the makeup of a true gentleman to be able to put together at least the kind of polite verse required at social functions, and poetry composition also figured in some types of government examinations. As a result, many men in public life who were neither particularly interested in nor temperamentally suited for the writing of poetry have left behind them

Translations of Li Po's poetry are found in Shigeyoshi Obata, *The Works of Li Po*, and Bynner and Kiang, *The Jade Mountain*. For a detailed discussion of Pound's famous translations from Li Po and other Chinese poets, see Wai-lim Yip, *Ezra Pound's Cathay*. Arthur Waley, in *The Poetry and Career of Li Po*, presents a brief and not very sympathetic biography of the poet.

Tu Fu's life and poetry are treated at length in William Hung, *Tu Fu, China's Greatest Poet*, 2 vols.; and David Hawkes, *A Little Primer of Tu Fu*. Tsu-lin Mei and Yu-kung Kao, "Tu Fu's 'Autumn Meditations': An Exercise in Linguistic Criticism," *Harvard Journal of Asian Studies*, 28 (1968), 44–80, focuses on one of Tu Fu's most important groups of poems. Other translations from Tu Fu are found in Rewi Alley, *Selected Poems of Tu Fu*; Bynner and Kiang, *The Jade Mountain*; A. C. Graham, *Poems of the Late T'ang*; and Kenneth Rexroth, *One Hundred Poems from the Chinese*. The Graham volume in my opinion is the most lively and exciting work of Chinese poetry translation to appear in recent years.

modest collections of verse, usually of the occasional kind demanded by etiquette. Because the works of 2,200 writers are preserved in the *Complete T'ang Poetry*, this by no means signifies that there were 2,200 genuine poets in the T'ang.

Similarly, although the great T'ang poets such as Li Po, Tu Fu, and Po Chü-i produced collections of over one or two thousand poems each, not every verse is infused with the intensity and seriousness one generally looks for in poetry today. The major poets, nearly all of them bureaucrats, were required to write their share of public poetry, to celebrate imperial outings and auspicious occurrences, to bid farewell to departing fellow officials or acknowledge the good wishes of friends when they themselves set off on a journey. Moreover, because they were recognized as masters in their own lifetime, they were undoubtedly pressed more often than lesser men to honor each occasion with a verse, as though T. S. Eliot had been importuned by his host to put together a poem each time he was invited out to dinner.

The Chinese, aware that profundity and originality are hardly to be expected under such conditions, have usually been content to settle for grace and technical skill in place of greatness, or to look for the kind of greatness that is diffused through a large number of works rather than concentrated in a few. Verse has been for many Chinese writers the medium for recording not only life's moments of intense feeling and conviction, but the countless minor events and scenes of everyday existence as well. They have used it as writers of other cultures have used the diary, the autobiography, or the sketchbook, and readers have been accustomed to read their verse with this in mind, not disturbed when they encounter much that is trivial or private in nature.

We do not always know how the works of the earlier Chinese poets came to be preserved. Copies of their poems circulated among friends and interested parties, and they themselves may have had little to say concerning which works were to be handed down to posterity and in what form. But, despite modest disclaimers, it would seem that they had no objection to most, if not all, of their work being transmitted. At least this is the feeling that prevails in the case of poets who are known to have collected and edited their own works. Mark Van Doren, writing of Robert Herrick, says: "And if when he published his own book he admitted many pieces he knew to be imperfect, I fancy it was for a human reason that I like in him as much as I like the best of his poetry: he was fond of the places and persons they were about."[1] Po Chü-i, in a letter to his friend Yüan Chen in which he describes how he has collected and arranged his own poems, remarks that, when it came to those pieces that had to do with friends and social gatherings, "I have not been able to throw any of them away," though he adds that some day, "if someone else should edit my writings for me, it will not matter if he omits them."[2]

T'ang poetry reached its first, and perhaps greatest, flowering during the reign of Emperor Hsüan-tsung. Though a generally judicious ruler and enthusiastic patron of the arts, his reputation in history has unhappily been marred by the infatuation for the beautiful Yang Kuei-fei that possessed him in his later years and the disastrous rebellion that broke out in 755, forcing him to flee the capital and resign the throne to his son. Two of the most famous poets of Emperor Hsüan-tsung's time, Li Po and Tu Fu, will be discussed here; a third, Wang Wei, will be treated in the chapter that follows. Because all three men held office at one time or another and were recognized in their own day, we possess considerable biographical information about them. It is understandably a temptation to use the poetry of the men to illustrate their biographies. Here I hope to confine myself to the opposite process, offering only as much biographical and historical data as seem to throw important light on the poetry. Readers desirous of fuller information may turn to the studies listed in the bibliographical note.

It is customary to picture Li Po as a thoroughgoing romantic, mystic, and libertine, and Tu Fu as a serious, sober man deeply committed to the Confucian ideals of humanism and public service. These stereotypes are not wholly without basis in truth, though they reflect more nearly what the poets would *like* us to believe

[1] "Robert Herrick Revisited," *The Happy Critic*, p. 172.
[2] "Letter to Yüan Chiu." For a discussion and partial translation of this famous letter, see Arthur Waley, *The Life and Times of Po Chü-i*, pp. 107–14.

about themselves—it is not at all certain that the two were really so very different. Actually, nearly every great Chinese poet turns out, on close examination, to embody within himself an amalgam of Taoist mysticism and Confucian sobriety, as though, in European literature, one were to find the Roman and the Celt joined in a single writer. But rather than attempt to characterize the personalities of the two poets, which must always remain to some degree uncertain and elusive, I prefer here to venture some generalizations about their poetry. If these are tentative as well, the reader will at least have before him examples of their poetry by which to test them.

## LI PO (701–62)

The first thing to note about Li Po's poetry, particularly in comparison to that of Tu Fu, is that it is essentially backward-looking, that it represents more a revival and fulfillment of past promises and glory than a foray into the future. In the matter of poetic form critics generally agree that Li Po introduced no significant innovations. He seems to have been content to take over and employ what his predecessors had left him, writing in all the ordinary verse forms of the time, including the *lü-shih* and *chüeh-chü*, though he showed a marked preference for the *ku-shih* or old-style form. The irregular line lengths of the *ku-shih*, the freedom from compulsory tonal and verbal parallelism, and the unlimited length were apparently to his liking, and he used the form to create a kind of wild, rhapsodic quality reminiscent of the poets of the *Ch'u Tz'u*. One of his best-known *ku-shih* poems, for example, the *Shu-tao-nan* or "Hard Roads in Shu," employs lines that range in length from four to eleven characters, the form of the lines suggesting by their irregularity the jagged peaks and bumpy mountain roads of Szechwan depicted in the poem.

In theme and content also, his poetry is notable much less for the new elements it introduces than for the skill with which it handles old ones. Of the approximately 1,000 poems attributed to Li Po, about one sixth are in *yüeh-fu* style, which means that they are reworkings of themes drawn from the folk song tradition of earlier times. Two of his best-known poems, familiar to English readers through Pound's translations as "The River-Merchant's Wife" and "The Jeweled Stairs' Grievance," are *yüeh-fu*, dealing with the age-old subjects of the neglected wife and the palace lady who has fallen out of favor. Another important group of 59 poems, meditations on political, social, and philosophical themes, is entitled *ku-feng* or "in the old manner," and expresses his admiration for the poetry of the past, particularly that of the late Han and Wei, and his longing to recapture its excellences.

In treating the traditional themes, Li Po often introduces a freshness of outlook or imagery, a narrative skill, a beauty of diction that make his poem the most memorable and satisfying statement on the subject, replacing in popularity the earlier models upon which he drew. But because his poems, particularly those in *yüeh-fu* style, are conventionalized or impersonal in feeling and rely for so much of their appeal on pure lyricism, they are often less interesting in translation than those of other, perhaps inferior, poets.

The second important characteristic of Li Po's poetry that must be pointed out is the fantasy and note of childlike wonder and playfulness that pervade so much of it. From the time of his youth Li Po was strongly attracted to the *tao-shih*, the Taoist recluses who lived in the mountains and, through alchemy and the practice of various austerities, sought to become *hsien* or immortal spirits. Men who had turned their backs on contemporary society and its values, they are described by Li Po in terms that make them sound like the "beats" of their day,

> sleeping on boulders, all under one quilt,
> chopping through the ice to drink from cold springs,
> three men sharing a single pair of clogs.[3]

It is clear that the life of the *tao-shih* attracted him greatly and many of his poems deal with mountains, often descriptions of ascents that midway modulate into journeys of the imagination, passing from actual mountain scenery to visions of the nature deities, immortals, and "jade maidens" of Taoist lore. In such poems

---

[3] "Seeing Off Han Chun, P'ei Cheng, and K'ung Ch'ao-fu on Their Way Back to the Mountains."

Li Po once more shows his affinities with the past, with the poets of the *Ch'u Tz'u* or the early *fu* tradition who in their writings ranged back and forth freely between the real world and the supernatural.

This same element of fantasy lies behind the hyperboles and playful personifications—rather rare in T'ang poetry as a whole—that have so long delighted readers of Li Po's poetry. His descriptions of nature are particularly rich in such ingenuous fancy, as when he unself-consciously talks to the moon, speaks of a mountain and himself as "looking at each other without either of us tiring,"[4] or tells us that the star T'ai-po or Venus, from which he took his courtesy name, Li T'ai-po, "talked with me,/and opened up for me the barriers of Heaven."[5]

Li Po spent most of his life in travel, part of it exile imposed by the court because of unsavory political connections. Just what kept him so constantly on the move it is difficult to say. The point to note is that, in spite of all this moving about and the hardships and loneliness that it must have entailed, his poetry is remarkably free from expressions of unmitigated woe. Partly this may be due to the fact, already mentioned, that his writing tends to be less personal, less revealing of inner emotion than that of many of his contemporaries. But it is also due to his own inimitable vigor and zest for life. We have noted his fondness for nature, particularly the mountain landscapes with their promise of spiritual delight and emancipation, and his relatively sunny view of a universe in which stars stop to talk to him, the moon is a companion, and, as he declares in a poem to be quoted shortly, "heaven and earth are my quilt and pillow." One more consolation remains to be mentioned, one inseparably linked with his name: the very real and lifelong enjoyment he appears to have derived from drinking. Nearly all Chinese poets celebrate the joys of wine, but none do so as tirelessly and with such a note of genuine conviction as Li Po. Though he wrote in a poetic tradition that condoned, even demanded, the frank expression of sorrow, and he himself often gave voice to such feelings, one imagines that he could never have been entirely desolate so long as he had his wine.

4 "Sitting Alone on Mount Ching-t'ing."
5 "Climbing Mount T'ai-po."

Because of the rather impersonal nature of Li Po's poetry and the relative paucity of biographical data that has been preserved, we are unable to date most of his works with any certainty. For this reason, I have arranged the examples of his work by subject and will discuss them in that manner, beginning with two examples of poems in *yüeh-fu* style. The first is entitled "Tzu-yeh Song #3" and uses a 5-character line. On the Tzu-yeh songs, see p. 9, where their frequently seasonal themes have already been noted. This poem deals with autumn, when cloth is customarily fulled to make uniforms to send to the soldiers stationed at the frontier. Jade Pass is in Kansu far to the west.

> Ch'ang-an—one slip of moon;
> in ten thousand houses, the sound of fulling mallets.
> Autumn winds keep on blowing,
> all things make me think of Jade Pass!
> When will they put down the barbarians
> and my good man come home from his far campaign?

The second, entitled "Bring the Wine," uses a 7-character line with occasional lines of other lengths. It is a rather strident poem— one can almost hear the poet pounding the table—and hardly original in either ideas or imagery. And yet, like so much of Li Po's work, it has a grace and effortless dignity that somehow make it more compelling than earlier treatments of the same theme.

> Have you not seen
>     the Yellow River waters descending from the sky,
>     racing restless toward the ocean, never to return?
> Have you not seen
>     bright mirrors in high halls, the white-haired ones lamenting,
>     their black silk of morning by evening turned to snow?
>     If life is to have meaning, seize every joy you can;
>     do not let the golden cask sit idle in the moonlight!
>     Heaven gave me talents and meant them to be used;
>     gold scattered by the thousand comes home to me again.
>     Boil the mutton, roast the ox—we will be merry,
>     at one bout no less than three hundred cups.

Master Ts'en!
Scholar Tan-ch'iu!
bring wine and no delay!
For you I'll sing a song—
be pleased to bend your ears and hear:
Bells and drums, foods rare as jade—these aren't worth prizing;
all I ask is to be drunk forever, never to sober up!
Sages and worthies from antiquity—all gone into silence;
only the great drinkers have left a name behind.
The Prince of Ch'en once feasted in the Hall of Calm Delight;
wine, ten thousand coins a cask, flowed for his revelers' joy.
Why does my host tell me the money has run out?
Buy more at once—my friends have cups to be refilled!
My dappled mount,
my furs worth a thousand—
call the boy, have him take them and barter for fine wine!
Together we will wash away ten thousand years of care.

"Scholar Tan-ch'iu": Yüan Tan-ch'iu, a Taoist friend of the poet; "Master Ts'en" in the preceding line has been tentatively identified as the poet Ts'en Ts'an (715–70).
"Prince of Ch'en": Ts'ao Chih (see p. 39); Li Po echoes the following lines from Ts'ao Chih's poem "City of Fame":

I return to feast in the Hall of Calm Delight,
with fine wine, ten thousand coins a cask.

The following two poems, in 7-character *chüeh-chü* form, belong to the category known as *huai-ku* or meditations on the past, already mentioned on p. 88. The first, entitled "At Su Terrace Viewing the Past," was written when the poet visited the site of the Ku-su Terrace, built by Fu-ch'a, king of Wu, in the region just south of the Yangtze delta. The king's extravagant ways and infatuation with the beautiful Hsi-shih—the "lady" of the poem—weakened his state and led to its overthrow in 472 B.C. by its rival, the state of Yüeh (see the next poem).

Old gardens, a ruined terrace, willow trees new;
caltrop gatherers, clear chant of songs, a spring unbearable;

and now there is only the west river moon
that shone once on a lady in the palace of the king of Wu.

"In Yüeh Viewing the Past." Kou-chien was the ruler of Yüeh who
overthrew King Fu-ch'a of Wu.

Kou-chien, king of Yüeh, came back from the broken land of Wu;
his brave men returned to their homes, all in robes of brocade.
Ladies in waiting like flowers filled his spring palace
where now only the partridges fly.

Li Po is particularly noted for his mastery of the *chüeh-chü* form.
Two examples have been given above, in which the form is used to
lament the vanished glories of the past. The following six record
scenes that the poet encountered in his travels or sum up his
thoughts. "Autumn Cove Song #5"; 5-character *chüeh-chü*.

At Autumn Cove, so many white monkeys,
bounding, leaping up like snowflakes in flight!
They coax and pull their young ones down from the branches
to drink and frolic with the water-borne moon.

"Viewing the Waterfall at Mount Lu"; 5-character *chüeh-chü*. The
second of two poems on the subject of Mt. Lu in Kiangsi; Incense
Stone is the name of one of its peaks.

Sunlight streaming on Incense Stone kindles a violet smoke;
far off I watch the waterfall plunge to the long river,
flying waters descending straight three thousand feet,
till I think the Milky Way has tumbled from the ninth height of
Heaven.

"Spring Night in Lo-yang—Hearing a Flute"; 7-character *chüeh-chü*.
On the willow-breaking song, see p. 62.

In what house, the jade flute that sends these dark notes drifting,
scattering on the spring wind that fills Lo-yang?
Tonight if we should hear the willow-breaking song,
who could help but long for the gardens of home?

"Still Night Thoughts"; 5-character *chüeh-chü*.

Moonlight in front of my bed—

I took it for frost on the ground!
I lift my eyes to watch the mountain moon,
lower them and dream of home.

"Summer Day in the Mountains"; 5-character *chüeh-chü*.

Too lazy to wave the white plume fan,
stripped to the waist in the green wood's midst,
I loose my headcloth, hang it on a stony wall,
bare my topknot for pine winds to riffle.

"Presented to Wang Lun"; 7-character *chüeh-chü*. Written at a
place called Peach Flower Pool in Anhwei and given at parting to a
friend of the poet, a local wine seller named Wang Lun.

Li Po on board, ready to push off,
suddenly heard the tramping and singing on the bank.
Peach Flower Pool a thousand feet deep
is shallower than my love for Wang Lun who sees me off.

The following, entitled "Seeing a Friend Off," is an example of a
*lü-shih* by Li Po, this one in 5-character lines. It is unusual in that
it violates the rule that the two middle couplets of a *lü-shih* must
observe strict verbal parallelism, the kind of violation, Chinese
critics hasten to add, that is permitted only to a genius like Li Po.
Note the richly symbolic use of the nature images "green hills,"
"white water," "drifting clouds," etc.

Green hills sloping from the northern wall,
white water rounding the eastern city:
once parted from this place
the lone weed tumbles ten thousand miles.
Drifting clouds—a traveler's will;
setting sun—an old friend's heart.
Wave hands and let us take leave now,
*hsiao-hsiao* our hesitant horses neighing.

The remainder of the poems to be quoted are all in *ku-shih* or old-
poetry form.

"A Night with a Friend"; 5-character *ku-shih*.

Dousing clean a thousand old cares,
sticking it out through a hundred pots of wine,

a good night needing the best of conversation,
a brilliant moon that will not let us sleep—
drunk we lie down in empty hills,
heaven and earth our quilt and pillow.

"Facing Wine with Memories of Lord Ho; Introduction and Two Poems"; 5-character *ku-shih*, the first of the two.

Lord Ho, a high official in the household of the Crown Prince, on our first meeting at the Tzu-chi Temple in Ch'ang-an at once dubbed me the "banished immortal." Then he took off his golden tortoise and exchanged it for wine for our enjoyment. He is gone now, and I face the wine, wrapped in thought, and write these poems.

Wild man of Ssu-ming Mountain,
Incomparable Ho Chi-chen,
in Ch'ang-an when we first met,
calling me a "banished immortal"—
He used to love the "thing in the cup"
    (now he's dust under the pine tree),
and traded the golden tortoise for wine—
    my robe wet with tears, remembering.

⽿ "Banished immortal": implying that Li Po was really an immortal spirit of Heaven who, because of some offense, had been condemned to take on human form and descend to earth.

"Golden tortoise": badge of high office.

"Ssu-ming Mountain": in Chekiang, where Ho lived after he left court and became a Taoist hermit.

"In Reply When Lesser Officials of Chung-tu Brought a Pot of Wine and Two Fish to My Inn as Gifts"; 5- and 7-character *ku-shih*.

Lu wine like amber,
fish from the Wen, the purple damask of their scales;
and Shantung's fine officials, in expansive mood,
their hands bearing gifts for a man from far away.
We've taken to each other—we hit it off;
the pot of wine, the pair of fish convey this thought.
Wine comes—I drink it;
fish to be carved at parting,

twin gills that gape and pant, back and body taut-finned,
they twitch and twitter on a silver plate, all but taking wing.
I call the boy to clear the cuttingboard; frosty blades whirl—
red flesh and pale: fallen flowers, a gleam of whitest snow.
With your leave I dip my chopsticks, eat my fill,
then climb into the golden saddle, still drunk, to set off home.

"Red flesh and pale": the red and white portions of the raw fish. Like the Japanese today, the Chinese in early times often ate their fish raw.

"Poem #19 in the Old Manner;" 5-character *ku-shih*, nineteenth in the set of fifty-nine poems "in the old manner" mentioned above. Lotus Flower Mountain is the highest peak of Mt. Hua, one of the five sacred mountains of China, on the border between Shansi and Shensi. In a lake on its summit were said to grow lotuses which had the power to transform one into an immortal spirit. Bright Star was a spirit who lived on Mt. Hua. Wei Shu-ch'ing, a man of the Han dynasty who became an immortal by drinking an infusion of mica, lived on Cloud Terrace, another peak of Mt. Hua. The last four lines refer to the forces of the rebel An Lu-shan, who led a body of Chinese and foreign troops west to attack Ch'ang-an in 755.

West ascending Lotus Flower Mountain,
far far away I saw the Bright Star maid;
with pale hands she plucked lotus blossoms,
with airy steps she walked the great clear void;
her rainbow skirts, their broad belt trailing,
dipped and fluttered as she strode up the sky.
She called me to climb with her to Cloud Terrace,
to lift hands in salutation to Wei Shu-ch'ing.
Dazed and enraptured, I went with her;
mounting a stork, we rode the purple gloom.
I looked down and saw the Lo-yang River,
barbarian troops marching in endless files;
streams of blood that stained the meadow grasses,
wildcats and wolves wearing the hats of men!

We know little about Li Po's family life. He seems to have married several times, and the following poem is evidence that he had children by at least one of these marriages. At the time it was written, Li Po had left his family in Jen-ch'eng in Shantung (referred to in the poem as Lu), and was traveling in the south (Wu) on his way to the capital. Mt. Kuei and the Wen-yang River are in Shantung, near where his family were living. The poem is entitled "Sent to My Two Little Children in the East of Lu" and is in 5-character *ku-shih* form.

> Wu land mulberry leaves grow green,
> already Wu silkworms have slept three times.
> I left my family in the east of Lu;
> who sows our fields there on the dark side of Mt. Kuei?
> Spring chores too long untended,
> river journeys that leave me dazed—
> south winds blow my homing heart;
> it soars and comes to rest before the wine tower.
> East of the tower a peach tree grows,
> branches and leaves brushed with blue mist,
> a tree I planted myself,
> parted from it these three years.
> The peach now is tall as the tower
> and still my journey knows no return.
> P'ing-yang, my darling girl,
> picks blossoms, leaning by the peach,
> picks blossoms and does not see me;
> her tears flow like a welling fountain.
> The little boy, named Po-ch'in,
> is shoulder high to his elder sister;
> side by side they walk beneath the peach—
> who will pat them with loving hands?
> I lose myself in thoughts of them;
> day by day care burns out my heart.
> On this piece of cut silk I'll write my far-away thoughts
> and send them floating down the river Wen-yang.

"Wu silkworms": the silkworms sleep and shed their skins four times before they weave their cocoons.

The last Li Po poem I shall quote is entitled "Song of a Dream Visit to T'ien-mu: Farewell to Those I Leave Behind." In *ku-shih* form and using lines that vary in length from four to nine characters, it is noteworthy for its rhapsodic air and easy, rushing rhythms, which conceal the great care and precision with which it is put together. It begins with a reference to the Isles of Ying, fairy islands in the eastern sea where the immortal spirits live, and an assurance that the poet will, by contrast, describe an actual mountain. But his visit to the mountain is made in a dream and, like the journey passages of the *Ch'u Tz'u* and Han *fu*, grows increasingly fantastic until the dream is shattered and the sleeper awakes. The work ends with the poet bidding farewell to the world and declaring his intention to become a recluse, dwelling among the white deer and green bluffs of the wilderness. The subject of the poem, T'ien-mu, or Matron of Heaven, is a mountain near the sea in Chekiang (here referred to by the old name Yüeh), northwest of the more famous Mt. T'ien-t'ai. Lord Hsieh is the Six Dynasties landscape poet Hsieh Ling-yün, who lived in the region. He is supposed to have invented for mountain climbing a special type of clogs with detachable teeth, the front teeth being removed for climbing uphill, the back teeth for coming down. Li Po at one point echoes a poem which Hsieh Ling-yün wrote on the subject of Mt. T'ien-mu, "Climbing the Peak at Lin-hai," particularly the following lines:

> At dawn setting out south of the clear river;
> evening, shelter in the midst of Shan,
> next day to climb T'ien-mu peak,
> high high among clouds and rainbows;
> who can say when I'll return?

Seafarers tell of the Isles of Ying,
shadowy in spindrift and waves, truly hard to seek out;
Yüeh men describe T'ien-mu,
in clouds and rainbows clear or shrouded, there for eyes to glimpse;
T'ien-mu touching the sky, surging toward the sky,
lord above the Five Peaks, shadowing the Red Wall;
T'ien-t'ai's forty-eight thousand fathoms
beside it seem to topple and sprawl to south and east.
I longed, and my longing became a dream of Wu-Yüeh;
in the night I flew across the moon of Mirror Lake;

the lake moon, lighting my shadow,
saw me to the Valley of Shan,
Lord Hsieh's old home there today,
where green waters rush and roil and shrill monkeys cry.
Feet thrust into Lord Hsieh's clogs,
body climbing ladders of blue cloud,
halfway up the scarps I see the ocean sun,
and in the air hear the cocks of heaven.
A thousand cliffs, ten thousand clefts, trails uncertain,
I turn aside for flowers, rest on rocks—suddenly it's night;
bear growls, dragon purrs in the din of cliffside torrents
shake the deep forest, startle the piled-up peaks;
clouds blue-dark, threatening rain,
waters soft-seething, sending up mists:
a rent of lightning, crack of thunder,
and hilltops sunder and fall;
doors of stone at grotto mouths
swing inward with a grinding roar,
and from the blue darkness, bottomless, vast and wild,
sun and moon shine sparkling on terraces of silver and gold.
Rainbows for robes, wind for horses,
whirling whirling, the Lord of the Clouds comes down,
tigers twanging zithers, *luan* birds to turn his carriage,
and immortal men in files thick as hemp—
    Suddenly my soul shudders, my spirit leaps,
    in terror I rise up with repeated sighs:
    only the mat and pillow where now I woke—
    lost are the mists of a moment ago!
All the joys of the world are like this,
the many-evented past a river flowing east.
I leave you now—when will I return?—
to loose the white deer among green bluffs,
in my wandering to ride them in search of famed hills.
How can I knit brows, bend back to serve influence and power,
never dare to wear an open-hearted face?

✣ "Cocks of heaven": another name for the golden pheasant.

"Lord of the Clouds": a deity addressed in the shaman songs of the *Ch'u Tz'u*.

## TU FU (712–70)

The Ming critic Wang Shih-chen (1526–90) speaks of the poetry of Li Po as being dominated by *ch'i* or spirit, and *tzu-jan*, spontaneity or naturalness. To these he contrasts the dominating qualities in Tu Fu's poetry, *yi*, purpose or meaning, and *tu-tsao*, originality or creativity (*I-yüan chih-yen* Ch. 4). I trust the reader will see how this description of Li Po accords with what has been said above. Wang's point, I believe, is that Li Po's poetry appears to possess a life or vitality of its own, and so well is its art concealed that it gives the impression of being quite artless and unpremeditated. Tu Fu's poetry, on the other hand, if we follow Wang, is above all serious in purpose and full of deep meaning. This way of putting it may seem rather unfair to Li Po, implying that he is mere froth and banality, but it is essentially just, as we shall see. *Tu-tsao*, literally "independent creation," is likewise an apt choice to suggest both the great care that Tu Fu expended on the composition of his poetry, and the innovations in technique and subject matter that he introduced. If Li Po's work looks to the past, that of Tu Fu may be said to face squarely into the future. As Tu Fu himself freely admitted, his aim is to startle the reader.

I have mentioned Li Po's preference for the *ku-shih* or old poetry forms, with their relative freedom and air of old-time simplicity. Tu Fu, by contrast, took up the "modern style" forms with enthusiasm, welcoming the technical demands they make upon the artist. Of the approximately 1,450 extant poems in his collected works, over 1,000 are in one or another of these forms. It was he, in fact, who brought the *chin-t'i* forms to full maturity and established them as a vehicle for serious poetic statement. This is particularly true of the *lü-shih* or regulated verse form, which before his time had been used mainly for displays of verbal dexterity.

The *lü-shih*, as mentioned earlier, is made up of four couplets, the two middle couplets observing strict syntactical parallelism. Earlier writers had for the most part been content to use the two lines of the parallel couplets to repeat an idea or to pair images that one might naturally associate. Tu Fu, on the other hand, while maintaining perfect verbal balance, worked to introduce all manner of variation into the parallelisms of his *lü-shih*. Sometimes he achieved novelty by linking two images that would not ordinarily be associated with one another. At other times he introduces a shift in focus from one line of the couplet to the other, a change from a distant view to a closeup, from something visually perceived to something aurally perceived, from an image involving motion to one involving stillness, or vice versa. In other words, he packed the utmost amount of skill and significance into the parallel couplets, using them not, as earlier writers had too often done, to display a series of essentially static tableaux, but to propel the poem forward by putting it through a succession of highly disciplined maneuvers.

This type of packing or compression of language, seen at its most intense in the parallelisms of the *lü-shih*, is characteristic of Tu Fu's poetry as a whole. Far from seeking the kind of "natural" expression we have seen attributed to Li Po, he deliberately condensed and distorted his language, in his later poems introducing what are almost surely intended to be calculated ambiguities, until some lines have to be completely taken apart and rearranged before one can make out what they are about at all. This is one of the principal reasons why Tu Fu is so difficult to translate effectively. By the time one has unraveled the mere surface meaning of a line of the original and written it all down in another language, he finds himself with something that more nearly resembles a paragraph than a line of verse.

Tu Fu's originality is evident not only in the way he handled poetic form, but in his wide choice of subject matter as well. He was a man of warmth, compassion, and strong reformist sentiments, and he often used his poetry to attack social injustice. We have already noted the Confucian view of poetry as a vehicle for political and social protest, as exemplified in the songs of the *Book of Odes* and the *yüeh-fu* ballads. Tu Fu, in writing his own protest pieces, was merely carrying on and giving new life to this tradition. But whereas most T'ang poets, such as Li Po or Po Chü-i, expressed their criticisms indirectly through the conventions of the *yüeh-fu* style, borrowing the guise of the soldier or the peasant and setting the poem in some distant era of the past, Tu Fu boldly described in his own words the abuses and sufferings that he and his contemporaries encountered.[6] He lived through the terrible years of the An Lu-shan rebellion and witnessed all the misery that warfare, famine, and civil disorder can inflict upon a nation. The experience roused his deepest concern and inspired him to works of a power and realism all but unknown in Chinese poetry since the equally grim days of the late Han.

The same realism finds expression in a quieter vein in the numerous poems he wrote on the scenes of everyday life, particularly those that concern the members of his family. Such mundane subjects, though occasionally treated earlier by men like T'ao Yüan-ming, were generally thought to be unsuited to poetry. Tu Fu worked to broaden the definition of poetry by demonstrating that no subject, if properly handled, need be unpoetic. He was greatly aided in these efforts by a minuteness of observation and keen eye for detail that discovered significance in whatever it examined. There is evidence to suggest that he was versed in the lore of herbs and medicinal plants, and perhaps this knowledge gave him a special appreciation for the humbler forms of natural life. Some of his poems display a compassion for birds, fish, or insects that would almost seem to be Buddhist inspired. Whatever the reason, he appears to have possessed an acute sensitivity to the small motions and creatures of nature, a sensitivity beautifully illustrated in the poem "Restless Night" on p. 167. Somewhere in all the ceaseless and seemingly insignificant activities of the natural world, he keeps implying, truth is to be found.

Some of the technical skill, freshness of image, and close observation which I have described above will, I hope, be apparent in the following sample of couplets taken from Tu Fu's *lü-shih*:

[6] Especially noteworthy are the so-called Three Li and Three Partings poems describing the harsh treatment of the *li* or officials and the partings forced on members of peasant families by conscription and warfare. Unfortunately these works are not represented in my selection because, in spite of repeated efforts, I have not been able to produce translations that I felt were satisfactory. The reader may consult good translations in Rewi Alley and other works listed in the bibliography.

"Visiting the Ho Family Again," #1:

> Blossoms fall—orioles shouldering butterflies;
> the stream grows noisy—otters chasing fish.

"River Stop":

> Rivers flow—my heart doesn't try to keep up;
> clouds remain—slow as my imagination.

"River Village":

> My aging wife draws on paper, making us a chessboard;
> my little boy pounds a needle, fashioning a fishhook.

"Freeing the Boat," a description of a river journey; note the irregular caesura occurring after the first character:

> Green—I hate to see the hilltops passing;
> yellow—I know that citrons are on the way.

"Written Aboard a Boat on the Day of Little Cold Food." "Little Cold Food" was a spring holiday; the second line refers to the poet's failing eyesight.

> A boat on the spring waters—like sitting on top of the sky;
> flowers of my old age—seen as though through mist.

The keen sensibility which such lines attest led Tu Fu in times of elation to a kind of mystical identification with all of creation. But in times of depression, which were frequent in his troubled late years, it resulted in a mood of morbid irritation. His repeated efforts to secure a post in the government that would allow him to put into effect his reformist ideals ended in failure, and his anger and dis- illusionment with the human situation at times spilled over into a very un-Chinese attack on nature. In 759, traveling over the arduous Sword Gate Pass into Szechwan, for example, he exclaimed in exasperation:

> I would like to punish the Creator;
> my wish would be to cut away these piled up peaks!

Once in Szechwan, settled in a cottage on the outskirts of Ch'eng- tu, he was able to enjoy a few years of relative calm and ease, which are reflected in his poetry in a feeling for the more benign qualities of nature. But civil unrest once more forced him to take to the road and he spent his remaining years in restless wandering, hounded by sickness and privation. The poetry of this final period, as one might expect, is darkest of all, permeated by a sense of the weird and shuddery aspects of nature, and a despair that in its totality is painful for even his most ardent admirers to contemplate. Hardship had earlier served to bring out the finest in Tu Fu's moral and artistic nature, but in the end it tried him beyond the limits that art can reasonably cope with.

The forward-looking nature of Tu Fu's poetry is attested by the fact that, as we shall see in the chapters that follow, it anticipates so many of the trends of later poetry, and that his reputation grew steadily in the centuries following his death. The men of his time certainly regarded him highly, but, whereas they could immediately perceive the greatness of Li Po's poetry, Tu Fu's they must have found in some respects baffling. A forecast of what was to come, however, may be seen in the case of Chang Chi, a poet of the early ninth century, who expressed his admiration with disarming direct- ness by burning a copy of Tu Fu's works, mixing the ashes with honey and eating them. The men of the succeeding Sung dynasty, when Confucianism reasserted its sway over the intellectual world, were strongly attracted to Tu Fu by the realism and social signifi- cance of his poetry, as well as by the moral soundness of his charac- ter, and did their best to emulate him. His apotheosis was completed in the twelfth century with the bestowal upon him of the epithet *shih-sheng*, the "Sage of Poetry," acknowledging him the artistic counterpart of Confucius himself.

Traditional Chinese critics have not always distinguished carefully between a writer's works and his moral character. In fact those who, like Dr. Johnson, believe that it is always a writer's duty to make the world better (and they are the majority) would consider such a distinction improper to begin with. Thus the vast admiration which the Chinese have in the past expressed for Tu Fu, and continue to express today, is founded certainly on a genuine appreciation of the literary value of his poetry, but at the same time is undoubtedly colored by the fact that he is known to have been a loving husband

and father, a loyal patriot, and a compassionate friend to the common people. Foreign readers may feel that a juster appraisal of the poet's worth is to be arrived at by judging him on the basis of his writing alone, though if they read him in translation only, they may have a somewhat misleading impression of ease and accessibility. My own feelings about Tu Fu are mixed; much of what he has to say I find moving and important, but I am often put off by the difficulties of the language, difficulties that do not always seem artistically justified. Perhaps I am too conscious of his ranking as "China's greatest poet." As in the case of Beethoven, I feel that if people would stop for a moment telling me how great he is, I might have a better chance of appreciating that fact for myself.

Tu Fu's poetry is intimately related to the ups and downs of his own eventful life and to the history of the period, and it seems best, therefore, to follow chronological order, insofar as it can be determined, in presenting examples of his work. As an artist, Tu Fu matured slowly and there is little important work that dates from the first forty years of his life. I will begin my selection with a poem probably written in 753 entitled "Song of the Beautiful Ladies," in seven-character *ku-shih* form. Ostensibly a description of a lively court picnic, the poem is in fact a veiled attack on the Yang family, relatives of Emperor Hsüan-tsung's favorite, Yang Kuei-fei. The scene is the springtime outing traditionally held on the third day of the third lunar month at Ch'ü-chiang or Winding River, a pleasure park in the southeast sector of Ch'ang-an. The gathering centers about the two elder sisters of Yang Kuei-fei (referred to in the poem as "the lady of cloud screens and pepper-scented halls"), who had been enfeoffed as the Ladies of Kuo and Ch'in respectively. The gentleman who arrives later is Yang Kuei-fei's cousin, Yang Kuo-chung, a high minister. There were rumors that he was carrying on an intrigue with the Lady of Kuo, and this is probably behind the reference to the bluebird, the traditional bearer of love messages.

Third month, third day, in the air a breath of newness;
by Ch'ang-an riverbanks the beautiful ladies crowd,
warm-bodied, modest-minded, mild and pure,
with clear sleek complexions, bone and flesh well matched,

in figured gauze robes that shine in the late spring,
worked with golden peacocks, silver unicorns.
On their heads what do they wear?
Kingfisher glinting from hairpins that dangle by sidelock borders.
On their backs what do I see?
Pearls that weight the waistband and subtly set off the form.
Among them, kin of the lady of cloud screens and pepper-scented
　　halls,
granted titles to the great fiefs of Kuo and Ch'in.
Humps of purple camel proffered from blue caldrons,
platters of crystal spread with slivers of raw fish;
but ivory chopsticks, sated, dip down no more,
and phoenix knives in vain hasten to cut and serve.
Yellow Gate horses ride swiftly, leaving the dust unstirred,
bearing from royal kitchens unending rare delights.
Plaintive notes of flute and drum, enough to move the gods;
throngs of guests and lackeys, all of highest rank;
and last, another rider, with slow and measured stride,
dismounts at the tent door, ascends the brocade carpet.
The snow of willow catkins blankets the white-flowered reeds;
a bluebird flies away, in its bill a crimson kerchief—
　　Where power is all-surpassing, fingers may be burned;
　　take care and draw no closer to His Excellency's glare!

The extravagance, corruption, and political intrigue hinted at in
the poem above, if they did not directly bring on the An Lu-shan
rebellion, at least created an atmosphere in which revolt might hope
to succeed. Toward the end of 755, as we have seen, An Lu-shan
began marching west from his base near present-day Peking, and it
was not many months before he was approaching the capital. The
following poem, in five-character *ku-shih* form, gives an account of a
journey made by Tu Fu and his family in 756 when they fled north
from Ch'ang-an to avoid the rebel armies. Entitled " Song of P'eng-
ya," it was written the following year.

I remember when we first fled the rebels,
hurrying north over dangerous trails;

night deepened on P'eng-ya Road,
the moon shone over White-water Hills.
A whole family endlessly trudging,
begging without shame from the people we met:
valley birds sang, a jangle of soft voices;
we didn't see a single traveler returning.
The baby girl in her hunger bit me;
fearful that tigers or wolves would hear her cries,
I hugged her to my chest, muffling her mouth,
but she squirmed and wailed louder than before.
The little boy pretended he knew what was happening;
importantly he searched for sour plums to eat.
Ten days, half in rain and thunder,
through mud and slime we pulled each other on.
There was no escaping from the rain,
trails slick, clothes wet and clammy;
getting past the hardest places,
a whole day advanced us no more than three or four li.
Mountain fruits served for rations,
low-hung branches were our rafter and roof.
Mornings we traveled by rock-bedded streams,
evenings camped in mists that closed in the sky.
We stopped a little while at the marsh of T'ung-chia,
thinking to go out by Lu-tzu Pass;
an old friend there, Sun Tsai,
ideals higher than the piled-up clouds;
he came out to meet us as dusk turned to darkness,
called for torches, opening gate after gate,
heated water to wash our feet,
cut strips of paper to call back our souls.
Then his wife and children came;
seeing us, their tears fell in streams.
My little chicks had gone sound to sleep;
he called them to wake up and eat from his plate,
said he would make a vow with me,
the two of us to be brothers forever.
At last he cleared the room where we sat,

wished us goodnight, all he had at our command.
Who is willing, in the hard, bleak times,
to break open, lay bare his innermost heart?
Parting from you, a year of months has rounded,
Tartar tribes still plotting evil,
and I think how it would be to have strong wings
that would carry me away, set me down before you.

꒛ "Strips of paper": an ancient rite used to call back the souls of travelers, dispersed in fright. Commentators disagree whether, in this case, the rite was actually performed, or whether it is alluded to here only as a figure of speech.

The poet, having settled his wife and children at a place called Fu-chou, north of Ch'ang-an near present-day Yenan, attempted to make his way alone to the headquarters of the crown prince, where loyalist forces were gathering. But he fell into the hands of the rebels and was taken to Ch'ang-an. In the following poem, "Moonlight Night," written in 756 when he was a prisoner in Ch'ang-an, he imagines how his wife and children are spending the autumn evening. The poem is in five-character *lü-shih* form.

From her room in Fu-chou tonight
all alone she watches the moon.
Far away, I grieve that her children
can't understand why she thinks of Ch'ang-an.
Fragrant mist in her cloud hair damp,
clear lucence on her jade arms cold—
when will we lean by chamber curtains
and let it light the two of us, our tear stains dried?

The next poem, a five-character *lü-shih*, was written early in 757 when the poet was still held captive in Ch'ang-an. It is entitled "Spring Prospect." In the second couplet I have attempted to preserve the ambiguity of the original by employing dangling participles. The subject, unexpressed in Chinese, is presumably the poet, who, viewing the usually joyful signs of spring, can only react with sorrow and alarm. Some commentators, however, would make the flowers the subject of the first line, interpreting the line as pathetic fallacy, that is, feeling the times, flowers shed tears.

The nation shattered, hills and streams remain.
A city in spring, grass and trees deep:
feeling the times, flowers draw tears;
hating separation, birds alarm the heart.
Beacon fires three months running,
a letter from home worth ten thousand in gold—
white hairs, fewer for the scratching,
soon too few to hold a hairpin up.

I have already discussed the *lü-shih* and *chüeh-chü* forms. There is
a third "modern style" form known as *p'ai-lü*, which observes the
same rules of tonal parallelism as the *lü-shih* but is unrestricted in
length. The following poem, entitled "Passing Chao-ling Again,"
is an example of a five-character *p'ai-lü*. It is also an example of an
important genre of Chinese poetry so far not illustrated, that of
patriotic poems written to pay tribute to the greatness of the ruling
dynasty. Chao-ling was the mausoleum of Emperor T'ai-tsung
(r. 627–48), the second ruler of the T'ang and the man who was
largely responsible for the actual founding of the dynasty. The
first eight lines describe T'ai-tsung's rise to power in the troubled
times at the end of the Sui. The "five-hued clouds" of the last line
are an auspicious omen appearing in response to T'ai-tsung's
greatness. The poem was written in 757, when the dynasty's fortunes seemed anything but glorious.

From rude darkness the heroes rose;
amid songs of praise, destiny chose him;
in wind and dust, his three-foot sword,
armor donned for the altars of the land;
wings to his father, pure in civil virtue;
heir of the great charge, wielder of war's might;
his holy vision wide and huge as heaven,
in service of ancestors more radiant than the sun.
The mound-side chamber lies wrapped in empty slopes;
warriors, bear-like, to guard the blue-green hill.
Once more I gaze up the pine and cypress road,
watching five-hued clouds drift by.

"The Lovely Lady," a poem in five-character *ku-shih* form written in 759, describes the fate of a woman whose family had been wiped out in the rebellion and whose husband had deserted her. The poet adopts the kind of impersonal tone usually associated with the *yüeh-fu*, though he is almost certainly basing his description upon an actual experience.

Lovely lady, fairest of the time,
hiding away in an empty valley;
daughter of a good house, she said,
fallen now among grasses of the wood.
"There was tumult and death within the passes then;
my brothers, old and young, were killed.
office, position—what help were they?
I couldn't even gather up my brothers' bones!
The world despises you when your luck is down;
all I had went with the turn of the flame.
My husband was a fickle fellow,
his new girl as fair as jade.
Blossoms that close at dusk keep faith with the hour,
mandarin ducks will not rest apart;
but he could only see the new one laughing,
never hear the former one's tears—"
Within the mountain the stream runs clear;
out of the mountain it turns to mud.
Her maid returns from selling a pearl,
braids vines to mend their roof of thatch.
The lady picks a flower but does not put it in her hair,
gathers juniper berries, sometimes a handful.
When the sky is cold, in thin azure sleeves,
at dusk she stands leaning by the tall bamboo.

✦ "Juniper": the juniper and the bamboo, which remain green all year, function here as symbols of the lady's unchanging fidelity.

The following five-character *ku-shih*, also written in 759, deals with the theme of friendship and is entitled "Presented to Wei Pa, Gentleman in Retirement."

Life is not made for meetings;
like stars at opposite ends of the sky we move.
What night is it, then, tonight,
when we can share the light of this lamp?
Youth—how long did it last?
the two of us grayheaded now,
we ask about old friends—half are ghosts;
cries of unbelief stab the heart.
Who would have thought?—twenty years
and once again I enter your house.
You weren't married when I left you;
now suddenly a whole row of boys and girls!
merrily greeting their father's friend,
asking me what places I've been.
Before I finish answering,
you send the boys to set out wine and a meal,
spring scallions cut in night rain,
new cooked rice mixed with yellow millet.
Meetings are rare enough, you say;
pour the wine till we've downed ten cups!
But ten cups do not make me drunk;
your steadfast love is what moves me now.
Tomorrow hills and ranges will part us,
the wide world coming between us again.

"Seven Songs Written During the Ch'ien-yüan Era While Staying at T'ung-ku-hsien" is the title of a series of seven-character *ku-shih* that records the experiences of the poet in 759 when, fleeing from famine, he had led his family west to the region of T'ung-ku in Kansu. The following, the first, second, third, fourth, and sixth of the series, tell of his search for food or for herbs that could be made into medicine to sell. Tzu-mei is Tu Fu's courtesy name.

1. A traveler, a traveler, Tzu-mei his name,
   white hair tousled, dangling below the ears,
     through the years gathering acorns in the wake of the monkey
         pack:
   cold skies at dusk within a mountain valley.

No word from the middle plain, no hope of going home;
hands and feet chilled and chapped, skin and flesh grown numb,
ah-ah, song the first, a song already sad;
mournful winds for my sake come down from the sky.

2. Long hoe, long hoe, handle of white wood,
  I trust my life to you—you must save me now!
  No shoots of wild taro where mountain snows drift high;
  robe so short, pull as I may it will not hide my shins.
  And so with you I go empty-handed home;
  the boy grumbles, the girls whine, my four walls are still.
  Ah-ah, song the second, the song at last breaks free;
  village lanes for my sake put on the face of pity.

*"Wild taro": or, following another text, "shoots of wild lily," used in medicine.

3. [Tu Fu had four brothers, the youngest with him in T'ung-ku;
      the others were living in the east.]

  I have brothers, younger brothers in a place far away,
  three of them sickly, not one of them strong;
  parted in life, to veer and turn, never to meet;
  barbarian dust blackens the sky, the road is long.
  Wild geese flying east, behind them the cranes—
  if they could only carry me to your side!
  Ah-ah, song the third, the singer's third refrain;
  if I should die here, how would you find my bones?

4. [Chung-li is in Anhwei south of the Huai River.]

  I have a sister, little sister, living in Chung-li,
  husband dead these many years, her orphan ones still young.
  On the long Huai the waves leap up, dragons and serpents rage;
  we haven't met for ten years—when will you come?
  I want to go in a little boat but arrows fill my eyes;
  far away in that southern land, banners of war abound.
  Ah-ah, song the fourth, four times I've sung;
  forest monkeys for my sake wail even at noon.

6. [Clearly a political allegory, though critics do not agree on exactly
   what the dragon and the vipers stand for.]

To the south there is a dragon living in a mountain pool,
where old trees, dark and lush, touch limb to bending limb.
When tree leaves yellow and fall, he goes to his winter sleep,
and from the east come vipers to play on the waters there.
Passing by, I marveled that they would dare come forth;
I drew a sword to slash them, but put it up again.
Ah-ah, song the sixth, its purpose long denied;
stream-cut valley, for my sake put on spring clothes again!

The following four poems date from the relatively sunny period
in Tu Fu's life when he was living in the outskirts of Ch'eng-tu.
The first, entitled "A Guest Arrives," a seven-character *lü-shih*, was
written in 760.

North of my lodge, south of my lodge, spring rivers all;
day by day I see only flocks of gulls convening.
Flower paths have not been swept for any guest;
my thatch gate for the first time opens to you.
For food—the market's far—no wealth of flavors;
for wine—my house is poor—only old muddy brew.
If you don't mind drinking with the old man next door,
I'll call across the hedge and we can finish off what's left.

"On the Spur of the Moment"; seven-character *lü-shih* written in 761.
Tu Fu tries to convince himself that he is contented in his life of
retirement. O-mei is a famous mountain southwest of Ch'eng-tu.

River slopes, already into the midmonth of spring;
under the blossoms, bright mornings again:
I look up, eager to watch the birds;
turn my head, answering what I took for a call.
Reading books, I skip the difficult parts;
faced with wine, I keep my cup filled.
These days I've gotten to know the old man of O-mei;
he understands this idleness that is my true nature.

"Restless Night"; five-character *lü-shih* written in 764, an evocation of the faint but incessant movement of nature, reflecting the "rest-lessness" of the title.

The cool of bamboo invades my room;
moonlight from the fields fills the corners of the court;
dew gathers till it falls in drops;
a scattering of stars, now there, now gone.
A firefly threading the darkness makes his own light;
birds at rest on the water call to each other;
all these lie within the shadow of the sword—
    Powerless I grieve as the clear night passes.

"*Chüeh-chü*"; first of two poems in five-character *chüeh-chü* form written in 764.

In late sun, the beauty of river and hill;
on spring wind, fragrance of grass and flower;
where mud is soft the swallows fly;
where sands are warm the mandarin ducks doze.

The following poem, a five-character *lü-shih* written in 766, bears the heading "My younger brother Feng is alone in the region east of the Yangtze and for three or four years I have had no word from him; I am looking for someone to take him these two poems." Tu Fu was in K'uei-chou on the upper Yangtze, the Chiang-han region mentioned in the poem; his brother was somewhere in the seacoast area south of the Yangtze delta. This is the second of the two poems.

They say you're staying in a mountain temple,
in Hang-chou—or is it Yüeh-chou?
In the wind and grime of war, how long since we parted!
At Chiang-han, bright autumns waste away.
While my shadow rests by monkey-loud trees,
my soul whirls off to where shell-born towers rise.
Next year on floods of spring I'll go downriver,
to the white clouds at the end of the east I'll look for you!

✦ "Shell-born towers": towerlike mirages at sea, believed to be formed from the breath of mollusks.

The last poem to be quoted, a five-character *lü-shih* entitled "A Traveler at Night Writes his Thoughts," is assigned by some

scholars to 765, by others to 767. In the second couplet, note the
ambiguity: is it the stars that sweep or the fields? is it the moon
that flows or the river? or both?

> Delicate grasses, faint wind on the bank;
> stark mast, a lone night boat:
> stars hang down, over broad fields sweeping;
> the moon boils up, on the great river flowing.
> Fame—how can my writings win me that?
> Office—age and sickness have brought it to an end.
> Fluttering, fluttering—where is my likeness?
> Sky and earth and one sandy gull.

# IX

## LATER TRENDS IN
## T'ANG POETRY

꿊

### BUDDHIST QUIETISM: WANG WEI AND HAN-SHAN

*How could you be so happy, now some thousand years
dishevelled, puffs of dust?*—JOHN BERRYMAN

IN THE PRECEDING section we have noted the Taoist-inspired
fantasy that is characteristic of much of Li Po's poetry, and the
Confucian idealism and social consciousness so important in that of
Tu Fu. A third element that played a major part in the intellectual
and spiritual life of the T'ang is represented in the poetry of Wang

Translations and studies of Wang Wei and Han-shan will be found in Chang
Yin-nan and Lewis C. Walmsley, *The Poems of Wang Wei*; Ch'en, *Poems of
Solitude;* Gary Snyder, "Han Shan: Cold Mountain Poems," *Evergreen Review*, 2
(no. 6, 1958), 69–80, reprinted in Birch, *Anthology*; Arthur Waley, "Poems by
Han-shan," *Encounter,* 3 (no. 3, Sept., 1954), reprinted in *Chinese Poems;* Burton
Watson, *Cold Mountain: 100 Poems by Han-shan*; and Wu Chi-yu, "A Study of
Han Shan," *T'oung Pao*, 45 (no. 4–5, 1957), 392–450.

Arthur Waley, *The Life and Times of Po Chü-i* provides an excellent study of the
poet. Other Middle T'ang poets are translated in Graham, *Poems of the Late
T'ang*; and Payne, *The White Pony.*

Margaret Tudor South, *Li Ho* is useful mainly for its biographical information;
James J. Y. Liu, *The Poetry of Li Shang-yin, Ninth Century Baroque Chinese Poet*
combines biography with extensive literary analysis. Further translations of
Late T'ang poetry will be found in Ch'en, *Poems of Solitude*; Graham, *Poems of
the Late T'ang*; and Payne, *The White Pony.*

THE QUOTATION ABOVE IS FROM "NOTE TO WANG WEI."

Wei (699–759), whose 400 extant works have been described as so many affirmations of the Buddhist faith.

The exact extent of Buddhist influence upon the cultural life of the T'ang is difficult to measure. In the plastic arts, there is no question of the enormous importance of Buddhist painting, sculpture, and architecture, though nearly all of this was swept away in the proscription of Buddhism carried out in the ninth century, or the wars that accompanied the fall of the dynasty. Because of the conservatism and deep-seated cultural pride of the Chinese men of letters, and the fact that almost none of them, even the most fervent Buddhist believers, ever took the trouble to learn any of the languages in which the scriptures of their religion were originally written, Buddhist influence in literature is much less marked, and when it does occur, is often inextricably fused with elements of Taoism. In T'ang poetry one frequently encounters terms taken from Buddhist philosophy, but this is no assurance that the poet who used them was a believer, or even understood the real meaning of the words. More often such terms were thrown in merely to lend an air of exoticism or modernity, as we find the words *bodhisattva, satori*, etc. at times bandied about in American letters today.

There were, however, a certain number of responsible poets such as Wang Wei, Liu Tsung-yüan, or Po Chü-i who were not only serious students of Buddhist thought, but who tried to some extent to give expression to their religious views and ideals in their poetry. This true Buddhist poetry, as distinguished from that which merely dabbles in Buddhist terminology, may be divided into two types. First is that which is overtly doctrinal. Most often it is cast in the *chi* or *gāthā* form, hymns of praise or devotional verses patterned after those found in the Chinese translations of Buddhist scriptures and most commonly employing a four-character line. These verses may deal directly with philosophical or religious concepts, as in Po Chü-i's eight *gāthā* on the subjects of contemplation, enlightenment, *samādhi*, etc.; or they may employ conventional Buddhist images such as the lion and the elephant, borrowed from Indian literature, the moon reflected in the water, or the *pa-chiao* (plantain). But when such images are used, they function solely on the symbolic level: the plantain, with its pulpy trunk, stands for the idea of physical frailty, the moon in the water for that of unreality, and so forth. The purpose of the poems in which they occur is to express ideas and concepts, not to describe scenes; in spite of any incidental interest that may attach to the imagery, their principal aim is doctrinal rather than literary.

The second type of Buddhist poetry is that in which the philosophical meaning lies much farther below the surface. The imagery functions on both the descriptive and the symbolic levels at once, and it is not often possible to pin down the exact symbolic content of an image. These poems make no doctrinal point or deliver no sermon; they are Buddhist only in their general tone or outlook, and in fact if one were unaware of the author's identity, or did not know that he was a believer, one might never think of them as Buddhist at all—which, of course, from the Buddhist point of view, would mark them as the highest type.

Wang Wei's poetry belongs to this latter category. Some of it has to do with visits to temples, though this fact is less significant than one might suppose. Temples were pleasant places to visit on an outing or to put up at for the night, and countless Chinese poets wrote of them who had no real interest in the doctrines they taught or the religious life conducted there. Of more importance are Wang Wei's descriptions of landscapes, particularly those at his country home at Lan-t'ien southeast of Ch'ang-an. These are the poems for which he is most famous and which best exemplify his outlook on life.

Religions such as Judaism, Christianity, or Islam, since they exhort their followers to cultivate an active faith, devotion, and love toward God, are in their literature free to make use of highly emotional language and symbolism, even that of sexual passion, provided it is understood allegorically. But because the aim of Buddhist teaching is to extinguish passion, to cut man loose from his emotional entanglements, it must choose its words with great circumspection when giving literary expression to its ideals. Chinese Buddhism, borrowing from Indian and Central Asian sources, offered vivid and highly emotional descriptions of the hells that await the sinner and the Western Paradise where the blessed are reborn. But these descriptions were intended mainly for the unlettered masses, who were not capable of understanding the higher subtleties of the doctrine. The more sophisticated believer would understand that such depictions of Heaven and Hell were in the end only an "expedient means" employed to draw men in the direction of salvation. When he himself came to express his religion in words, he sometimes composed modest hymns or poems of doctrine such as have been described above. But more often he sought simply to convey in his writing the calmness, detachment, and purity that characterize the enlightened mind.

These are precisely the qualities embodied in Wang Wei's poetry. He seems to have carefully excluded from his poems, most of them descriptions of nature or rustic life, every element that could be considered wild, dramatic, grandiose, or stirring—all, in fact, that lies at the heart of the nature poetry of the Romantic Movement in the West. In Wang Wei, nothing is left of the earlier Chinese attitude of fear or awe in the presence of nature, or even of Hsieh Ling-yün's ideal of active appreciation. Instead he gives the impression of viewing the landscape with perfect Buddhist passivity, not seeking to see anything at all, but merely allowing whatever may lie within the scope of vision to register upon his mind. Concealing the care he has taken to create such an impression, he would have us believe that he is a mirror, that favorite symbol in both Taoist and Buddhist literature, reflecting existence without partiality or prejudice.

The typical Wang Wei poem, couched in terms of extreme simplicity, presents a broad, generalized view. The title may identify it as a description of some particular spot, but in the poem itself details are so sparingly offered that the effect of such particularization is largely nullified. As in so much T'ang nature poetry, the focus is less often upon land areas or the immediate foreground than upon light and aerial effects, lending a tone of evanescence and insubstantiality. Signs of human existence and activity are neither sought out nor fastidiously excluded. A mark of true enlightenment, one feels, is the way in which Wang Wei manages to avoid making any comment upon the subject of man's relationship to nature, or of even recognizing that a distinction exists between the two. Wang Wei's poetry, in fact, is almost totally free of overt philosophizing, and, far from containing any element of the consciously picturesque or quaint, as descriptions of it sometimes suggest, it is actually plain to a degree that is the despair of translators. Yet it is this very plainness, which in the end is a kind of purity, that gives it true value.

Such statements, admittedly vague, will become clearer and more meaningful, I hope, when we turn to the poetry itself. The first three poems, all in 5-character *chüeh-chü* form, are part of a famous set entitled "Twenty Views of Wang-ch'uan," which describes various parts of the poet's country estate at Lan-t'ien. In the first poem, the poet, having acquired a villa there on the Wang River, near the site of an old settlement called Meng-ch'eng, muses on the men who have owned the property in the past and planted willows which are now old and decayed, and on the future owners who will in the same way think back pityingly on his own days of ownership.

"Meng-ch'eng Hollow"

A new home at the mouth of Meng-ch'eng;
old trees—last of a stand of dying willows:
years to come, who will be its owner,
vainly pitying the one who had it before?

"Bamboo Mile Lodge"

Alone I sit in dark bamboo,
strumming the lute, whistling away;
deep woods that no one knows,
where a bright moon comes to shine on me.

"Deer Fence"

Empty hills, no one in sight,
only the sound of someone talking;
late sunlight enters the deep wood,
shining over the green moss again.

"Duckweed Pond"; 5-character *chüeh-chü*; the fifth of a set of five poems written at a place called Cloud Valley for the poet's friend Huang-fu Yüeh.

By the spring pond, deep and wide,
you must be waiting for the light boat to return.

Supple and soft, the green duckweed meshes,
till dangling willows sweep it open again.

"Joys of the Country: Seven Poems"; the fourth of the series, an
example of a 6-character *chüeh-chü*. I hope the rather jerky rhythm
typical of this unusual form will be apparent even in translation.

Lush lush, fragrant grasses in autumn green;
tall tall, towering pines in summer cold;
cows and sheep come home by themselves to village lanes;
little boys know nothing of capped and robed officials.

"Seeing Someone Off"; 5-character *ku-shih*. There is no way to
identify the person whom the poet is sending off to retirement in
Southern Mountain—probably Chung-nan, the range just south
of Ch'ang-an. Critics have suggested that the poem is in fact an
imaginary dialogue of the poet with himself.

We dismount; I give you wine
and ask, where are you off to?
You answer, nothing goes right!—
back home to lie down by Southern Mountain.
Go then—I'll ask no more—
there's no end to white clouds there.

The fifth line, because of its lack of pronouns, is open to various
interpretations, depending upon whether one takes it as the words
of the poet or his friend. Such is the ambiguity of Chinese verse
that any of the following alternative translations might be correct:

Go then, and ask [about the world] no more—
I'll go then, and ask [about the world] no more—
I'll go then—ask me no more—

"At My Country Home in Chung-nan"; 5-character *lü-shih*.

Middle age—I grow somewhat fond of the Way,
my evening home at the foot of southern hills.
When moods come I follow them alone,
to no purpose learning fine things for myself,
going till I come to where the river ends,
sitting and watching when clouds rise up.

By chance I meet an old man of the woods;
we talk and laugh—we have no "going-home" time.

᠊ᡐ᠊ "To no purpose" translates *k'ung*, "void" or "empty," one of Wang Wei's favorite words. The surface meaning is "in vain," that is, I see these beautiful sights in vain because I have no companion to enjoy them with—the conventional belief that joys are real joys only when shared with a like-minded friend. On a different level is the philosophical meaning of *k'ung*: I know these fine things "emptily," without trying to grasp or hold on to them, indeed without even in the end recognizing them as "fine things."

"Visiting the Temple of Accumulated Fragrance;" 5-character *lü-shih*.

I didn't know where the temple was,
pushing mile on mile among cloudy peaks;
old trees, peopleless paths,
deep mountains, somewhere a bell.
Brook voices choke over craggy boulders,
sun rays turn cold in the green pines.
At dusk by the bend of a deserted pond,
a monk in meditation, taming poison dragons.

᠊ᡐ᠊ "Peopleless paths": most translators take the phrase *wu-jen-ching* to mean "no people-paths," i.e., no paths for people to walk on; I prefer to take it as "no-people paths."

"Monk in meditation": *an-ch'an*, "composed meditation," *ch'an* representing the Sanskrit *dhyāna*. The poison dragons are the passions and illusions that impede enlightenment. At the same time they recall the tale of a poison dragon that lived in a lake and killed passing merchants until it was subdued by a certain Prince P'an-t'o through the use of spells. The dragon changed into a man and apologized for its evil ways. According to another interpretation, the last line should read "Let me sit in meditation, taming poison dragons."

"Weeping for Yin Yao"; 7-character *chüeh-chü*. Yin Yao, poet and official, was a close friend of Wang Wei; in a longer poem on the same subject, Wang Wei mentions that the two men studied Buddhism together. Yin's family was very poor and had to rely on the generosity of Wang Wei and other friends to meet the expenses of the funeral.

We send you home to a grave on Stone Tower Mountain;
through the green green of pine and cypress, mourners' carriages
return.

Among white clouds we've laid your bones—it is ended forever;
only the mindless waters remain, flowing down to the world of
men.

Though ostensibly this is a lament for the dead, we find that the
deceased friend has in fact gone "home" to a mountaintop world
of white clouds, symbols of freedom and purity, and eternally green
trees. The real lament, it would appear, is for the living, who must
leave the mountain and return again to "the world of men." The two
worlds are linked by the flowing stream, whose "mindlessness"—
its utter freedom from ego and purposeful activity—points the way
for man's salvation.

Wang Wei, a well-to-do official and accomplished painter,
calligrapher, and musician who spent most of his life in the region
of the capital, is typical of the genteel, upper-class Buddhist believer
of the north. Another important Buddhist poet, Han-shan or the
Master of Cold Mountain, represents a very different type. Though
nothing is known of him for certain, he is said to have been a
recluse who lived at a place called Cold Mountain on the T'ien-t'ai
range in Chekiang, the wild and beautiful region we have already
found described in the poetry of Hsieh Ling-yün and in Li Po's
"Visit to T'ien-mu" on p. 151. We possess a collection of some
300 poems attributed to him and to an equally mysterious companion, Shih-te, the Foundling. The earliest known references to the
poems date from the ninth century and they would appear therefore
to be the product of a writer or writers of the late eighth or early
ninth century, though they may be somewhat earlier.

Some of the poems are little more than crude sermons in verse, of
the kind frequently used among the masses to popularize Buddhist
teachings such as vegetarianism and the doctrine of karma. Others
resemble the *yüeh-fu* ballads, describing the hardships of the soldier
or the peasant or lamenting the swiftness with which youth and
beauty fade. Some deal with Buddhist doctrines through the conventional type of symbolism I have mentioned above. Such, for
example, is the following five-character *ku-shih* which employs the
image of the moon reflected in the water:

My mind is like the autumn moon

shining clean and clear in the green pool.
No, that's not a good comparison.
Tell me, how shall I explain?

There are other poems in which the images, though almost
certainly intended to function symbolically, are less certain in
meaning, such as the following five-character *ku-shih* which begins
with the image of the setting sun. The setting sun stands for many
things in T'ang poetry: the passing of time, the approach of death,
the awareness that things are often most beautiful just before the
moment of extinction. To turn back to Wang Wei for a moment,
we know that he, like many men of the T'ang, was a worshiper of
the Buddha Amida, and in a hymn he wrote he speaks of his desire
to be reborn in Amida's Western Paradise. It has been suggested
that the image of the setting sun may, in Wang Wei's poetry, be a
symbol of devotion to Amida and the Western Paradise, or be
associated with the practice, enjoined in the *Kuan-wu-liang-shou
ching*, of meditating on the sun as it goes down.[1] In the Han-shan
poem to be considered here, the conjunction of "late sun" and
"western hill" seems to suggest old age and approaching death.
The "dark and gloomy place," like Dante's *selva oscura*, would appear
to represent spiritual crisis, though I am unable to cite any specific
evidence in Buddhist literature to support this, or to illuminate the
symbolism of the tigers and the knife.

In the late sun I descended the western hill,
light streaming over the grass and trees,
till I came to a dark and gloomy place
where pines and creepers grew thick together.
Within crouched many tigers;
when they saw me, their fur stood on end.
Not so much as a knife in my hand,
did I not gasp with fear?

More famous, and of greater merit as literature, are those poems
which, like the best of Wang Wei, combine description of the actual

[1] See postface by Ogawa Tamaki to Ō I [*Wang Wei*], tr. by Tsuru Haruo,
*Chūgoku shijin senshū* #6 (1958).

landscape with the delineation of mental and spiritual states. The landscape of Han-shan's poetry is that of the T'ien-t'ai Mountains, far more rugged and isolated than that of Wang Wei's villa in the hills south of Ch'ang-an. Moreover, to judge from his poetry, Han-shan was a follower of the southern branch of the Ch'an or Zen sect, which placed great emphasis upon individual effort and was less wary of emotionalism than earlier Buddhism had been. As a result Han-shan's poetry has little of the tone of dry, bland understatement we have seen in Wang Wei. Though he writes at times in a mood of serenity, at other times he appears despondent, angry, arrogant, or wildly elated, and he delights in emphasizing both the incomparable beauty of his mountain retreat and its frightening strangeness. Wang Wei saw in the gentle landscape of the north an embodiment of the peace and anonymity that he sought, and he was content to lose himself in it. Han-shan's home in Chekiang was a ruder, more savage place, and his Buddhism, though its ultimate goal was the same tranquillity that Wang Wei cultivated, placed greater stress on the experiential life of the individual. Something of the highly personal flavor of Han-shan's eremitic poetry will, I hope, be apparent in the following examples, four poems in five-character form. The third is a *ku-shih*, the remainder are *lü-shih*. All of Han-shan's poems are untitled.

I climb the road to Cold Mountain,
the road to Cold Mountain that never ends.
The valleys are long and strewn with boulders,
the streams broad and banked with thick grass.
Moss is slippery though no rain has fallen;
pines sigh but it isn't the wind.
Who can break from the snares of the world
and sit with me among the white clouds?

Cold Mountain is full of weird sights;
people who try to climb it always get scared.
When the moon shines, the water glints and sparkles;
when the wind blows, the grasses rustle and sigh.
Snowflakes make blossoms for the bare plum,
clouds in place of leaves for the naked trees.

At a touch of rain the whole mountain shimmers—
but only in good weather can you make the climb.

Last night in a dream I returned to my old home
and saw my wife weaving at her loom.
She held her shuttle poised, as though lost in thought,
as though she had no strength to lift it further.
I called. She turned her head to look
but her eyes were blank—she didn't know me.
So many years we've been parted
the hair at my temples has lost its old color.

Among a thousand clouds and ten thousand streams
here lives an idle man,
in the daytime wandering over green mountains,
at night coming home to sleep by the cliff.
Swiftly the springs and autumns pass,
but my mind is at peace, free of dust and delusion.
How pleasant, to know I need nothing to lean on,
to be still as the waters of the autumn river!

## MIDDLE T'ANG: HAN YÜ AND PO CHÜ-I

Tu Fu, particularly in his late works, pushed Chinese poetry about
as far as it could profitably go in the direction of richness and compression of meaning. Many of the poets who followed him in the
Middle T'ang (roughly 765–835), perhaps because they did not
fully understand or appreciate what he had been trying to do, perhaps because they felt he had already exhausted the possibilities of a
style of such extreme refinement and density, began deliberately
working back toward a freer, looser, more colloquial diction and
syntax. In doing so, they opened up a new avenue of growth for
Chinese poetry, though its potentialities were not completely realized
until several centuries later, in the time of the Sung dynasty.

One of the most important leaders in this new poetic movement
was Han Yü (768–824), also famous as a Confucian thinker and
creator of the *ku-wen* or old prose style. His efforts to introduce

reforms both in prose and in poetic style were in many ways motivated by the same ideals. In prose, he sought to break away from
the *p'ien-wen* or parallel prose style, with its extreme attention to
formal regularity and rhetorical flourish, and to substitute a style
embodying the simplicity, naturalness, and respect for speech
rhythms that, it was claimed, had characterized the writings of the
ancients. In poetry he made a similar effort to do away with stale or
contrived diction and to restore freshness to the language of the
poem. In addition, he worked to liberate the *shih* from its tight formal
regularity by using a freer line, one that was not end-stopped in the
traditional fashion, or that departed from the norm in length or
placing of the caesura. He also tried employing the kind of deliberate
repetition of words or phrases heretofore used frequently in the *fu*
but frowned upon in the *shih*.

Such innovations in form and diction can hardly be adequately
illustrated in translation. A third contribution which Han Yü made
to the new poetic style should, however, be immediately apparent
from the examples to be quoted. As he worked to instill new vigor
into the *shih* by introducing formal elements from the *fu*, he enriched its content in a comparable fashion by developing its narrative
and descriptive possibilities, essaying subjects that had previously
been regarded as proper for prose or the *fu* form alone, and sounding
a more openly philosophical note.

In undertaking these innovations, he ran the risks usual to a
reformer, and not all of his experiments were an unqualified success.
The move toward greater formal freedom and simplicity, combined
with the introduction of more prosaic subject matter, often robbed
the poem of its necessary tautness, allowing it to relax almost into
prose pure and simple. The fondness for philosophizing led at times
to poetry that was all but barren of images (as in the tenth poem in
the series entitled "Autumn Thoughts"). Such philosophizing and
psychological analysis, had it been of greater intrinsic interest,
might well have compensated for the absence of images. But Han
Yü's musings, alas, were those of the typical T'ang writer: gloomy,
fretful, and inclined to self-pity. It remained for the Sung poets,
with their more complex outlook on life, to produce really interesting philosophical poetry.

Many of Han Yü's experiments, as I have said, were unsuccessful. Others, though interesting enough to the modern reader, did not impress his contemporaries and successors or inspire them to emulation, and his work stands outside the mainstream of the T'ang poetic tradition. Nevertheless, in a culture as given to imitation of the past as that of China, imitation that is often vapid and mindless when it is not downright servile, one ought to bestow special praise on innovation and experimentation of any kind. And, in judging Han Yü, it is well to remember that he was in the unhappy position of following immediately on the heels of a group of poetic geniuses such as his country had never known before. It is surely to his credit that, uncowed by their greatness, he was able to shape his own artistic destiny, enlarging and enriching the poetic tradition in ways that were quite distinct from those of his predecessors.

The following poem, written in seven-character *ku-shih* form and entitled "The Girl of Mt. Hua," will give some idea of Han Yü's narrative style, while at the same time displaying his well-known contempt for Buddhism and Taoism. The poem begins with a description of the immense popularity of the Buddhist preachers of Ch'ang-an, who had drawn the crowds away from their Taoist rivals, and of a sudden reversal of the situation when the "girl of Mt. Hua," a beautiful young Taoist priestess, appeared in the capital to attract the attention even of the emperor himself. In the closing section, the poet chides the rich young men of the capital who flock about the priestess for other than spiritual reasons, and hints that her favors are reserved for more exalted personages. The bluebird in the last line, bearer of love notes, is the messenger of the immortal spirit Hsi-wang-mu, the Queen Mother of the West, to whom the priestess is compared. We have no way of knowing whether Han Yü's insinuations were justified, though it might be recalled that Yang Kuei-fei, the renowned favorite of Emperor Hsüan-tsung, originally entered the palace as a Taoist priestess.

In streets east, streets west, they expound the Buddhist canon,
   clanging bells, sounding conches, till the din invades the palace;
"sin," "blessing," wildly inflated, give force to threats and
   deceptions;

throngs of listeners elbow and shove as though through duckweed
    seas.
Yellow-robed Taoist priests preach their sermons too,
but beneath their lecterns, ranks grow thinner than stars in the
    flush of dawn.
The girl of Mount Hua, child of a Taoist home,
longed to expel the foreign faith, win men back to the Immortals;
she washed off her powder, wiped her face, put on cap and shawl.
With white throat, crimson cheeks, long eyebrows of gray,
she came at last to ascend the chair, unfolding the secrets of
    Truth.
For anyone else the Taoist halls would hardly have opened their
    doors;
I do not know who first whispered the word abroad,
but all at once the very earth rocked with the roar of thunder.
Buddhist temples were swept clean, no trace of a believer,
while elegant teams jammed the lanes and ladies' coaches piled
    up;
Taoist halls were packed with people, many sat outside;
for latecomers there was no room, no way to get within hearing.
Hairpins, bracelets, girdle stones were doffed, undone, snatched
off, till the heaped-up gold, the mounds of jade glinted and glowed
    in the sunlight.
Eminent eunuchs from the heavenly court came with a summons
    to audience;
ladies of the six palaces longed to see the Master's face.
The Jade Countenance nodded approval, granting her return;
dragon-drawn, mounting a crane, she came through blue-dark
    skies.
These youths of the great families—what do they know of the
    Tao,
milling about her a hundred deep, shifting from foot to foot?
Beyond cloud-barred windows, in misty towers, who knows
    what happens there,
where kingfisher curtains hang tier on tier and golden screens are
    deep?

The immortal's ladder is hard to climb, your bonds with this world
    weighty;
vainly you call on the bluebird to deliver your passionate pleas!

The remaining poems show the more personal side of Han Yü's
poetry. The first is number eight in a set of eleven poems entitled
"Autumn Thoughts," in five-character *ku-shih* form. It was probably
written in 812, and the boy in the poem would seem to be the poet's
son Han Ch'ang, about fourteen at the time.

Leaves fall turning turning to the ground,
by the front eaves racing, following the wind;
murmuring voices that seem to speak to me
as they whirl and toss in headlong flight.
An empty hall in the yellow dusk of evening:
I sit here silent, unspeaking.
The young boy comes in from outdoors,
trims the lamp, sets it before me,
asks me questions I do not answer,
brings me a supper I do not eat.
He goes and sits down by the west wall,
reading me poetry—three or four poems;
the poet is not a man of today—
already a thousand years divide us—
but something in his words strikes my heart,
fills it again with an acid grief.
I turn and call to the boy:
    Put down the book and go to bed now—
    a man has times when he must think,
    and work to do that never ends.

The following three poems are the first, third, and fifth in a set
of five seven-character *chüeh-chü* entitled "A Pond in a Jardiniere."

Old men are like little boys:
I draw water, fill the jardiniere to make a tiny pond.
All night green frogs gabble till dawn,
just like the time I went fishing at Fang-k'ou.

My ceramic lake in dawn, water settled clear,
numberless tiny bugs—I don't know what you call them;
suddenly they dart and scatter, not a shadow left;
only a squadron of baby fish advancing.

Pond shine and sky glow, blue matching blue;
a few bucketfuls of water poured is all that laps these shores.
I'll wait until the night is old, the bright moon set,
then count how many stars come swimming here.

Better known than Han Yü, and far more influential in the later development of Chinese poetry, is Po Chü-i (772–846), the other major figure of the Middle T'ang. Like Han Yü, he worked to develop a style that was simple and easy to understand, and posterity has requited his efforts by making him one of the most well-loved and widely read of all Chinese poets, both in his native land and in the other countries of the East that participate in the appreciation of Chinese culture. He is also, thanks to the translations and biographical studies of Arthur Waley, one of the most accessible to English readers, and I shall therefore not discuss him in detail or quote extensively from his work.

One reason Po Chü-i cultivated a plain, easily intelligible style was that he placed great value upon the didactic function of literature. Of all his works—and he was the most prolific of the T'ang poets—he regarded as most significant the series of 50 poems entitled "New *Yüeh-fu*." Drawing their inspiration from the homiletic works of the *Book of Odes* and the early *yüeh-fu*, as well as later works of social and political criticism by men like Li Po, Tu Fu, and Han Yü, the poems comment on a wide range of contemporary problems. Though a few appear to praise, their aim is mainly ironic; condemnation is the poet's real end and he pursues it with passion. Some of the poems employ allegory, others broach the matter directly, mixing historical allusions and examples from the distant past with references to T'ang history and the writer's own time. Like Tu Fu, Po Chü-i condemns the extravagance of the emperor and his officials and the burdensome taxes and military conscriptions that bring suffering to the common people, describing in vivid detail the plight of the frontier soldier, the farmer, the weaving woman, or the

charcoal seller. But he extends his censure to less obvious or weighty
ills, attacking the whole T'ang infatuation with foreign goods and
manners, laxity in marriage customs, ostentation in funerals, the
costliness of Buddhist establishments, or the absurdity of women's
fashions in make-up and hair style.

The present-day American reader, accustomed to works such as
"Tentative Description of a Dinner to Promote the Impeachment
of President Eisenhower," or "Blowin' in the Wind," will have no
difficulty understanding the concept underlying such protest
poetry, though the particular targets may strike him as unfamiliar.
It is not so certain, however, that the poetry in the poems, as distinct from the message, can be gotten across successfully in translation since, like many similar poems of social and political outcry
in other languages, they tend to sound shrill and petulant when they
are not being merely prosy. This is particularly true of works such
as these of Po Chü-i, where the element of humor is wholly lacking.
The following example, #32 in the series, while not concerned with
the most flagrant of social injustices, will, because of its rich imagery,
give some impression, I hope, of Po Chü-i's enormous skill and
facility of language. It is entitled *Liao-ling*, the name of a type of silk,
and is in seven-character *ku-shih* form.

*Liao-ling*, sheer patterned silk—what is it like?
Not like poorer silks, *lo, shao, wan,* or *chi*,
but the forty-five-foot waterfall
that leaps in the moonlight of Mount T'ien-t'ai;
woven with wonderful designs:
on a ground clothed in white mist, clustered snowflake flowers.
Who does the weaving, who wears the robe?
A poor woman in the glens of Yüeh, a lady in the palace of Han.
Last year eunuch envoys relayed the royal wish:
patterns from heaven to be woven by human hands,
woven with flights of autumn geese clearing the clouds,
dyed with hue of spring rivers south of the Yangtze,
cut broad for making cloak sleeves, long for sweeping skirts,
hot irons to smooth the wrinkles, scissors to trim the seams,
rare colors, strange designs that shine and recede again,

patterns to be seen from every angle, patterns never in repose.
For dancing girls of Chao-yang, token of profoundest favor,
one set of spring robes worth a thousand in gold—
to be stained in sweat, rouge-soiled, never worn again,
dragged on the ground, trampled in mud—who is there to care?
The *liao-ling* weave takes time and toil,
not to be compared to common *tseng* or *po*;
thin threads endlessly plied, till the weaver's fingers ache;
clack-clack the loom cries a thousand times but less than a foot is
    done.
You singers and dancers of the Chao-yang Palace,
could you see her weaving, you'd pity her too!

More famous than the "New *Yüeh-fu*," though less esteemed by
their author, are the long narrative poems "Lute Song" and "Song
of Everlasting Regret" that have been so often translated. But
perhaps of greatest importance, particularly in the later development
of Chinese poetry, are the countless poems which Po Chü-i wrote
describing himself, his family and friends, and the simple, quiet
griefs and pleasures of everyday life. It was in these poems, deliberately relaxed and undramatic in theme and treatment, that he
used the plain style for which he is famous. In a work called, in
Waley's translation, "Illness and Idleness," he speaks of such poems
and their style:

When the poem is made it is slight and flavourless,
A thing of derision to almost every one.
Superior people will be pained at the flatness of the metre;
Common people will hate the plainness of the words.[2]

The following poem, in five-character *chüeh-chü* form, is a good
example of this extremely simple, quiet style. Entitled "A Question
Addressed to Liu Shih-chiu," it is noteworthy for the tact and
restraint with which it extends its invitation:

Green bubbles—new brewed wine;
lumps of red—a small stove for heating;

[2] Waley, *Chinese Poems,* p. 136.

evening comes and the sky threatens snow—
Could you drink a cup, I wonder?

With a combination of Buddhist detachment and Confucian scorn for fame and material possessions, Po Chü-i makes much of the joys of idleness and simple living. In a poem entitled "Doing As I Please," written when he was living in the country and observing mourning for his mother, he declares:

I get up in the morning only when I've had enough sleep,
lie down at night only when I've drunk my fill.

Other poems show him going about his official duties—he had a long and distinguished official career—with the same casualness, as in that entitled "Back Office of the Imperial Library," written when he held a post in the Imperial Library at Lo-yang. He describes himself in the third person:

All day in the back office, nothing whatever to do;
the old librarian, white-haired, asleep with his head on a book.

As this last quotation suggests, Po Chü-i is the poet not only of idleness but of old age, and many of his most moving works were written in the decade or two before his death at the age of seventy-four. Lionel Trilling singles out Yeats as perhaps "the first writer ever to make his own representation of himself as an aging man a chief element in his creation."[3] Chinese poets, however, though they may not have made it the chief element in their work, had from early times come to accept the subject of old age—their own as well as that of man in general—as one of the most important themes of poetry. True, many of their treatments of the theme, though couched in the first person, hardly went beyond the kind of stereotyped lament that might be expected from any man of sensibility. But for other poets, maturing rather late, as was so often the case in China, it constituted one of their principal subjects. Far less inclined than their Western counterparts to sing of the youthful joys of love or the hunt or to describe the excitement of battle, many of them seemed to find their true voice only with the onset of old age

[3] *The Experience of Literature* (1967), p. 110.

and the opportunity for quiet introspection that it occasioned. Tu Fu's late poems, many of them on the subject of his senescence, are, as we have seen, of great literary importance and merit, though often painfully downcast in tone. Han Yü, in the poems on the jardiniere quoted above, strikes a lighter note, suggesting that old men enjoy something of the carefree delight of children, and many of Po Chü-i's poems on his old age are similar in vein, dwelling not upon the inevitable aches and inconveniences but the unexpected compensations of the aged. Even in the works written just before his death, he maintains the same note of calm joy, as may be seen in these lines from a work entitled "Poem on My Aging Self To Show to My Household"; Waley, who calls the lines "Last Poem," translates them as follows:

> They have put my bed beside the unpainted screen;
> They have shifted my stove in front of the blue curtain.
> I listen to my grandchildren reading me a book;
> I watch the servants heating up my soup.
> With rapid pencil I answer the poems of friends,
> I feel in my pockets and pull out medicine-money.
> When this superintendence of trifling affairs is done,
> I lie back on my pillows and sleep with my face to the South.[4]

## THE TWILIGHT AGE: LI HO AND LI SHANG-YIN

While the Chinese poetic tradition, led by men like Han Yü and Po Chü-i, moved in the direction of a simpler, more relaxed style, greater variety of subject matter, and more discursive or philosophical treatment, bringing it momentarily, as Graham notes, much closer to our own,[5] a young writer of promise named Li Ho (791–817) was busily forging ahead on a wholly different course. He has traditionally been described as a *kuei-ts'ai* or man of "devilish talent," a term that points up both the uncanny brilliance he showed even at an early age, and the weird, otherworldly quality

---

[4] *Chinese Poems,* p. 174.
[5] *Poems of the Late T'ang,* p. 72.

that informs much of his important work. We have noted this eerie quality appearing in the late works of Tu Fu; Li Ho explored it to the full, filling his more daring poems with images drawn from mythology and folk religion or the shaman songs of the *Ch'u Tz'u*. From the late poetry of Tu Fu he took also a fondness for extreme compression of language, which in his own work assumes the form of a deliberately disjoined, nonlogical manner of presentation. To increase the effect of shock and surprise which such a style was clearly designed to arouse in the reader, he employed odd diction, new and peculiar expressions that he invented to replace conventional ones. Finally, from the late Tu Fu he took a highly personal tone and a mood of unrelieved pessimism that in time was to become characteristic of nearly all poetry of the closing years of the T'ang.

Had Li Ho lived beyond his twenty-sixth year, he might have matured into a figure of major importance and influenced the entire course of later Chinese poetry. As it is, his work stands as something of an isolated oddity in the literary tradition. Though praised by T'ang writers, its mood of eeriness and violence seemed to repel later readers, who allowed it to sink into relative neglect. Recently there has been a considerable revival of interest, the oddness and obscurity that were once regarded as the defects of Li Ho's poetry being now very much in fashion. Its greatest asset remains its vivid, haunting imagery, which can be appreciated without undue concern for what it all may mean.

The following poem, entitled "For the Examination at Ho-nan-fu: Song of the Twelve Months (with Intercalary Month)," is one of a set of 13 poems written for a preliminary government examination which the poet took, and passed, in 810 at Lo-yang. It deals with the seventh month, the first month of autumn by the lunar calendar, and is in five-character *ku-shih* form. In the eighth couplet, the presence of a person is implied, though no subject is expressed in the Chinese. I have tried to reproduce the anonymity of the original, though the pronoun "one" is conspicuous in English in a way that the lack of a subject is not in Chinese.

Stars rest cold by shoals of cloud;
dew spatters round into the plate.

From tree tips fair flowers unfold;
in deserted gardens fading orchids grieve.
The evening sky seems flagged with jade;
on the pool, lotus leaves, huge coins of green bronze.
With annoyance one finds the single dancing cloak too thin,
gradually grows aware of a chill on flowered mats.
Dawn winds—how they sough and sigh!
Blazoned in brightness, the Little Dipper gleams.

"Song of the Sacred Strings," a seven-character *ku-shih* in *yüeh-fu* style, borrows its title from a third-century song used to accompany religious ceremonies. It is a deliberately mysterious succession of images suggesting the music and dance of shamannesses, the gods they serve, and other unexplained—and perhaps unexplainable—manifestations of the supernatural.

On western hills the sun dies, eastern hills are dusking;
whirlwinds buffet the horses, horses that prance on cloud.
Patterned strings and plain white flute—a shallow, dinning sound;
flowered skirts that rush and rustle, pacing the autumn dust.
Cassia leaves torn in the wind—the cassias drop their fruit;
blue badgers wail in blood, cold foxes die.
Painted dragons on the old wall, tails glued with gold;
the Rain God rides them, down into the waters of an autumn
        pool.
The hundred-year-old owl puts on a tree sprite's form,
the voice of laughter, jade-green fire from the midst of his nest
        ascending.

"The Northland in Cold," seven-character *ku-shih*, an example of the highly elaborate, often contrived descriptive style of Li Ho.

The blackness of one quarter lights up the mauve of three:
the Yellow River in a weld of ice, its fish and dragons die.
Bark of the three-foot trees splits into scar and crackle;
carts, strong beneath a hundred-weight, ascend the river's flow.
Blossoms of frost upon the grass, huge as copper coins;
brandished swords could not pierce these meshed and low-slung
        skies.

Ocean's wrest and tumble grows loud with hurtling ice;
mountain cascades are voiceless, dependent rainbows of jade.

The last two poems, in five-character *chüeh-chü* form, were written at
the poet's country home in Ch'ang-ku west of Lo-yang, probably
a short while before his death. The first is entitled "At Ch'ang-ku,
Reading: To Show to My Man Pa."

Echo of insects where the lamplight thins;
the cold night heavy with medicine fumes:
because you pity a broken-winged wanderer,
through bitterest toil you follow me still.

The second, the poet's conception of how his servant might answer,
is entitled "My Man Pa Replies." Note how it picks up the heavily
melancholic tone of the first poem and gently mocks it.

Big-nose looks best in mountain-coarse clothes;
bushy-brows should stick to his poetry toils!
Were it not for the songs you sing,
who would know the depths of autumn sorrow?

Though Li Ho, because of his untimely death, technically belongs
to the Middle T'ang period, his work in many ways foreshadows
the poetry of the period to follow. His pessimism, as we have seen,
became in time the prevailing mood, his fondness for compressed,
highly polished language, the ideal in diction. But what in Li Ho
had been a search for new and striking effects devolved into mere
fussiness and preoccupation with surface ornament. Whereas he
had, like Han Yü, experimented in the irregular forms of the
*ku-shih*, delighting in the deliberate repetition of words which they
allow, the Late T'ang poets turned once more to the *lü-shih* and
other modern style forms. They no doubt hoped in this way to
recapture something of the brilliance that Tu Fu and others had
earlier achieved in these forms. Unfortunately, they succeeded for
the most part in reproducing only the ornateness and technical
dexterity of the earlier age. In theme and feeling their works seemed
unable to rise above a shallow and world-weary mannerism.

The age was one of increasing turmoil and political disintegration.
The dynasty was clearly sinking and it is hardly surprising that the

poets, feeling their hopes and fortunes sinking with it, should have
written in a mood of foreboding. One of the few who, in the face of
such odds, still succeeded in producing poetry of genuine depth and
vitality is Li Shang-yin (813?–58). Like Li Ho, he is a poet who
often trembles on the brink of meaning, particularly in the love
poems called *wu-t'i* or "untitled." These poems, marked by indirection and extreme ambiguity, have been thought to be at least
partially autobiographical, and commentators have long labored to
unravel their allusions and enigmas. As in the case of Li Ho's
obscurer works, the reader can perhaps best approach them by
setting aside the question of precise meaning and noting instead the
richness and beauty of their imagery and the striking skill with
which they are put together.

   The first example, a seven-character *lü-shih* entitled "Spring Rain,"
shows us the poet dreaming of a lady to whom he is for some reason
denied access. The wild goose in the last line is the traditional bearer
of letters.

   Lying disconsolate in new spring white wadded robes,
   by white gates lost and lonely, my wish too much denied:
   a red pavilion beyond the rain—we watch each other coldly;
   pearl blinds, a torch that flickers—she comes home alone.
   A long road is grief enough in spring dusk and evening;
   what's left of the night still offers me phantoms of a dream.
   Jade earrings, a sealed letter—how to get them through?
   Ten thousand miles of cloud gauze, a wild goose winging.

In the next poem, a five-character *lü-shih* entitled "Thoughts in the
Cold," we have no way of determining the sex of the speaker, or
whether the poem deals with romantic love or friendship; the
interpretation of individual lines is also open to much question.

   When he left, the waves were flush with the railing;
   now cicadas are silent and branches full of dew,
   and I keep on remembering at a time like this,
   leaning here while seasons pass.
   For the North Star too, spring is far away;
   too late to send couriers to your southern hill.

At the sky's edge, over and over I question my dreams,
wondering if you haven't found someone new.

"Untitled"; 7-character *lü-shih*. A young official recalls a party of the evening before at which he drank and played guessing games before returning to his duties at the Orchid Terrace, the government archives.

Last night's planets and stars, last night's wind,
by the painted tower's west side, east of Cassia Hall—
for us no nearness of phoenixes winging side by side,
yet our hearts became as one, like the rhino's one-thread horn.
From opposing seats, we played pass-the-hook; spring wine was
    warm.
On rival teams, we played what's-under-it? wax candles shone red.
When I heard the drums that called me back to work,
I raced my horse to Orchid Terrace like tumbleweed torn loose.

"Untitled"; 5-character *ku-shih*.

At eight stealing a mirror glance,
already she knew how to paint long eyebrows.
At ten off to roam the green,
lotus flowers made skirts for her.
At twelve learning to play the lute,
never would she put the silver pick down.
At fourteen she hid from her six relations,
knowing their thoughts, though not yet a bride.
At fifteen in the spring wind she cried,
under the swing, her face turned away.

The works quoted above, typical of the sensuous and mildly erotic poems for which Li Shang-yin is most famous, draw upon the conventions of love poetry we have already examined in the earlier discussion of the *Yü-t'ai hsin-yung* in Chapter VI. The loved one's beauty and desirability are suggested through articles of clothing and furniture or architectural detail rather than directly described, and the physical excitement of love is largely ignored in favor of evocations of its sorrow, frustration, and essential transience. In Li Shang-yin's hands the indirectness and faint preciosity of the imagery and languid melancholy of mood are controlled with such skill that they do not become offensive, though in the work of less adroit and intelligent followers these qualities quickly degenerate into trite sentimentalism.

That Li Shang-yin was a poet of major status is seen not only in the superiority of his love poetry to that of his imitators, but in the fact that, unlike them, he could handle other themes and styles with equal success. Some of his most impressive poems are passionate works of social criticism. The following, also in a wholly different vein from his love poetry, is entitled "Poem for My Little Boy" and is in five-character ku-shih form. Its title is an imitation of Tso Ssu's "Poem for My Little Girls," that has been mentioned on p. 78. In the first section he contrasts the intelligence of his boy with that of the not so bright boys described in T'ao Yüan-ming's poem "Blaming My Sons," who could not tell six from seven and thought only of hunting pears and chestnuts.

> My little boy Kun-shih,
> no finer, no handsomer lad;
> in bellyband, less than one year old,
> already he knew six from seven;
> at three he could tell you his name,
> had eyes for more than chestnuts and pears.
> My friends come to look him over,
> call him the phoenix of Cinnabar Cave;
> at former courts where looks were prized,
> he'd have rated first, they say;
> but no, he has the style of an immortal spirit,
> the swallow-throat, the crane-walk of a nobleman!
> Why do they praise him so?
> His father poor and talentless, they hope to comfort me thus.
> In green spring, the warm and gentle months,
> cousins all, his companions in play,
> he runs round the hall, threads the wood:
> a rush of bronze caldrons bubbling over.
> Elderly gentlemen come to the gate;
> at once he dashes out to greet them;

in front of the guests, asked what he would like,
he mumbles shyly and won't speak up.
Guests gone, he mimics their faces,
bursting through the door, snatching his father's staff,
now aping Chang Fei's outlandish face,
now making fun of Teng Ai's stutter.
A brave hawk on high wings soaring,
a noble horse with fierce snorting breath,
he cuts stout green bamboo for a pony,
gallops wildly, banging into things.
Suddenly he is the General in a play,
in stage voice summoning his groom;
now beside the gauze-veiled lamp
he bows his head in evening obeisance to Buddha.
Whip upraised, he bats at spider webs;
head bent down, he sucks nectar from the flower,
so nimble he outruns the swallowtail butterfly,
so swift he hardly lags behind the flying willow catkins.
By the terrace stairs, he comes on Elder Sister,
rolls dice with her, loses all he has;
sneaks in to play with her vanity case,
prying at the golden clasp till he breaks it off.
Try to hold him—he wiggles and squirms;
threaten and scold—he will not be ruled.
Crouching down, he drags on the window netting;
with globs of spit he polishes the lacquer lute.
Sometimes he watches while I practice calligraphy,
standing bolt upright, knees never moving;
old brocade book cover—can he cut it up for clothes?
the scroll's jade spindle—he begs for that too;
pleads with me to make him a spring garland,
spring garland fit for spring days,
when plantain leaves angle up—furls of letter paper;
and magnolia buds droop—writing brushes proffered.
Your father once was fond of reading books;
sweating, slaving, he wrote some of his own;
going on forty now, worn and tired,

no meat for his meals, cringing from fleas and lice—
Take care, my son—do not copy your father,
studying, hoping for first or second on the exam!
Jang-chü's *Rules of the Marshal*,
Chang Liang's *Yellow Stone Strategy*,
these will make you a teacher of kings;
waste no time on trash and trifles!
Much less now when west and north
barbarian tribes rise in defiance,
when neither force nor bribes will bring them to heel
and the burden of them saps us like an old disease.
My son, grow to manhood quickly,
seek out the cubs in the tiger's cave;
make yourself lord of ten thousand households—
Don't huddle forever over some old book!

◄§ Chang Fei and Teng Ai: historical figures of the second and third centuries,
noted respectively for swarthy bearded face and a stutter.

"Spring garland": neck ornaments of figured silk worn by boys and girls at
the festivities celebrating the beginning of spring.

*Rules of the Marshal*; *Yellow Stone Strategy*; works on military science of the
late Chou and early Han respectively.

# X

# POETRY OF THE SUNG
# DYNASTY

*Sainte-Beuve, as he grew older, came to regard all experience
as a single great book, in which to study for a few years ere
we go hence; and it seemed all one to him whether you should
read in Chapter XX, which is the differential calculus, or in
Chapter XXXIX, which is hearing the band play in the
gardens.*—ROBERT LOUIS STEVENSON

♋

I HAVE TRACED the development of the five-character and seven-
character *shih* form from its brilliant beginnings in the late Han
through the troubled period of disunity and the long centuries of
T'ang rule. The final collapse of the T'ang in 907 was followed by
decades of strife and warfare that allowed little time for devotion to
the arts. Unity was restored by the Sung dynasty, founded in 960,
but, as in the case of the T'ang, it was some time before a new style
of poetry developed that was in any way distinct from what had
gone before. The first 70 or 80 years of Sung rule saw instead a
prolongation of Late T'ang style—mannered, morose, with all the

For a general discussion of Sung poetry in the *shih* form, see Yoshikawa Kojiro,
*An Introduction to Sung Poetry*. Su Tung-p'o, one of the leading Sung poets, is the
subject of Lin Yutang, *The Gay Genius*. Translations of Sung poets will be found
in Gerald Bullett, *The Golden Years of Fan Ch'eng-ta;* Clara Candlin, *The Rapier
of Lu: Patriot of China* (translations from Lu Yu); Rexroth, *One Hundred Poems
from the Chinese*; and Burton Watson, *Su Tung-p'o*.

faults of Li Shang-yin and none of his compensations. All this was changed when, in the course of the eleventh century, a succession of highly gifted and original poets appeared on the scene to inject new vigor into the *shih* tradition and create what in time would come to be recognized as the typical style of Sung poetry.

I have spoken earlier of the formal innovations and developments carried out in the T'ang. By contrast, the Sung is totally lacking in technical innovation. The Sung poets took over the old style and modern style forms—the *ku-shih*, *lü-shih*, and *chüeh-chü*—just as they found them, and in the thirteenth century passed them on to the Yuan in exactly the same state. Apparently they saw no possibility for further refinement or change.

When it came to content, however, the Sung poets were highly venturesome—much more so, on the whole, than their predecessors in the T'ang. To be sure, many of the innovations in subject matter had already been anticipated in T'ang poetry, but usually only in works of highly original writers like Tu Fu, Han Yü, or Po Chü-i, who in many ways were in advance of their time. The Sung in effect took up certain traits and attitudes that in T'ang times had appeared only sporadically, and made them the foundation for a whole new style.

The broadening of subject matter and richness of content that mark Sung poetry result at least in part from the larger number of men writing poetry and the fact that individual poets wrote greater numbers of poems. The same trends we have noted in the T'ang continued: verse composition became an increasingly popular pastime among members of the educated class, and men wrote more frequently, taking care to preserve even their most casual productions. Historical accident, it must be admitted, has helped to foster this impression—the fact that printing became widespread during the Sung, and hence aided the preservation of a larger volume of poetry. Yet, even making allowances for such accidents, it seems certain that there were more poets in the Sung and that they were on the whole more prolific. We have 2,800 of Po Chü-i's poems, and this seems to be close to his total output. But 10,000 poems from the hand of Lu Yu (1125–1210), the most productive of the Sung poets, have been preserved, and these represent almost entirely the work written after his fortieth year. With so many men writing such quantities of poetry, it is only natural to expect a greater variety of subject matter; had there not been, the monotony would have become unendurable.

There is one subject, relatively important in Six Dynasties and T'ang poetry, that was less often treated in Sung *shih*, the subject of romantic love, particularly as it is expressed in the stock figure of the neglected wife or concubine. The reason would seem to be that the Sung poets had available to them a new poetic form, the *tz'u*, originally a song form developed in late T'ang times and from the first closely associated with singing girls and suggestive lyrics. Characterized by lines of varied lengths and intricate tonal patterns, it gained great popularity in Sung times and absorbed much of the attention of the poets of the period. They used it mainly to describe the same amorous peasant girls or languishing ladies of the bed-chamber who had earlier been the subject of *yüeh-fu*, though in time they broadened it to include the treatment of many other themes as well.

The existence of the *tz'u* form, therefore, abetted, perhaps, by the influence of Confucian prudery, seems to have deprived Sung *shih* of some of the romantic element it might otherwise have possessed, and in this respect to have narrowed its thematic scope. With this exception, however, the Sung shows, in comparison with previous eras, a decided broadening in the subject matter of the *shih*.

It is often stated that the An Lu-shan rebellion and the years of unrest and decay of centralized government that followed it marked the downfall of the old aristocracy that had dominated China from early Six Dynasties times. Their power, we are told, had now passed into the hands of a new class of scholar-bureaucrats who in time formed the backbone of the Sung government. Like so many theories of social change, this one doubtless involves contradictions and oversimplifications, and is difficult to corroborate at every point. Nevertheless, if valid, it would certainly help to explain, among other things, the contrasts between T'ang and Sung poetry that are so noticeable. With the broadening of content in Sung poetry came an attention to subjects that, according to earlier, more aristocratic canons of taste, would have been considered too undignified, mundane, or intrinsically prosy for treatment in verse. Tu Fu, as so often the pioneer in these matters, had written a poem on chicken raising, and Han Yü and Po Chü-i had followed with works on equally "unpoetic" themes. In the Sung such poems appeared with increasing frequency, as though writers were determined to prove that no subject was too drab or lowly for the poet to take up.

Many of their poems were works of social protest, distinguished by the kind of stark realism we have already seen in the Chien-an poets and men of the T'ang like Tu Fu or Po Chü-i. Some were couched in the old *yüeh-fu* style, such as Su Tung-p'o's "Farm Wife of Wu" quoted on p. 215; others, like the poem by Wang An-shih on salt production on p. 213, speak out boldly in the poet's own voice. The Sung saw a great resurgence of Confucian thought, and this movement, known as Neo-Confucianism, gave new life and encouragement to the old ideals of social consciousness. The poetry of protest once more began to flourish, though, as we shall see in the case of Su Tung-p'o, the Sung government, for all its professed adherence to Confucian principles, often proved as intolerant as its predecessors in the face of overt attack.

The Sung poets wrote of the humdrum realities of everyday existence, and, when they wished to expose injustice or voice a criticism, they did not hesitate to depict the harshest, meanest aspects of life. They even at times seemed to delight in dirt and sordidness, chatting about rats and lice, describing a nauseous hangover or a case of piles. In this respect their work strikingly resembles the poetry of our own culture and time. There is one important point, however, in which it differs from ours: they made no attempt to treat the subject of sex with any degree of frankness. Some scholars argue that the Chinese of these and earlier times were so wholesomely free of any puritanical attitude toward sex that they were simply not interested in dwelling upon the subject to the extent that we are. Others claim that, far from being free of puritanism, the Chinese were bound by it to such an extent that, at least in their less furtive types of literature, they could not even entertain the possibility of discussing sex openly. Without presuming to decide which theory is correct, I will only note here that the Sung poet, while he gives us a most thorough picture of his home, his family, and his daily activities, keeps his sex life discreetly out of sight. We have seen that, when treated at all, erotic themes are likely to be assigned to the *tz'u* rather than the *shih* form, but even here their handling is so clouded by stylization and ambiguity that, if there is a confessional element present, it is all but impossible to identify, at least at this far remove.

The Sung poet, if he remains for the most part silent on the subject of sex, is nevertheless voluble in his descriptions of all other varieties of human activity, the myriad ways, however humble or trivial, in which men labor or pass their time. There is, in fact, in Sung poetry as a whole a delight in diversity and detail that, as we shall see later, is almost certainly related to the philosophical currents of the time. The same attitude may be seen in the treatment of nature. Whereas the T'ang poets had for the most part been content to view the landscape from a distance, or to evoke it through the naming of a few symbolic plants or creatures, those of the Sung seem much more disposed to examine the components of the natural scene and render an accurate, detailed report of what they find. There is, for example, a greater interest in and compassion for animals. Earlier poets, when writing of horses, had usually noticed only the sleek and well-groomed thoroughbred; Mei Yao-ch'en (p. 211) portrays a very different kind of horse and reveals his own involvement in its plight.

As the humblest activities of man engage the poet's concern, so do the smallest, most insignificant creatures of nature. Tu Fu had written with warmth and appreciation of a species of little white fish that he saw sold in the market:

Spread out on the stall, a jumble of silver blossoms;
dumped from a basket—snowflakes disappearing;

and begged that, though the full-grown fish be taken for sale, the spawn be left unharmed ("White Little"). Here is a poem by a Sung writer of the twelfth century, Yang Wan-li (1127–1206), on the subject of a fly. Observe how the poet carefully avoids making the fly a symbol of anything or drawing a moral from its behavior, as earlier writers would almost surely have done.

Noted outside the window: a fly, the sun on his back,
rubbing his legs together, relishing the morning brightness.
Sun and shadow about to shift—already he knows it,
suddenly flies off, to hum by a different window.

Because Sung poetry tries to record the moods and minor happenings of everyday life as well as the moments of great passion, to wander from the path of earlier poetic convention and poke about among the minutiae of existence, it often strikes one, particularly in comparison with T'ang poetry, as rambling, discursive, and almost excessively low-keyed. For one thing, it is more likely to be cast in the freer *ku-shih* form, unrestricted in length, than in the compact and highly regulated, modern style forms. Of the 33 poems quoted in my selection below, all but seven are in *ku-shih* form. The diction of Sung poetry reflects the same tendency, being simpler and less ornate than that of the T'ang. We have seen this striving for a plainer, more colloquial style in a few T'ang writers such as Po Chü-i. The Sung poets carried on the search, introducing an even larger number of colloquialisms (though the language of their works remained classical Chinese, which is quite different from the actual spoken language of the period). Su Tung-p'o, perhaps the finest of the Sung poets, is reported to have said, "Everyday words, the language of the streets—all can be used in poetry. The only thing that is required is skill in using them" (*Chu-p'o shih-hua* ch. 2). And a late Sung poet, writing in praise of Lu Yu's verse, says:

Using what is plain and simple, he fashioned subtle lines;
taking the most ordinary words, he changed them into wonders.[1]

It would be easy enough merely to note these differences that seem to distinguish Sung poetry from what went before, and rest the discussion there. But the literary historian shirks his task, I believe, if he does not venture some suggestion, no matter how tentative or impressionistic, as to why such differences exist. Before concluding, therefore, I would like to outline in brief some of the influences that appear to have contributed to the formation of this distinctive style of Sung poetry.

[1] Tai Fu-ku (b. 1167), "Reading the *Chien-nan shih-kao* by Mr. Fang-weng."

For the student of Chinese intellectual history, the Sung represents first of all an era of revitalized Confucianism. Though the Neo-Confucian movement had its roots in the T'ang, it was carried forward and brought to fruition by the Sung scholars and constituted the dominant factor in the philosophical climate of the time. It is natural, therefore, to see the humanism of Sung poetry, its deep-felt concern with man and his activities, and in particular its note of social protest, as inspired by Confucian ideals. But there are other elements in Sung poetry not so readily accounted for. The Han, especially that part known as the Eastern Han, was likewise committed to Confucian values and ideals, but its poetry, as we have seen in the "Nineteen Old Poems" and the *yüeh-fu*, though passionately concerned with man and society, is pervaded by an air of brooding fatalism. Sung poetry, on the other hand, is relatively free of this kind of encompassing sorrow; is, in fact, sunnier than anything to be found in the poetic tradition of the preceding millennium. Either the poetry of the Han or that of the Sung is not truly Confucian at all, or else the Confucianism of the two periods is in some essential way different.

Han Confucianism speaks much of a trinity of Heaven, earth, and man, but never really explains how the three are related. Though positing an elaborate series of rather mechanical correspondences among the super-natural, natural, and human spheres, it offers no organic theory that would link them together. Man is enjoined to keep his attention fixed upon human concerns and goals, to harmonize with the workings of the other two members of the triad, but not to pry too sedulously into their affairs. Such a doctrine may suffice in times of relative peace and social stability, but clearly it provides little comfort or guidance in the face of adversity. The sorrow apparent in so much of late Han and Six Dynasties poetry is in part the despair of men who have lost faith in the possibility of attaining the ideal Confucian society and at the same time can find nothing in Confucianism to solace or excuse them in their failure.

By contrast, Taoism, and later Buddhism, offered the Chinese a much more complex and sophisticated explanation of the relationship between the One and the many, the absolute and the relative, the universe and man. In Taoism, the explanation was couched mainly in poetic and rhetorical terms; in Buddhism, in the language of Indian philosophy. Greatly simplified, it consisted in effect of a flat assertion that the One is identical with the many, that the Tao is inherent in all beings, and that to be in the world of samsara is to be in the world of nirvana. Once this identification is made in the mind of the believer, he is freed from all attachment to time or place, from all need to strive for a goal, and can never again fall victim to failure and frustration.

Neo-Confucianisms's avowed aim was to do away with this kind of transcendentalism and to restore validity to the ideals of benevolence, righteousness, and decorum. It thus put man back on the path of moral striving again, with all the possibilities for earnest optimism and crushing despair which that entailed. In order to be able to challenge Buddhism and Taoism with any hope of success, however, it had perforce to take over much of their metaphysical and mystical vision. As a result it became incomparably richer, more subtle, and at least in its early stages, a more satisfying creed than early Confucianism had ever been. But because of this fusion of Buddhist, Taoist, and Confucian thought that took place, often unconsciously, in the Sung, it is frequently impossible to say whether a particular writer or poet is deriving his ideas directly from Buddhist or Taoist sources, or indirectly through the medium of Neo-Confucianism.

To take an example already touched upon above, I may mention the relative freedom from attachment to place that is found in Su Tung-p'o and other Sung poets. Though Confucius himself had hinted at such a freedom in the *Analects*, the great majority of Chinese in ancient times unquestionably felt a profound attachment to their native region, the place where their ancestors were buried and where they themselves prayed to be buried in turn. Moreover, since early Confucianism placed such great emphasis upon music, ritual, and the study of classical texts, a Chinese could not help feeling that he was moving away from all that was good and beautiful in life as he moved away from the geographical centers of traditional learning and culture. The Taoists attempted to combat this idea with their attacks upon the artificiality of human culture and their glorification of the life of the wilderness. The Buddhists came forward with assurances that believers who fell in no matter what remote region would be reborn in the Western Paradise as surely as those who died in the bosoms of their families. And for the more select group who could comprehend the teachings of the Zen sect, they sought to make clear, through sermon and paradox, that relative concepts such as time and place are wholly without reality, that in Buddha there is no north or south.

These mystic views of Taoism and Buddhism passed all but unquestioned into Neo-Confucianism, as may be seen in the following sentences from the famous "Western Inscription" of Chang Tsai (1021–77), one of the leading early Sung Confucian thinkers: "That which extends throughout the universe I regard as my body and that which directs the universe I consider as my nature. All people are my brothers and sisters, and all things are my companions." [2] We need not be surprised, therefore, in a poem to be quoted below, to find Su Shih (Su Tung-p'o) assuring his brother that it will be all right to "bury me anywhere on the green hills," or describing the scenery in the remote southern regions with as much interest and enthusiasm as he does that of his native Szechwan or the ancient centers of Chinese civilization in the north. As Andrew March in his article "Self and Landscape in Su Shih" notes, "To Su the point was that all landscapes, in experience, are essentially the same, and that therefore one need have no attachment to particular landscapes." [3]

But if Buddhist and Taoist ideas added metaphysical richness and breadth of vision to the old Confucian world view, Confucianism in turn modified these ideas in the direction of greater warmth and accessibility. I have noted above the compassionate attitude toward animals and other lesser creatures that is so characteristic of Sung poetry. One would expect such an attitude to flourish naturally under the influence of Taoism and Buddhism, with their assertions of the Tao present even in the lowly ant, or the belief that men may be reborn in animal form. But Buddhism and Taoism were more often found exhorting men to renounce all emotion rather than to extend it to the lower forms of life, and when, for the sake of the masses, they consented to speak in terms of human feeling, it was usually to describe in lurid detail the fearful punishments meted

[2] W. T. de Bary, ed. *Sources of Chinese Tradition*, p. 524.
[3] *Journal of the American Oriental Society*, 86 (no. 4, Oct.–Dec. 1966), 378.

out in the afterlife to those who eat meat or otherwise inflict suffering upon living creatures. It remained for the Neo-Confucians, it would seem, with their dedication to the ideal of positive love and goodness, to take these negative injunctions and transmute them into the kind of tenderness and concern we see in such works as Mei Yao-ch'en's poem on the dappled horse or the eulogy to his dead cat.

This same combination of Buddhist and Taoist immanentistic concepts with a cheery Neo-Confucian humanism may perhaps account for the distinctive manner in which Sung poets so often speak of nature. In the poetry of the *Book of Odes*, as we have seen, nature and its activities were important mainly because they were attempting to tell man something, to give him clues as to how best to proceed on his way. But once this primitive magico-religious view was outgrown, a gulf opened between man and nature and they were seen as unrelated and essentially indifferent to one another. Thus, pathetic fallacy is relatively rare in the poetry of late Han, Six Dynasties, and T'ang times, and when it does occur, the emphasis, as one might expect, is upon the coldness or actual hostility of nature and the inanimate world. Thus, for example, a sixth-century poet named Chiang Tsung describes in these words an unhappy lady whose grief is compounded by the indifference and ill will of the objects surrounding her:

The screen makes a point of blocking out the moonlight;
the lamp, unfeeling, shines on her sleeping alone.
                                    ("Bedchamber Grievance")[4]

The poets of the T'ang likewise, when they stopped to consider the matter at all, usually saw nature as *wu-ch'ing*, "heartless" or "unfeeling," as in "Scene of Chin-ling" by Wei Chuang (836–910),

---

[4] An unusual example of the opposite view—nature's empathy for human emotions—is expressed in the following couplet by Liu K'un (270–317), from his dolorous "Fu-feng-ko." It is important to note, however, that it is man's grief, rather than some other emotion, that wakes the sympathy of the clouds and the birds:

The drifting clouds for my sake come together;
the homing birds for my sake wheel about.

describing the willows planted by rulers of the Liang dynasty which
live on long after their masters have vanished:

> Most heartless of all are these willows of T'ai-ch'eng,
> as of old mist-shrouded along the ten-mile dike.

Or "Thoughts of a Traveler on a Spring Evening" by Ts'ui T'u
(b. 854):

> Waters flow on, flowers fade, both of them heartless.

Characteristically, Po Chü-i was among the first to sound a new
note of optimism, as in his poem "Traveler's Moon," where,
consciously challenging the popular view, he asks:

> Who says the moon has no heart?
> A thousand long miles it has followed me.[5]

This is the attitude taken up by Su Tung-p'o and the other major
Sung poets, an attitude which, though often intended as no more
than a playful turn of speech, prefers to envision the universe as
essentially benign, rather than cold or inimical. This does not mean
that the Sung poets were all pollyannas. They did not hesitate to
write sad poetry when they felt honestly sad, but they did not woo
sadness, as one so often feels that earlier poets had done, or invariably wait until it was upon them before writing their poems. And
though they were as keenly aware of human frailty and the fleeting
nature of life as their predecessors, they did not insist upon seeing
every change as a change for the worse. Theirs was a broader,
calmer, more historical-minded view of existence, much like that
suggested in the epigraph at the beginning of this chapter, which
could find value in all varieties of experience and look upon them all
as fit material for artistic creation.

The qualities described above will, I trust, be evident in the poems
to be quoted. Rather than attempt a general selection of Sung
poetry, I have concentrated upon the works of five major poets,
Mei Yao-ch'en, Wang An-shih, Su Tung-p'o, Huang T'ing-chien,

[5] Li Po, as already noted, expressed a similar sunny view, though his is more the
outlook of the adept who has established a special relationship with nature, one
not shared by the ordinary individual.

and Lu Yu. The selection does not pretend to cover all the schools and genres of Sung poetry, but only tries to represent those aspects that seem to mark it off from what has gone before and make it of lasting importance in the history of Chinese literature.

Mei Yao-ch'en (1002–60), "My Neighbor to the South, the Office Clerk Hsiao, Came in the Evening To Say Goodby," 5-character *ku-shih*; written in 1038, probably in the capital, K'ai-feng.

> Remember a while ago we happened to meet,
> met—and were like old friends?
> You said you lived in a different alley,
> but the house is right in back of mine;
> behind the wall, lamplight shines through;
> under the fence we share the same well.
> You ask me over, serve me fish for dinner;
> sometimes when you call I'm too poor to offer wine.
> But it's settled you're to leave tomorrow,
> and here's a whole cask to ladle from.
> The night is long—suppose you do get drunk!
> Once on the road, it will be no use looking back.

Mei Yao-ch'en, "Back from Green Dragon, Presented to Hsieh Shih-chih," 7-character *ku-shih*. Hsieh Shih-chih was a nephew of the poet's first wife. The poem, on the familiar friendship theme, is a mixture of homely, almost clinical realism, and fantasy. The "banished immortal" of the last line is Li Po (see p. 148), who, according to legend, drowned when drunkenly attempting to embrace the reflection of the moon in a river. The "rush-grown shore" of line 22 appears to be a private symbol and has never been explained.

> Away from you three or four years,
> tall and skinny exactly as before,
> only your beard a bit bushier and blacker,
> in learning long ago a shoulder above me;
> and I—old now, no more use,
> white hair stringy, the top about to go—
> the things I write are out of tune with the times;
> a peaked wife, babies bawling, no more money—
> luckily with the Classics I can while away the bright days;

wealth and power—why aim for the blue sky?
Drinking wine these days, I never take much;
before the cup's filled again my belly starts to churn.
Last night you and I drank and joked;
a few rounds and I'd nodded off.
Cocks crow, dogs bark, in my ears a buzzing;
I raise my head—the whole room spins around.
Up, I pull at my headcloth but it won't stay straight.
Hoist sail, let's be off to the gray sea's border!
or better, climb a whale and ride ten thousand li—
but I have no lightning, no whip of crackling thunder;
courage stumbles, my heart quails—should I take a nap?
In dreams at once I come to a rush-grown shore.
I'll not be staying to drink with you again,
and who can manage to die drunk like the banished immortal?

Mei Yao-ch'en, "Sharing Lodging with Hsieh Shih-hou in the
Library of the Hsü Family and Being Much Bothered by the Noise
of Rats," 5-character *ku-shih*; written at K'ai-feng in 1044. Hsieh
was a nephew of the poet's wife, who had died earlier in the year;
he was married to a daughter of the Hsü family. The poet and his
two little children were spending the night at the Hsü home.

The lamp burns blue, everyone asleep;
from their holes the hungry rats steal out:
flip-flop—a rattle of plates and saucers;
clatter-crash!—the end of my dream.
I fret—will they knock off the inkslab on the desk?
worry—are they gnawing those shelves of books?
My little son mimics a cat's miaowing,
and that's a silly solution for sure!

Mei Yao-ch'en, "Shih-hou Pointed Out to Me that from Ancient
Times There Had Never Been a Poem on the Subject of Lice, and
Urged Me To Try Writing One," 5-character *ku-shih*; Shih-hou is
identified in the poem above.

A poor man's clothes—ragged and easy to get dirty,
easy to get dirty and hard to keep free of lice.

Between the belt and the lower robe is where they swarm,
ascending in files to the fur collar's margin.
They hide so cleverly, how can I ferret them out?
dining on blood, making themselves at home—
My world too has its sallies and withdrawals;
why should I bother to pry into yours?

Mei Yao-ch'en, "Sad Remembrance," 5-character *ku-shih*, 1045.
Memories of the poet's first wife, a daughter or a relatively well-to-do
family, who had died the year before.

From the time you came into my house
you never seemed to mind being poor,
every evening sewing till midnight,
lunch ready a little past noon.
Ten days and nine we ate pickles;
one day—a wonder—we dined on dried meat.
East and west for eighteen years,
the two of us sharing bitter and sweet,
counting all along on a hundred years' love—
who'd have thought you'd be gone in one night!
I still remember when the end came,
how you held my hand, not able to speak—
this body, though it lives on,
at the last will join you in dust.

Mei Yao-ch'en, "Out and Back on the Fifteenth Night of the First
Month," 5-character *ku-shih*. On the night of the fifteenth, the first
full moon of the new year, the people of the capital, usually forbidden
by curfew from going out at night, packed the streets dressed in
their best clothes and amused themselves at street stalls and entertainments. The year before, the poet's wife and second son had
died, leaving him with a small son and daughter to raise alone.

If I don't go out I'll only mope;
a stroll outside might ease my mind.
Rich man, poor man, each with his companion—
I alone feel no special joy.
Growing older, my spirits quickly flag;
I start to go and already feel depressed.

Back home I face my boy and girl;
before they speak the sour smell of grief is in my nose.
Last year they went out with their mother,
aping her with smears of lipstick and rouge;
now she's gone to the springs below,
and dirt is on their faces, their clothes in rags.
But I remember that you are still young,
and hide my tears—I can't let you see them.
I push the lamp aside, lie facing the wall,
a hundred worries cramped in my chest.

Mei Yao-ch'en, "The Dappled Horse," 5-character *ku-shih*; written on a journey by river boat. Tu Fu had expressed great pity for tired and ailing creatures such as the horse described here, though he could think of no immediate way to help them. This picture of a scholar-gentleman not sipping wine, poring over texts, or strumming a lute, but trying ineffectually to scare off a flock of birds by pitching clods across a river, however, is, so far as I know, something new in Chinese literature.

The boat moored, lunch in a lonely village;
on the far bank I see a dappled horse,
in lean pasture, gaunt with hunger;
scruffy birds flocking down to peck his feed.
Pity is powerless—I have no bow;
again and again I try to pelt them with clods
but I haven't the strength to manage a hit,
face sweaty and hot with chagrin.

Mei Yao-ch'en, "Marrying Again," 5-character *ku-shih*; 1046.

Some days ago I remarried,
delighting in now, sorrowful for the past;
someone to entrust the household to,
no more my lone shadow under the moon.
Force of habit—I call the wrong name;
as of old, something weighing on my heart.
How lucky I am—gentle and mild:
to have found two women with natures like this!

Mei Yao-ch'en, "Aboard a Boat at Night, Drinking with My Wife," 5-character *ku-shih*.

The moon appears from the mouth of the sheer bluff,
its light shining behind the boat over there.
I sit drinking alone with my wife;
how much better than facing some dreary stranger!
The moonlight slowly spreads over our mat,
dark shadows bit by bit receding.
What need is there to fetch a torch?
We've joy enough in this light alone.

Mei Yao-ch'en, "At Night, Hearing Someone Singing in the House Next Door," 5-character *ku-shih*. Line four is an allusion to the story of a famous singer of Han times whose voice was so beautiful that the very dust on the rafters stirred in response.

Midnight: I still haven't gotten to sleep
when I hear faint sounds of singing next door.
I picture to myself the red lips moving;
the dust stirs on the rafters, I know.
She makes a mistake and laughs to herself.
I get up to listen and put on my robe;
put on my robe, but the song has ended.
The moon in the window shines a little while longer.

Mei Yao-ch'en, "An Offering for the Cat," 5-character *ku-shih*; written on a river journey.

Since I got my cat Five White
the rats never bother my books.
This morning Five White died.
I make offerings of rice and fish,
bury you in mid-river
with incantations—I wouldn't slight you.
Once you caught a rat,
ran round the garden with it squeaking in your mouth;
you hoped to put a scare into the other rats,
to clean up my house.
When we'd come aboard the boat

you shared our cabin,
and though we'd nothing but meager dried rations,
we ate them without fear of rat piss and gnawing—
because you were diligent,
a good deal more so than the pigs and chickens.
People make much of their prancing steeds;
they tell me nothing can compare to a horse or donkey—
enough!—I'll argue the point no longer,
only cry for you a little.

Mei Yao-ch'en, "Lunar Eclipse," 5-character *ku-shih*. When a lunar
eclipse occurred, it was the custom to make an offering of wheat
cakes and pound on bronze mirrors to scare away the evil influences
that were swallowing up the moon. "Cassia hare" is another name
for the moon.

The maid comes into the hall
bringing word of the weird event:
in a sky made of blue glass,
the moon like a piece of blackened crystal;
now when it ought to be ten parts round,
only a thumb-length of brightness showing!
My wife is off with baked wheat cakes,
the children make a racket pounding on mirrors,
and though such beliefs are foolish and shallow,
I honor in them the spirit that seeks to save.
    Night deepens and the cassia hare comes forth,
    crowds of stars trailing it down the west.

Wang An-shih (1021–86), "Confiscating Salt," 7-character *ku-shih*.
Salt was a government monopoly and the officials made every effort
to prevent people living on the seacoast from boiling water and
extracting salt for private profit. The poem attacks these attempts to
deprive the people of a possible livelihood and compete with them
for profit.

From the local office, orders flying thicker than comb's teeth;
along the seacoast, salt confiscation stricter than ever.
Poverty moans and sobs under a broken roof
while boatloads of inspectors patrol back and forth.

Islands of the ocean, from times past lean and barren;
island folk struggling just to keep alive:
boil sea water or starve to death;
who can sit unmoving, not try to escape?
And now they say there are pirates hereabouts
who murder traveling merchants, scuttle their boats—
The life of one subject weighs heavier than the realm!
What true man would vie with others for a hairbreadth's gain?

Wang An-shih, "Two Poems Written on the Wall of Pan-shan
Temple," 5-character *ku-shih*; the second poem. Pan-shan, "Halfway-
to-the-Mountain," where Wang lived in retirement, took its name
from the fact that it was exactly halfway between the eastern gate
of Nanking and Mount Chung. In 1084 Wang suffered a severe
illness; on his recovery, he requested that his home be made into
a temple. The emperor granted the request and bestowed on it the
name Pao-ning Ch'an-ssu (Zen Temple of Requited Peace).

Cold days sit where it's warm,
hot days walk in the cool.
All beings—no different from Buddha;
Buddha—just the same as all beings.

Wang An-shih, "Twenty Poems in Imitation of Han-shan and
Shih-te," 5-character *ku-shih*; the second of the series. For Han-shan
and Shih-te, see p. 176.

Once I was a cow, a horse;
the sight of hay and bean stalks pleased me;
another time I was a woman;
men were what I liked to see.
And if in truth I am this I,
it will be like this always.
But if, unresigning, I love and hate,
I know I will become the slave of things.
Solemn, solemn, the man of full stature
will not look on things as self.

Wang An-shih, "Fresh Flowers," 5-character *ku-shih*.

Old age has little joy,
less when you're lying sick in bed.
Dip water, fix fresh flowers,
take comfort from this drifting scent;
drifting scent gone in a moment;
and I—will I be here for long?
Fresh flowers and an old I—
so!—best forget each other.

Su Tung-p'o (1037–1101), "Lament of the Farm Wife of Wu,"
7-character *ku-shih* in *yüeh-fu* style. Wu is the region around the
mouth of the Yangtze. The last line contains a reference to the old
custom of sacrificing a young girl each year as a "bride" to the
River Lord, the god of the Yellow River.

Rice this year ripens so late!
We watch, but when will frost winds come?
They come—with rain in bucketfuls;
the harrow sprouts mold, the sickle rusts.
My tears are all cried out, but rain never ends;
it hurts to see yellow stalks flattened in the mud.
We camped in a grass shelter a month by the fields;
then it cleared and we reaped the grain, followed the wagon
        home,
sweaty, shoulders sore, carting it to town—
the price it fetched, you'd think we came with chaff!
We sold the ox to pay taxes, broke up the roof for kindling;
we'll get by for a time, but what of next year's hunger?
Officials demand cash now—they won't take grain;
the long northwest border tempts invaders.
Wise men fill the court—why do things get worse?
I'd be better off bride to the River Lord!

Wise men: literally, Kung (Sui) and Huang (Pa), officials of the Han who
worked for the welfare of the peasants.

Su Tung-p'o, "On the Road to Hsin-ch'eng," 7-character *lü-shih*.

The east wind, knowing I plan to walk through the hills,
hushed the sound of endless rain between the eaves.

On peaks, fair-weather clouds—cloth caps pulled down;
early sun in treetops—a copper gong suspended.
Wild peach smiles over low bamboo hedges;
by clear sandy streams, valley willows sway.
These west hill families must be happiest of all,
  boiling cress and roasting shoots to feed spring planters.

Su Tung-p'o. The following two poems, in seven-character *lü-shih*
form, were written a short while apart and employ the same rhyme
words. The first, as the poet explains in an introduction, was addressed to his brother, Tzu-yu, and was written when the poet was in
prison on charges of "slandering the emperor," that is, writing
poetry that was considered too critical of the government. As may be
seen, Su fully expected to die before the year was out. The second,
written a few days before the end of the year, celebrates his unexpected release from prison. It is typical of Su's attitude toward life that
he should cast two poems so completely different in mood and cir-
cumstance in the same form and employ the same rhyme words in
both, indicating his awareness of the continuity behind change, his
sense of the eventual equality of sorrow and joy, life and death.

Under the heaven of our holy ruler, all things turn to spring,
but I in dark ignorance have destroyed myself.
Before my hundred years are past, I'm called to settle up;
my leaderless family, ten mouths, must be your worry now.
Bury me anywhere on the green hills
and another year in night rain grieve for me alone.
Let us be brothers in lives and lives to come,
mending then the bonds that this world breaks.

A hundred days, free to go, and it's almost spring;
for the years left, pleasure will be my chief concern.
Out the gate, I do a dance, wind blows my face;
our galloping horses race along as magpies cheer.
I face the wine cup and it's all a dream,
pick up a poem brush, already inspired.
Why try to fix the blame for troubles past?
Years now I've stolen posts I never should have had.

Su Tung-p'o, "Eastern Slope," 5-character *ku-shih*; two of a series of eight poems describing a small farm at a place called Eastern Slope in Huang-chou, Hupeh, where the poet lived in exile after his release from prison.

A little stream used to cross my land,
came from the mountain pass back there,
under city walls, through villages—
the current sluggish and choked with grass—
feeding finally into K'o Clan Pond,
ten *mou* stocked with fish and shrimp.
Drought this year dried it up,
its cracked bed plastered with brown duckweed.
Last night clouds came from hills to the south;
rain soaked the ground a plowshare deep.
Rivulets found the channel again,
knowing I'd chopped back the weeds.
In the mud a few old roots of cress
still alive from a year ago.
If white buds will open again,
when spring doves come I'll make a stew!

I planted rice before Spring Festival
and already I'm counting joys!
Rainy skies darken the spring pond;
by green-bladed paddies I chat with friends.
Transplanting takes till the first of summer,
delight growing with wind-blown stalks.
The moon looks down on dew-wet leaves
strung one by one with hanging pearls.
Fall comes and frosty ears grow heavy,
topple, and lean propped on each other.
From banks and dikes I hear only
the sound of locusts like wind and rain.
Rice, newly hulled, goes to the steamer,
grains of jade that light up the basket.
A long time I've eaten only government fare,
old rusty rice no better than mud.

Now to taste something new—
I've already promised my mouth and belly.

Su Tung-p'o, "Beginning of Autumn: A Poem To Send to Tzu-yu,"
5-character *ku-shih*; 1083. The poet recalls when he and his brother,
Tzu-yu, were studying for the examination that launched them on
their careers as government officials and brought about their long
separation.

The hundred rivers day and night flow on,
we and all things following;
only the heart remains unmoved,
clutching the past.
I recall when we stayed at Huai-yüan Stop,
door shut against fall heat,
eating boiled greens, studying,
wiping away the sweat, you and I.
The west wind suddenly turned cold;
dried leaves blew in the window.
You got up for a heavier coat
and took hold of my hand:
We won't be young for long—
I needn't tell you.
Probably we'll have to part,
hard to tell when success may come—
Even then I felt a chill of sorrow,
and now when both of us are old—
Too late to look for a lost road,
too late, I'm afraid, to study the Way.
This fall I began talks to buy some land;
if I build a house, it should be done by spring.
Nights at Snow Hall, in wind and rain,
already I hear you talking to me.

Su Tung-p'o, "Days of Rain; the Rivers Have Overflowed,"
7-character *lü-shih*; written in 1095 at Hui-chou, near present-day
Canton, where the poet was living in exile.

Drenching rain hisses down, cooling the evening;
I lie and listen to banyan noise echo on the porch.

By feeble lamp shine, I shake off a dream;
curtains and blinds, half soaked, breathe old incense.
High waves shake the bed, spray blows from the cistern;
dark wind rocks the trees—they clink like jade.
Even if it clears I have no place to go—
let it keep on all night pelting the empty stairs.

Huang T'ing-chien (1045–1105), "Song of the Clear River," 7-character *ku-shih*.

River gulls bob and toss in reed-flower autumn;
eighty-year-old fisherman, not a worry in a hundred:
by clear dawn he works the scull, picking lotus pods;
by evening sun hauls in the net, letting the boat drift.
His little boys are learning to fish—not bad at all;
his old woman, white-haired, has pleasures still ahead.
The whole family, wine-drowsy, sleep beneath the thatch,
their boat on the cold sand where night tides run out.

Huang T'ing-chien, "Once More Following the Rhymes of Pin-lao's Poem 'Getting Up after Illness and Strolling in the Eastern Garden,'" 5-character *ku-shih*; to match a poem by the poet's friend Huang Pin-lao. Ho Ch'ü-ping was a famous general of the Former Han. The poem displays the rather eccentric diction and fondness for Zen for which Huang is famous.

West wind slaughters the lingering heat,
deadly as General Ho Ch'ü-ping,
unclogging ditches to flood the lotus pond,
sweeping leaves, brightening up the bamboo lane.
In the midst, a man calm and sedate
knows for himself the nature of perfect understanding;
the monkey of the mind, just now waking up,
gives a laugh—all six windows wide open!

"Monkey of the mind": the mind is often compared in Buddhist writings to a monkey romping in the trees of desire. The "six windows" are the six organs of sense, the eye, ear, nose, tongue, body, and mind. The poet alludes to the story found in *Ching-te ch'uan-teng lu* ch. 6: "The Zen master Yang-shan Hui-chi (814–890) asked, 'How can I get to see my true nature?' The Zen master Chung-i said, 'It's as though there were a room and the room had six windows and inside was an ape. You begin on the east side shouting *shan-shan!* and the answer comes *shan-shan!* You do this at all the six windows till you've gotten a response at each!' Yang-shan bowed his thanks and got up to go. 'It's not that I don't understand the analogy you have favored me with, Reverend,' he said. 'But there's one thing more. Suppose the ape on the inside is sound asleep— then how is the ape on the outside going to get to see him?' The Master climbed down from his chair, took Yang-shan by the hand, and began to dance with him, saying '*Shan-shan*—I see you!'"

Huang T'ing-chien, "To Go with Shih K'o's Painting of an Old Man Tasting Vinegar," 7-character *ku-shih*. Shih K'o was a tenth-century painter noted for his treatment of humorous and super-natural subjects; the painting, as we know from other sources, actually depicted an elderly couple. (See Arthur Waley, *Introduction to the Study of Chinese Painting,* pp. 227–30). Master Wu is Wu Tao-tzu, the famous T'ang painter.

Old lady Shih, braving acerbity, pokes in her three-foot beak; old man Shih, vinegar-tasting, face in a hundred wrinkles: who knows how it feels to scrunch up your shoulders, shivering
    clear to the bone?
A painting not to be surpassed even by the brush of Master Wu!

Lu Yu (1125–1209), "Border Mountain Moon," 7-character *ku-shih* in *yüeh-fu* style; the title originally designated a war song of the western region. Written in 1177, fourteen years after the Sung had made peace with the Chin, which had invaded and occupied north and central China. Vermilion gates in line three refers to the man-sions of the nobles and high officials; the kettles mentioned in line five were pounded at night in army camps to signal the hour.

Fifteen years ago the edict came: peace with the invader; our generals fight no more but idly guard the border.
Vermilion gates still and silent; inside they sing and dance; stabled horses fatten and die, bows come unstrung.
From garrison towers the beat of kettles hurries the sinking moon; lads who joined the troops at twenty, white-haired now.
In the sound of the flutes who will read the brave man's heart?
Above the sands emptily shining, moon on warrior bones.
Spear-clash on the central plain—this we've known from old.
But when have traitorous barbarians lived to see their heirs?

Our captive people, forbearing death, pine for release,
even tonight how many places stained with their tears?

Lu Yu, "The Merchant's Joy," 7-character *ku-shih* in *yüeh-fu* style.

The wide wide Yangtze, dragons in deep pools;
wave blossoms, purest white, leap to the sky.
The great ship, tall-towered, far off no bigger than a bean;
my wondering eyes have not come to rest when it's here before me.
Matted sails: clouds that hang beyond the embankment;
lines and hawsers: their thunder echoes from high town walls.
Rumble rumble of ox carts to haul the priceless cargo;
heaps, hordes to dazzle the market—men race with the news.
In singing-girl towers to play at dice, a million on one throw;
by flag-flown pavilions calling for wine, ten thousand a cask;
the Mayor? the Governor? we don't even know their names;
what's it to us who wields power in the palace?
Confucian scholar, hard up, dreaming of one square meal;
a limp, a stumble, prayers for pity at His Excellency's gate;
teeth rot, hair falls out—no one looks your way;
belly crammed with classical texts, body lean with care—
See what Heaven gives me—luck thin as paper!
Now I know that merchants are the happiest of men.

Lu Yu, "Sitting Outdoors," 7-character *lü-shih*. The poet, seventy-three at the time, had retired from government office and was living in the country and receiving a pension in the form of grain.

Cap tipped back, propped by a window, still can't settle down;
haul out the cane of Ch'iung bamboo, take a turn in the garden.
Clear autumn coming on—dew soaks the grass;
bright moon not yet risen—stars crowd the sky.
Barges shove through lock gates, racing for dawn markets;
men on treadmills watering fields—no night's sleep for them!
Plain people sweating like this for one square meal,
and I sit eating government dole—wince whenever I think of it.

Lu Yu, "Sending Tzu-lung Off to a Post in Chi-chou," 5-character *ku-shih*; written in 1202, when the poet was seventy-seven. Tzu-lung was his second son, who was on his way to the post of judge in

Chi-chou in Kiangsi. A long Polonius-type poem that reflects the basic optimism, stern public morality, and familial affection typical of much of Sung poetry.

I'm old and you're going far away—
you have no choice, I know.
From the carriage I see you off,
brushing away tears I can't hold back.
Who likes to say good-by?
But we're poor and have to do these things.
You will brave the billows of Hsü,
from there cross Lake P'eng-li,
waves alive with boat-swallowing fish,
forests shrill with one-legged goblins.
Rice you eat in fields—what inn will cook it?
Scull of your lone boat—by what banks will it rest?
A judge—better than T'ang times;
at least you'll be spared the whip.
Line up and bow with others—no shame in that;
to slack your job—that's the only disgrace.
You'll be an official of Chi-chou;
see you drink no more than Chi-chou water!
When you know where every penny goes,
who can find excuse for talk?
Set aside a little for A-hsi's wedding,
find a good tutor for Yüan-li.
I can keep myself in food;
don't worry about fancy things for me.
My robe wears through?—let the elbows stick out;
shoes come apart?—leave the toes showing;
out the gate I may be laughed at;
back home, I'll sleep better for it.
Lord Yi, a man of name and station,
solid—stands out like a mountain peak:
his family and ours have been friends for generations—
perhaps he'll grant you an interview.
If so, count that honor enough—

in no way must you seem to be courting favor!
Again there's Yang Ch'eng-chai;
no one these days his match for integrity;
the kind who hears one stupid word
and spends three days washing out his ears.
You may go and see how he's getting on,
but end it there—no further talk!
Hsi-chou I've known for years,
Ching-ssu comes from our home town;
not only do they excel in letters;
in action and character equally fine.
Study and learn all you can from them—
achievement lies in piling up!
"Benevolence," "righteousness"—take them where you find
     them;
in practice they make the gentleman.
Three years and you'll be home again;
who knows—I may still be here.
There are carp in the rivers where you're going—
give them a letter to carry now and then.

"Billows of Hsü": high waves of the Ch'ien-t'ang River, where the body of the loyal minister Wu Tzu-hsü was cast in ancient times. According to legend, he became the god of the waves and his anger causes the tidal bore that rages up the river.

"Spared the whip": in T'ang times the head of the local government could whip his subordinate officials but this was forbidden under the Sung.

"A-hsi," "Yüan-li": Tzu-lung's daughter and eldest son, the poet's grandchildren.

Lord Yi: Chou Pi-ta, friend of the poet and former prime minister, living in retirement in Chi-chou.

Yang Ch'eng-chai: the poet and statesman Yang Wan-li (see p. 201), also living in retirement.

Hsi-chou; Ching-ssu: Ch'en Hsi-chou and Tu Ssu-kung, friends of the poet who were apparently serving as officials in Chi-chou.

"Give them a letter": allusion to an old yüeh-fu ballad that tells of a gift of a pair of carp, in the belly of one of which was found a letter. In T'ang times, letters were folded into the shape of a pair of fish.

Lu Yu, "Farm Families," 5-character lü-shih; sixth in the series.

It's late, the children come home from school;
braids unplaited, they ramble the fields,
jeering at each other—guess what's in my hand!
arguing—who won the grass fight after all?
Father sternly calls them to lessons;
grandfather indulgently feeds them candy.
We don't ask you to become rich and famous,
but when the time comes, work hard in the fields!

Lu Yu, "Sitting Up at Night," 7-character *chüeh-chü*; written when the poet was over eighty.

Spinners' lights from house to house brighten the deep night;
here and there new fields have been plowed after rain.
Always I feel ashamed to be so old and idle.
Sitting close by the stove, I hear the sound of wind.

# BIBLIOGRAPHY

Acker, William. *T'ao the Hermit*. New York: Thames and Hudson, 1952.

Aldington, Richard, ed. *The Portable Oscar Wilde*. New York: Viking Press, 1946.

Alley, Rewi. *Selected Poems of Tu Fu*. Peking: Foreign Languages Press, 1962.

Binyon, Laurence. *Landscape in English Art and Poetry*. London: Cobden-Sanderson, 1931.

Birch, Cyril, ed. *Anthology of Chinese Literature*. New York: Grove Press, 1965.

Bullett, Gerald. *The Golden Years of Fan Ch'eng-ta*. Cambridge: Cambridge University Press, 1946.

Bynner, Witter, and Kiang Kang-hu. *The Jade Mountain*. New York: Knopf, 1929; Doubleday Anchor Book 1964.

Candlin, Clara. *The Rapier of Lu: Patriot Poet of China*. London: J. Murray (Wisdom of the East series), 1946. (Translations from Lu Yu.)

Chang Yin-nan, and Lewis C. Walmsley. *The Poems of Wang Wei*. Rutland, Vt.: Tuttle, 1959.

Chang, Lily, and Marjorie Sinclair. *The Poems of T'ao Ch'ien*. Honolulu: University of Hawaii Press, 1953.

Chen, Shih-hsiang. "In Search of the Beginnings of Chinese Literary Criticism," *Semitic and Oriental Studies*. Berkeley, Calif.: University of California Press, 1951, pp. 45–63.

Ch'en, C. J., and Michael Bullock. *Poems of Solitude*. London: Abelard-Schuman, Ltd., 1960.

Chow, Tse-tsung. "The Early History of the Chinese Word *Shih* (Poetry)." In Chow, ed., *Wen-lin*, pp. 151–209.

——, ed. *Wen-lin: Studies in the Chinese Humanities*. Madison, Wisc.: University of Wisconsin Press, 1968.

Davidson, Martha. *A List of Published Translations from the Chinese into English, French and German*, Part II, Poetry. Ann Arbor, Mich.: J. W. Edwards, 1957.

Davis, A. R. "The Double Ninth Festival in Chinese Poetry." In Chow, ed., *Wen-lin*, pp. 45–64.

——, ed. *The Penguin Book of Chinese Verse*. Tr. by Robert Kotewell and Norman L. Smith. London: Penguin Books, 1962.

de Bary, Wm. Theodore, *et al. Sources of Chinese Tradition*. New York: Columbia University Press, 1960.

Demiéville, Paul, ed. *Anthologie de la Poésie Chinoise Classique*. Paris: Gallimard, 1962.

Diény, Jean-Pierre. *Aux origines de la poésie classique en Chine*. Leiden: Brill, 1968.

——. *Les dix-neuf poèmes anciens*. Paris: Presses Universitaires de France (Bulletin de la Maison franco-japonais 7/4), 1963.

Dingle, Herbert. *Science and Literary Criticism*. London: Thomas Nelson & Sons, 1949.

Frankel, Hans F. "Fifteen Poems by Ts'ao Chih: An Attempt at a New Approach." *Journal of the American Oriental Society*, 84 (no. 1, Jan/March, 1964), 1–14.

Frodsham, J. D. *The Murmuring Stream: The Life and Works of Hsieh Ling-yün*. Kuala Lumpur: University of Malaya Press, 1967. 2 vols.

——, and Ch'eng Hsi. *An Anthology of Chinese Verse: Han Wei Chin and the Northern and Southern Dynasties*. Oxford: Clarendon Press, 1967.

Graham, A. C. *Poems of the Late T'ang*. Baltimore: Penguin Books, 1965.

Hawkes, David. "Chinese Poetry and the English Reader." In Raymond Dawson, ed., *The Legacy of China* (Oxford: Clarendon Press, 1964), pp. 90–115.

——. *Ch'u Tz'u: The Songs of the South*. Oxford: Clarendon Press, 1959; Boston: Beacon Press (paperback), 1962.

——. *A Little Primer of Tu Fu*. Oxford: Clarendon Press,-1967.

Hightower, James R. "T'ao Ch'ien's 'Drinking Wine' Poems." In Chow, *Wen-lin*, pp. 3–44.

——. *Topics in Chinese Literature: Outlines and Bibliographies*. Cambridge, Mass.: Harvard University Press, 1950; rev. ed., 1953.

Huizinga, Johan. *Men and Ideas: Essays of Johan Huizinga*. Tr. by James S. Holmes and Hans van Marle. New York: Meridian Books, 1959.

Hung, William. *Tu Fu, China's Greatest Poet*. Cambridge, Mass.: Harvard University Press, 1952. 2 vols.

Lin Yutang. *The Gay Genius*. New York: John Day, 1947. (Biography of Su Tung-p'o.)

Liu, James J. Y. *The Art of Chinese Poetry*. Chicago: University of Chicago Press, 1962; paperback ed., 1966.

——. *The Poetry of Li Shang-yin, Ninth-Century Baroque Chinese Poet*. Chicago: University of Chicago Press, 1969.

March, Andrew L. "Self and Landscape in Su Shih." *Journal of the American Oriental Society*, 86, (no. 4, Oct.–Dec., 1966), 377–96.

Mather, Richard B. "The Landscape Buddhism of the Fifth Century Poet Hsieh Ling-yün." *Journal of Asian Studies*, 18 (no. 1, Nov., 1958), 67–79.

Mei, Tsu-lin, and Yu-kung Kao. "Tu Fu's 'Autumn Meditations': An Exercise in Linguistic Criticism." *Harvard Journal of Asiatic Studies*, 28 (1968), 44–80.

Obata, Shigeyoshi. *The Works of Li Po*. New York: Dutton, 1922.

Payne, Robert, ed. *The White Pony*. New York: John Day, 1947; New American Library (Mentor), 1960.

Rexroth, Kenneth. *One Hundred Poems from the Chinese*. New York: New Directions, 1956.

Roy, David. "The Theme of the Neglected Wife in the Poetry of Ts'ao Chih." *Journal of Asian Studies,* 19 (no. 1 [1959]), 25–31.

Schafer. Edward H. "Mineral Imagery in the Paradise Poems of Kuan-hsiu." *Asia Major* 10 (no. 1, 1963), 73–102.

———. *The Vermilion Bird: T'ang Images of the South*. Berkeley, Calif.: University of California Press, 1967.

Shih, Vincent Yu-chung. *The Literary Mind and the Carving of Dragons*. New York: Columbia University Press, 1959. (Liu Hsieh's *Wen-hsin tiao-lung*.)

Snyder, Gary. "Han Shan: Cold Mountain Poems." *Evergreen Review,* 2 (no. 6, 1958) 69–80; reprinted in Birch, *Anthology*.

South, Margaret Tudor. *Li Ho*. Adelaide: Libraries Board of South Australia (Occasional Papers in Asian and Pacific Studies 1), 1967.

Trilling, Lionel. *The Experience of Literature*. New York: Holt, Rinehart & Winston, 1967.

Van Doren, Mark. *The Happy Critic*. New York: Hill and Wang, 1961.

Waley, Arthur. *Chinese Poems*. London: Allen and Unwin, 1946; paperback 1961. (Selected from three earlier books: *The Temple and Other Poems, a Hundred and Seventy Chinese Poems,* and *More Translations from the Chinese*.)

———. *An Introduction to the Study of Chinese Painting*. Originally published 1923; New York: Grove Press, 1958.

———. *The Life and Times of Po Chü-i*. London and New York: Allen and Unwin, 1949.

———. "Poems of Han-shan." *Encounter,* 3 (no. 3, [Sept., 1954]); reprinted in Waley, *Chinese Poems*.

———. *The Poetry and Career of Li Po*. New York: Macmillan, 1950.

Watson, Burton. *Cold Mountain: 100 Poems by Han-shan*. New York: Grove Press, 1962; reissued, New York: Columbia University Press, 1970; London: Jonathan Cape, 1970.

———. *Early Chinese Literature*. New York: Columbia University Press, 1962.

———. *Su Tung-p'o*. New York: Columbia University Press, 1965.

Wu Chi-yu. "A Study of Han Shan," *T'oung Pao,* 45 (nos. 4–5 [1957]), 392–450.

Wu, John C. H. "The Four Seasons of T'ang Poetry," *T'ien Hsia Monthly,* Apr., May, Aug., Nov., 1938; Feb., Aug., 1939.

Yevtushenko, Yevgeny. *A Precocious Autobiography*. Tr. by Andrew R. MacAndrew. New York: Dutton (paperback), 1964.

Yip, Wai-lim, *Ezra Pound's Cathay*. Princeton: Princeton University Press, 1969.

Yoshikawa Kojiro. *An Introduction to Sung Poetry*. Tr. by Burton Watson. Cambridge, Mass.: Harvard University Press, 1967.

# INDEX